Community, Economic Crea

Community, Economic Creativity, and Organization

Edited by
Ash Amin and Joanne Roberts

OXFORD
UNIVERSITY PRESS

OXFORD
UNIVERSITY PRESS

Great Clarendon Street, Oxford OX2 6DP

Oxford University Press is a department of the University of Oxford.
It furthers the University's objective of excellence in research, scholarship,
and education by publishing worldwide in

Oxford New York

Auckland Cape Town Dar es Salaam Hong Kong Karachi
Kuala Lumpur Madrid Melbourne Mexico City Nairobi
New Delhi Shanghai Taipei Toronto

With offices in

Argentina Austria Brazil Chile Czech Republic France Greece
Guatemala Hungary Italy Japan Poland Portugal Singapore
South Korea Switzerland Thailand Turkey Ukraine Vietnam

Oxford is a registered trade mark of Oxford University Press
in the UK and in certain other countries

Published in the United States
by Oxford University Press Inc., New York

British Library Cataloguing in Publication Data

Data available

Library of Congress Cataloging in Publication Data

Data available

Typeset by SPI Publisher Services, Pondicherry, India
Printed in Great Britain
on acid-free paper by
CPI Antony Rowe, Chippenham, Wiltshire

ISBN 978–0–19–954549–0 (hbk.)
 978–0–19–954550–6 (pbk.)

1 3 5 7 9 10 8 6 4 2

Contents

Contents

Acknowledgements

This book stems from a workshop held at Durham University in October 2006 hosted by the Institute of Advanced Study and Department of Geography. The workshop gathered scholars from different disciplines, practitioners and policymakers, and research postgraduates to debate the role of communities of practice and situated knowledge in general in driving innovation, competitive advantage, and regional development. The workshop formed part of a 6th Framework EU Network of Excellence – Dynamics of Institutions and Markets in Europe (DIME) – tackling the economic and social consequences of increasing globalization and the rise of the knowledge economy. We are grateful to DIME for funding the workshop and for incorporating an interest in communities of practice as a major research strand of the initiative. The workshop was an immensely creative two-day event, widely appreciated among the delegates for its open and critical discussion on the merits and limitations of a perspective stressing situated knowing. Along with the people who revised their papers to contribute to the volume, we would like to thank Göran Anderson, Marc Coenders, Alessia Contu, Phil Cooke, Silvia Gherardi, Nathalie Lazaric, Edward Lorenz, Peter Maskell, Paul Muller, and David Stark for speaking at the workshop. Other delegates also contributed actively to the workshop, and we are especially grateful to Frida Andersson, Simon Turner, and Zilia Iskoujina for their excellent summaries of the discussion. Credit for the flawless organization of the workshop goes to Veronica Crooks and Hamzah Muzaini, who spent weeks and months supporting the Durham end of the DIME network. Thanks also go to Taylor & Francis for permission to reprint Chapter 3 ' "The Art of Knowing": Social and Tacit Dimensions of Knowledge and the Limits of the Community of Practice' by Paul Duguid, originally published in *The Information Society*, Volume 21, Issue 2, April 2005, pages 109–18 (available from: http://www.informaworld.com). Finally, a warm thanks to David Musson at Oxford University Press for soliciting and staying with this publication.

Ash Amin and Joanne Roberts
Durham, November 2007

List of Figures

List of Tables

Notes on Contributors

Ash Amin is Professor of Geography at Durham University and Executive Director of the university's Institute Advanced Study. His current research interests lie in the areas of knowledge practices, the social economy, race and multiculturalism, social and spatial theory, urbanism, and political invention. His most recent books include *Cities: Reimagining the Urban*, with Nigel Thrift (Polity, 2002); *Placing the Social Economy*, with Angus Cameron and Ray Hudson (Routledge, 2002); *Architectures of Knowledge*, with Patrick Cohendet (Oxford University Press, 2004); *Cultural Economy: A Reader*, edited with Nigel Thrift (Blackwell, 2005). He is completing a book with Nigel Thrift on reimagining the Left political thought and practice.

Patrick Cohendet is Professor of Economics at the University Louis Pasteur of Strasbourg (France), presently at HEC Montreal (Canada) as Visiting Professor. His research focuses on the economics and management of innovation, economics of knowledge, knowledge management, and theory of organizations. He is co-founder and member of the BETA research laboratory in Strasbourg. He has carried out numerous studies on the economic impacts of innovation, the transfer of technologies, and knowledge-based policies for public agencies such as the EU, the European Space Agency, and the OECD. Amongst his recent publications is *Architectures of Knowledge: Firms, Capabilities and Communities* with Ash Amin (Oxford University Press, 2004).

Aurélie Delemarle is a C'Nano IdF post-doctoral fellow at the Technical Laboratories, Territories and Societies, Ecole National des Ponts et Chausses (ENPC), Marne la Vallée, France. Her research is focused on understanding the emergence of the Minatec innovation pole in micro- and nanoelectronics in Grenoble and on the collective engagements of firms in creating market infrastructures for nanotechnology-based products. She is a member of the PRIME network of excellence. Her research interests include: regional innovation and cluster policies, institutional theories and governance, science and technology policies, disruptive innovations, temporal management of science and technology, and science and society interactions.

Paul Duguid is Adjunct Professor in the School of Information at the University of California, Berkeley; a professorial research fellow at Queen Mary, University of London; and an honorary fellow of the Institute for Entrepreneurship and Enterprise Development at Lancaster University School of Management. From 1989 to 2001 he was a consultant at the Xerox Palo Alto Research Center. His interest in multidisciplinary, collaborative work has led him to work with social scientists, computer scientists, economists, linguists, management theorists, and social psychologists. His writing has appeared in a broad array of scholarly fields and journals.

Meric S. Gertler holds the Goldring Chair in Canadian Studies, in the Department of Geography and Program in Planning, University of Toronto. His research interests include: regional and national systems of innovation; technology production and use in its spatial context; relations between Canadian users and overseas producers of advanced technologies; political economy of technological change and industrial reorganization in its geographical context; local and regional economic development policy and planning; economic change in the Toronto region. Recent publications include: *Manufacturing Culture: The Institutional Geography of Industrial Practice* (Oxford University Press, 2004) and with D.A. Wolfe (eds.) *Innovation and Social Learning: Institutional Adaptation in an Era of Technological Change* (Macmillan/ Palgrave, 2002).

Philippe Larédo is Director of Research at the University of Paris-Est in the Ecole Nationale des Ponts et Chausses (ENPC), France. He is also Visiting Professor at the University of Manchester in the Manchester Business School (Manchester Institute of Innovation Studies). He has published in areas of: public intervention in higher education, innovation and research policy; strategic management of research and technology; European research policy; evaluation; research collectives and their dynamics; RD&I activities of large firms and breakthrough innovation. He is coordinator of the EU's PRIME European network of excellence (Policies for Research and Innovation in the Move towards the European Research Area 2004–2008).

Jean Lave is a social anthropologist at the University of California, Berkeley. Much of her ethnographically based research concentrates on the re-conceiving of learning, learners, and everyday life in terms of social practice. She has published several books on the subject: *Cognition in*

Practice (1988); *Situated Learning: Legitimate Peripheral Participation* (with E. Wenger, 1991); and *Understanding Practice* (co-edited with S. Chaiklin, 1993). More recently her work has taken a historical turn with a collaborative, ethno-historical project, edited with Dorothy Holland, *History in Person: Enduring Struggles, Contentious Practice, Intimate Identities* (2000). She is currently finishing a book on Vai and Gola tailors' apprenticeship in Liberia, *Apprenticeship in Critical Ethnographic Practice*, and continues to write about social practice theory.

Juan Mateos-Garcia is a research officer and doctoral researcher at CENTRIM, in the University of Brighton. His research interests include communities of practice and the social organization of knowledge production, particularly in the contexts of open-source software development and the Creative Industries.

Bart Nooteboom is Professor of Innovation Policy at Tilburg University. He is author of *Inter-firm Collaboration, Learning and Networks: An Integrated Approach* (2004), *Trust: Forms, Foundations, Functions, Failures and Figures* (2002), *Learning and Innovation in Organizations and Economies* (2000), *Inter-firm Alliances: Analysis and Design* (1999), and some 250 articles on small business, entrepreneurship, innovation and diffusion, innovation policy, transaction cost theory, inter-firm relations, and organizational learning. He is a member of the Royal Netherlands Academy of Arts and Sciences. He was awarded the Kapp Prize for his work on organizational learning and the Gunnar Myrdal Prize for his work on trust. In 1988–1990 he was member of a government committee on technology policy. In 1995–1999 he was director of a research institute/PhD school for economics, business, and geography. In 2006–2007 he was a member of the (Dutch) Scientific Council for Government Policy (WRR).

Joanne Roberts is Senior Lecturer in management at Newcastle University Business School. Her research interests include knowledge-intensive services, new information and communication technologies and knowledge transfer, inter- and intra-organizational knowledge transfer and the internationalization of business services. She is a participant in the Dynamics of Institutions and Markets in Europe, Network of Excellence, Honorary Associate Fellow at the Centre for Research on Innovation and Competition, University of Manchester, and co-founder and co-editor of the international journal, *Critical Perspectives on International Business*.

Harry Scarbrough is a professor in Warwick Business School, at the University of Warwick, UK, and Director of the ESRC Evolution of Business

Knowledge (EBK) research programme. Harry's research interests focus on the management of knowledge and learning in organizations.

Laurent Simon is Associate Professor in the Department of Management, HEC Montréal (Canada); DESC (management), Rouen; MSc (management); PhD (administration-management), HEC Montréal. His research interests include: management, new technologies and knowledge economy; knowledge-intensive firms and creativity; management of 'techno-creative' firms, with a strong qualitative and empirical focus.

W. Edward Steinmueller is a professorial fellow at Science and Technology Policy Research (SPRU), Sussex University. He has published widely in the field of the industrial economics of information and communication technology industries including integrated circuits, computers, telecommunications, software and the economic, social policy issues of the Information Society. Professor Steinmueller has been an advisor to the European Commission, National Academies of Science and Engineering (USA), Ministry of Economic Affairs (the Netherlands), Department of Trade and Industry and Office of Telecommunications (UK), and the United Nations University Institute for New Technologies (UNU-INTECH) as well as other private, public, and third-sector organizations.

Michael Storper is Professor of Economic Geography at the London School of Economics; Professor of Regional and International Development in the Department of Urban Planning, School of Public Affairs, UCLA; and Professor of Economic Sociology at Institut d'Etudes Politiques de Paris. His pioneering research work on the socio-economic and political reasons for unequal economic development processes in cities and regions have attracted a major international response. He is the author of *The Regional World: Territorial Development in a Global Economy* (Gilford Press, 1997) and (with Robert Salais) *Worlds of Production: The Action Frameworks of the Economy* (Harvard University Press, 1997).

Jacky Swan is Professor of Organizational Behaviour at Warwick Business School, University of Warwick, UK. She is Director of ikon – research centre in Innovation Knowledge and Organizational Networks. Her current research focuses on the translation of innovation in the biomedical industry in the UK and USA, and on the management and organization of knowledge during the clinical trials process. Jacky is author of numerous papers on innovation, knowledge management, and learning in project-based environments and co-author of *Managing Knowledge Work*.

Nigel Thrift is Vice Chancellor and Professor at the University of Warwick. He is also a visiting professor of geography at Oxford University and an emeritus professor of geography at Bristol University. Professor Thrift is maintaining his research career alongside his role as Vice Chancellor. His current research spans a broad range of interests, including international finance; cities and political life; non-representational theory; affective politics; and the history of time.

Prologue: Community of Practice Then and Now

Paul Duguid

On the last morning of the workshop from which this book emerged, the participants were asked to give their understanding of a community of practice. The request was not unreasonable. We had been discussing the topic for two days; presumably we knew what we were talking about. Yet, as is not uncommon in academic gatherings, the responses suggested that we had not all been talking about quite the same thing.[1] Among the range – and there was quite a range – let me pick three that strike me as fairly representative of current thought about communities of practice:

A group of people bound together by their interest in a common working practice.
Social groups organized around a certain activity (practice).
Groups sharing a same practice and oriented towards the resolution of common problems.

While these responses reflect current usage, it seems to me that they have come a long way from the early discussions of the concept, and in this brief preface, I shall try to plot some of that journey. So saying, I am not trying to say these definitions are in any way wrong. As another response to the question noted, a community of practice 'is nothing more than a construction of the academy'. As an active construct, the community of practice is susceptible to constant change and redirection. (In passing, it is worth noting how remarkable it is, given the short life of many academic constructs, that this one is still under active construction.) Those who are currently engaged in the work of construction (and I do not count myself among them) are entitled to use the term as they find it. Indeed, it would be a denial of the situated, transformational character of human learning, which community of practice theorizing has stressed so strongly, to maintain that the concept could be held to a timeless definition.

What Was the Community of Practice?

What I can do, however, is draw on my twenty or so years around this concept to map some of its route across the territory that lies between its inception and the present, and then, very briefly, to suggest what might be gained by travelling back to its earlier positions.

The three definitions evidently have a lot in common. The concept still turns on social groups. They also give prominence to practice. (So doing, as I shall note below, they are slightly unrepresentative of broader uses.) But for me, most noticeably, these accounts encapsulate the way *interest*, *intention*, and *instrumentality* have become all but inseparable from current use. Many of the papers I see using the concept are preoccupied with groups brought together by their shared interests in a topic. This approach excludes much of the workforce in most jobs, who are brought together by their shared interest in making a living. Papers also tend to make a lot of the purposefulness with which organizations create or manage communities of practice. So doing they tend to make communities of practice the outcome of management fiat, and not of practice. And many papers highlight the problems that such communities can be created to solve. In a significant portion of the literature, then, the community of practice is seen as a useful, management-controlled, problem-solving tool that nonetheless comprises people with an interest or even a 'passion' for their work.

In reaching this point, the concept has travelled a fair distance from its early days and bridged some remarkable chasms (Lave and Wenger 1990). After all, the theory first developed as a theory of learning at the Institute for Research on Learning in Palo Alto. It escaped seminars and personal presentations in a report written by Jean Lave and Etienne Wenger published by the Institute in 1990. I had the task of editing the Institute's report series then, so I had the opportunity to work closely with Lave and Wenger and saw their ideas develop through multiple drafts of the report and its transformation into the 1991 book of the same name, *Situated Learning: Legitimate Peripheral Participation*.[2]

Surprising as it may seem, learning was (and remains) remarkably undertheorized. To be unfair, but not too unfair, cognitive psychology, which tended to dominate the field, portrayed the learner as little more than a 'tabula rasa' (a phrase that suggests how old this way of thinking was), a passive recipient on whom, when learning was successful, knowledge or information were inscribed. You judged success by the extent to which what was imparted by teachers was received and could be retransmitted unadulterated by learners. Learning, from this perspective, is the mirror of teaching.

Lave in her prior work and Lave and Wenger in *Situated Learning* argued by contrast that learning was not the process of replicating what others think – where what is to be learned and whether it has been learned are judged from the perspective of those 'others'. Rather, it involved deploying through practice the resources – cognitive, material, social – available to you to participate in society, a process which, Lave and Wenger argued, was inseparable from the development of a social identity through legitimate peripheral participation in particular social forms.

To understand learning from this perspective, attention needed to shift, Lave and Wenger showed, from teaching and pedagogy, to engagement in practice. Taking into account the learner's perspective – and making teaching all but epiphenomenal for most learning – is not an easy shift to make, particularly in the academy, where teaching is so important and its success judged by the production of intellectual clones. It is also a hard shift for other kinds of formal organization, where learning is assumed to be manifest in the ability to follow rules.

If the central focus of the theory has often been ignored, so has its central concept: practice. Instead, attention tended to focus on what Raymond Williams called the 'warmly persuasive' concept of community. The group, and in particular, the small cohesive group, became the appealing centre of attention. But community of practice theory is nothing at all without practice.

Indeed, the shifting of attention from, more broadly, production (the perspective of teaching, instructing, and rule giving) to consumption (the perspective of learners and employees) plays a significant part in practice theory more generally, evident, for example, in the work of Bourdieu (1977) and de Certeau (1988). In Bourdieu's case the connection to Lave is direct. His *Outline of a Theory of Practice* had influenced Lave's work since *Cognition in Practice* and his work was much discussed in the Institute for Research on Learning. Connections to de Certeau's *The Practice of Everyday Life* are less direct. The parallel is nonetheless evident, particularly in his powerful critique of Foucault for attempting to understand history from the point of view of texts, as if social practice simply mirrored textual precepts. If, however, learning is replaced by the idea of engagement in social practice, then communities of practice represent the social loci of that engagement and, as is too often overlooked in discussions of Lave and Wenger's work (my own included), the site of a continuous power struggle over 'continuity and displacement'.

As the three definitions with which I began suggest, construction of this academic concept today seems to be focused elsewhere. I regularly read papers and hear talks in which people explicitly or implicitly use the concept to endorse cognitive theory, to describe workplace teams, to define groups brought together by shared interests or common problems, and so on. Of course, as I have suggested, with a theory under constant, situated construction, this sort of repositioning is inevitable. It is only misleading when such repositioning is presented as a seamless continuation of Lave and Wenger's initial ideas. Using the terms in such diverse ways may be a sign of healthy transformation, but it should place some obligation on authors to indicate how they get from Lave and Wenger's 1991 argument to their own positions. No doubt, some authors simply fail to understand the difference between their individualist, cognitivist, thoroughly conventional accounts of learning (worthy though all those may be) and the original concepts mapped out by Lave and Wenger. Others, I suspect, have simply failed to read Lave and Wenger (1991), gaining their knowledge by proxy. As one of the chief proxies, it is probably time for me to explain my part in the redirection of the original concept.

Turning Right

In *Situated Learning*, five 'studies of situated learners' follow the outline of the theory, which opens the book. These involve Yucatec midwives, Liberian tailors, naval quartermasters, American butchers, and alcoholics. The choice is very deliberate and the examples are fascinating. These particular examples, however, rarely come up in discussions of community of practice theory. Instead, if called upon to summon an example from the past, most authors discuss Xerox technicians.

The link from Lave and Wenger's theory to Julian Orr's (1996) study of the Xerox 'reps', going from what might be seen as relatively marginal communities to the heart of corporate America, is made neither in Lave and Wenger's work nor in Orr's book, which studiously avoids a discussion of Lave and Wenger. Rather, it was made for better or for worse in an article I wrote with John Seely Brown, thus I have to take some responsibility for this redirection of the theory (Brown and Duguid 1991).[3]

4

That article set out, however ineptly, to address through juxtaposition gaps in both of the sources it drew upon so heavily. Orr seemed to have at the time almost no theory of learning, yet learning was critical to understanding the working of the Xerox reps. Lave and Wenger could contribute that theory, yet they seemed to have no theory of institutions or organizations. Bringing together the two – the learning theory, on the one hand, and the workers with their complicated relationship to the corporation as the dominant source of what they should know, on the other – seemed a worthwhile thing to do.

Theory passed effortlessly from learning research to business-school syllabus and a practice perspective became a managerial perspective in good part because the story exemplifying the theory and elaborating practice, the story of the reps, had a happy ending. The reps, as Orr had shown, helped save the corporation from its own ineptitude. With hindsight it is quite clear that absent explicit arguments to the contrary (and even with them), readers familiar with the solution-obsessed literature of management reviews could assume that we were claiming that all communities of practice would be beneficial to corporations and so communities of practice are inherently a good thing from a management perspective. I must concede that such a reading of the paper is plausible. It was not one that I had foreseen, but there the fault is mine. Indeed, so complete was my lack of foresight that I was at first surprised when people began to tell me that they had found a corporate community with a dark side. By this they meant that robust communities of practice did not always further managerial goals and, at times, they might even thwart those goals. People told me this with kindness and tact, assuming that I might be heartbroken to discover that one of my sunny little brood might be a wolf in sheep's clothing. To deflect such unrequited acts of kindness, I found it necessary for a while to include among my list of exemplary communities of practice, intravenous drug users, mafia families, and ruling cadres of genocidal governments. These examples did not deflect the managerial trajectory for communities of practice. I did notice, though, that it dried up the stream of invitations I had been receiving to take part in managerial conferences and reviews.

In sum, in the context of management studies (and most organization studies now are primarily management studies), the inversion that Lave and Wenger and Orr had achieved – shifting attention from the perspective of managerial precept to the perspective of work practice – was ignored. Instead of a challenge to managerial theory and practice, the

5

community of practice too easily came to be seen as a new, tractable management tool.

One question then comes to the fore: if instead of the Xerox reps, we had used a disruptive community of practice as our prime example, might we have avoided this comforting, functionalist reading of the concept? I suspect we might have. More to the point, we probably would not have been read at all. Indeed, we might not have been published, and certainly would not have drawn so much attention. But these concerns aside, there were, I still believe, good, discomfiting reasons for highlighting Orr's group of reps.[4]

As I have argued elsewhere, both Lave and Wenger's theory and Orr's ethnography raise the issue of workplace improvisation (Duguid 2006). Management research, still very much in the tradition of Taylor, has tended to see improvisation as damaging deviance. More surprisingly, but in a similar vein, radical critique has also tended to see spontaneity as inherently oppositional, exposing the contradictions of capital and preventing its smooth working. From a quite different perspective, then, both champions of the capitalist workplace and its critics would seem to agree that crude conformity makes the work go better, even if one perspective seeks to enhance that conformity and the other to disrupt it.

This conclusion, with its support from opposing directions, makes it easy to argue that agency, autonomy, and improvised learning among the workforce are only problematic. From here we are led to ideas of work as rule following and workplace learning as ingesting those rules. This is a crude but not, I believe, too unjust summary of ideas that run along a canonical path from Taylorism to modern Enterprise Resource Planning, with an odd Althusserian detour along the way. Though Taylor is a symbol of this tradition, he is hardly its origin. Perhaps it would be better to invoke the first Admiral Troubridge (1758–1807) as its patron saint. He apparently ran his ships with the view that 'Whenever I see a fellow look as if he was thinking, I say that's mutiny'. Implicit in such rule-driven ideas is the conclusion that good managers should stamp out improvisation and demand obedience: good work entails following rules.

Neither Lave and Wenger, nor Orr, or, I believe, Brown and Duguid allow such easy conclusions. Lave and Wenger's theory suggests that even organizationally compliant learning is to a significant degree at the disposition of the workforce. Orr's study showed that, in certain conditions, rule-breaking improvisation can be better for organizational success than rule-following obedience. So, in the rep's case, it was better for the company that the rules be broken than that the reps observe them. If that does not quite rise to the level of capitalist contradiction, it presents an intriguing dilemma. There is no simple rule for management to follow either. Insist on conformity, and you inhibit learning and your organization might thus fall victim of the frailty of its own rules; encourage learning, and you encourage autonomy and might face mutiny in response to those own rules.

To put this argument another way, it seems reasonable to argue that Lave and Wenger's (1991) view of learning is agonistic. It involves wrestling to situate cultural signals of one sort or another in the context of local practice and collective identity formation. Despite the agonism and attendant transformation, most such learning nevertheless conforms broadly with the general assumptions of those initiating the communication. From this conformity comes coordination. We also get a theory that appeals strongly not only to business schools, but also to management consultants: it is instrumental, operational, and promises only beneficial results. Successfully install a community of practice, the theory seems to say, and you will advance organizational goals. But there is no guaranteeing or predicting where resilient communities of practice will emerge, who will be members, and whether they challenge or undermine organizational assumptions rather than conform with them. The strongest challenges are not merely agonistic but antagonistic, subverting the best-laid business plans, undermining business processes, and making consultants look a little foolish. The community of practice is, to use an old cliché, an interestingly double-edged sword. Such a view is widely accepted in discussions of corporate research. Scientists, in service both of a discipline and a corporation are assumed to and allowed to think for themselves. So doing they contain both threat and promise. The same view is generally not accepted of line workers. One outcome of the community of practice perspective is that as quasi-autonomous social groups with their own interests and imperatives, such workers are not very different from either management or researchers – hence John Seely Brown and I talked in the subtitle of our 1991 essay of 'learning, working, and innovation' and suggested in the argument that these were indivisible.

These implications of the attempt to synthesize the two important bodies of work on which they drew – Lave and Wenger's, on the one hand, and Orr's, on the other – should, to my mind, present standard management and organizational theory and practice with a challenging dilemma. In truth, it rarely did. The community of practice was rapidly domesticated. An account intended to challenge assumptions about organizational learning was quickly turned into a comforting homily for the established church. A means to analyse the tensions with which organizational structure must live has been deployed to hide those tensions. The diagnostic power of the concept has been lost in claims for its healing potential. As the concept became more widespread, it took on the guise of those medical studies (and advertisements in the United States) that highlight the beneficial potential of medicines while suppressing the more problematic side effects. Such an approach quickly turned the concept into little more than a placebo. Communities of practice were something to be 'cultivated'; 'leveraging' rather than learning became the central concern.

What's Left for Community of Practice?

Today, the concept rests, as I say, in the hand of current practitioners, some of whose diverging interests I have tried to set out above. But, clinging to my naive faith, I would like to suggest that, set free from its instrumental constraints, it could once again become an incisive analytical concept. Furthermore, there are some signs that, as with most managerial concepts, its status is in decline and thus it might be ripe for emancipation. Early in the concept's life, for example, Nonaka embraced the concept. His endorsement helped to make it a nostrum in the field of knowledge management (Nonaka and Takeuchi 1995). More recently, without quite explaining his reversal, he has set aside the idea, preferring the more enigmatic concept of *Ba* and dismissing communities of practice as places for people 'gradually memorising jobs' (Nonaka et al. 2000, p. 15; Nonaka et al. 2006). Once again, we have come a long way from Lave and Wenger (and, I would hope, from Brown and Duguid) without much guidance as to how the difference was covered. Such dismissal might encourage the more instrumentally minded to leave the concept alone. We will all gain by taking the concept where it will lead us, rather than pushing it where we would like it to go. There are many places where it can usefully go. Let me in closing suggest a couple of directions.

First, as I argue in my chapter (Chapter 3) later in this volume, the community of practice presents a useful check on economic oversimplifications, which too readily reduce knowledge to information and social practice to individual utility maximization. Economists tend to dislike concepts of community, and the community of practice, with its account of how knowledge circulates, questions, in particular, ideas about perfect or complete information, as if the mere circulation of information could bring about completeness and perfection. In theory (if not always in practice, as I suggest), some economists seek to make the concepts of community no more than epiphenomena of individual action. Social theorists inevitably fight back. The struggle between the two is good for both fields.

Second, by extension, the concept raises issues about the geography of knowledge. Ideas of an information economy and an information society have led to remarkable claims about the death of distance and the earth being 'flat' (Cairncross 1997; Friedman 2006), or, in more sophisticated form, to Paul Romer's claim that the economic disparity once reflected an 'object gap' but is now the result of an 'idea gap', and that such gaps are 'relatively easy to solve' (Romer 1993, p. 556). If that is indeed the problem, then we can turn our back on questions of economic inequality, which will dissolve before evermore efficient technologies for circulating information. Yet, localization of knowledge, described by Marshall (1890) more than a century ago, remains tenacious, particularly in those very places, like Silicon Valley, where information technologies are at their most developed. If we want to understand such localization and if we want to overcome it (though it is not always clear that we do), we might do well to consider the community of practice, with its insights into learning, as it was envisaged in 1990.

References

Bourdieu, P. (1977). *Outline of a Theory of Practice*, trans. R. Nice. New York: Cambridge University Press.

Brown, J. and Duguid, P. (1991). 'Organizational learning and communities of practice: Towards a unified view of working, learning, and innovation', *Organization Science*, 2(1): 40–58.

Brown, J. S., Collins, A., and Duguid, P. (1989). 'Situated cognition and the culture of learning', *Education Researcher*, 18(1): 32–42.

Cairncross, F. (1997). *The Death of Distance: How the Communications Revolution Will Change Our Lives*. Boston, MA: Harvard Business School Press.

De Certeau, M. (1988). *The Practice of Everyday Life*, trans. S. Randall. Berkeley, CA: University of California Press.

Duguid, P. (2006). 'What *talking* tells us', *Organization Studies*, 27(12): 1794–804.

Friedman, T. L. (2006). *The Word is Flat: A Brief History of the Twenty-First Century*. New York: Farrar, Straus, & Giroux.

Lave, J. and Wenger, E. (1990). *Situated Learning: Legitimate Peripheral Participation* IRL Report IRL90 – 0013, February, Institute for Research on Learning, Palo Alto, CA.

——— (1991). *Situated Learning: Legitimate Peripheral Participation*. New York: Cambridge University Press.

Marshall, A. (1890). *Principles of Economics: An Introductory Volume*. London: Macmillan.

Nonaka, I. and Takeuchi, H. (1995). *The Knowledge-Creating Company: How Japanese Companies Create the Dynamics of Innovation*. New York: Oxford University Press.

Nonaka, I., Toyama, R., and Konno, N. (2000). 'SECI, Ba, and leadership: A unified model of dynamic knowledge creation', *Long Range Planning*, 33: 3–54.

Nonaka, I., von Krogh, I. G., and Voelpel, S. (2006). 'Organizational knowledge creation theory: Evolutionary paths and future advances', *Organization Studies*, 27(8): 1179–208.

Orr, J. (1996). *Talking about Machines: An Ethnography of a Modern Job*. Ithaca, NY: IRL Press.

Romer, P. (1993). 'Idea gaps and object gaps in economic development', *Journal of Monetary Economics*, 32(3): 543–73.

Wenger, E. (1998). *Communities of Practice: Learning, Meaning, and Identity*. Cambridge: Cambridge University Press.

—— McDermott, R., and Snyder, W. (2002). *Cultivating Communities of Practice*. Boston, MA: Harvard Business School Press.

Notes

1. I am grateful to Elizabeth Shove for both raising the question and providing me with the answers she received. I do not know who wrote what. My own definition reflected fairly closely footnote 1 of my chapter (Chapter 3) later in this book.
2. One other paper did appear before these, but as the ideas are clearly marked there as Lave and Wenger's, it claims only temporal priority (Brown, Collins, and Duguid 1989).
3. I have set aside here both Wenger (1998) and Wenger, McDermott, and Snyder (2002), though the unexplained distance between these two further exemplifies the question I am trying to explore here.
4. I do not mean only discomfiting to myself, though there was a certain challenge to telling the company that pays you how dysfunctional it is.

1

The Resurgence of Community in Economic Thought and Practice

Ash Amin and Joanne Roberts

1.1 Introduction

In their pioneering book, Jean Lave and Etienne Wenger (1991, p. 98) defined a community of practice (CoP) as 'a system of relationships between people, activities, and the world; developing with time, and in relation to other tangential and overlapping communities of practice'. They saw these relationships as central to learning, steadily incorporating 'peripheral participants' such as apprentices within a community of common expertise or focus. Wenger (1998, 2000) went on to explain the link between community and organizational learning, arguing that three factors – mutual engagement, joint enterprise, and shared repertoire – could be considered as key sources of social learning, through their encouragement of joint activity; sense of place, purpose, and shared identity; and the reconciliation of difference. Wenger was keen to stress that not all forms of joint work could be labelled as CoPs, which are marked by quite distinctive characteristics of situated practice contributing to learning (see Table 1.1).

Since the publication of Lave and Wenger's book there has been an explosion of research on CoPs and similar practice-based learning environments. For example, a database search in August 2007 for the term 'communities of practice' identified 543 publications, marked by a rapid rise in interest since the start of this decade (see Figure 1.1). Much of this literature works with definitions that are some way off the original formulations and intentions of the pioneers. The outcome, inevitably, has been a blurring of the specificities of CoPs (Mutch 2003), along with less precise explanation of the dynamics of learning and

Table 1.1: Characteristics of a community, of practice

- Sustained mutual relationships
- Shared ways of doing things together
- Rapid flow of information and propagation of innovation
- Absence of introductory preambles, conversations, and interactions as the continuation of an ongoing process
- Quick setup of a problem to be discussed
- Substantial overlap in participant awareness of who belongs
- Knowing what others know, what they can do, and how they can contribute to an enterprise
- Mutually defining identities
- Ability to assess the appropriateness of actions and products
- Specific tools, representations, and other artefacts
- Local lore, shared stories, inside jokes, and knowing laughter
- Jargon and shortcuts to communication as well as the ease of producing new ones
- Styles recognized as displaying membership
- Shared discourse reflecting a certain perspective on the world

Source: Compiled from Wenger (1998, pp. 125–6).

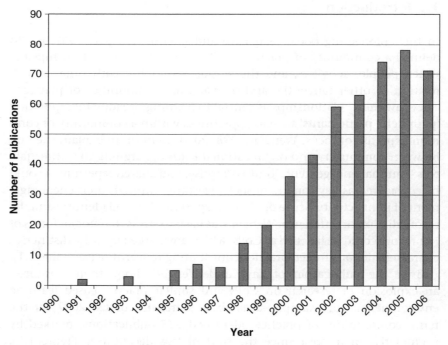

Figure 1.1: The rapid rise of publications on 'communities of practice'.

Source: *EBSCO Business Source Premier* (EBSCO), August 2007.

Note: *EBSCO Business Source Premier* provides full text for more than 2,300 journals, including full text for more than 1,100 peer-reviewed business publications. This database offers information in nearly every area of business (http://web.ebscohost.com).

knowledge formation (Handley et al. 2006) and more casual use of the word community (Lindkvist 2005; Roberts 2006). More significantly, situated practices of all manner and setting that more or less correspond to Wenger's list of characteristics are being seen as sources of learning and knowledge generation, local or spatially distributed, path-breaking or incremental, deliberate or non-intentional. How far and fast meanings and uses have changed is captured in the reflections that open and close this book by two of the founding figures, Jean Lave and Paul Duguid.

CoPs dominate the current literature, on economic creativity, organizational innovation, and local economic regeneration, as a key resource to tackle these challenges. The aim of this book is to put CoPs in their place. It does so in three senses. First, the book explores whether the knowledge and learning generated by CoPs is of a specific nature, oriented, for example, towards tacit knowing and incremental learning, rather than codified knowledge and path-breaking innovation. Second, it situates the interest in CoPs in a wider economic debate, to ask why at this particular historical conjuncture a discourse of creativity and innovation rooted in community has arisen, as well as to understand the corporate and organizational challenges raised by knowledge generation based on situated practice. Third, the book examines the spatial dynamics of CoPs and other forms of 'knowing in action' in order to address whether situated practice implies spatial proximity, and if not, what this might mean for managing spaces of creativity and maximizing returns for both local and global advantage.

An important reason for placing CoPs in context, which this chapter tackles by addressing the above-mentioned three dimensions, is that there is a paradox that needs to be explained. On the one hand, the rising interest in communities among academic researchers and practitioners has blunted the emphasis of original writing on CoPs as a distinctive kind of learning environment – one making masters out of apprentices, riddled with ambiguity, conflict, difference, and disagreement, and nurtured through everyday social practice, as Jean Lave reiterates in her contribution to this book. Different types of situated practice are now being read in the language of community, along with the assumption that CoPs are capable of generating many different types of knowledge. The complex, heterogeneous, and uncertain world of corporate and spatial creativity – a world requiring many modes of thinking and knowing and many modes of exploratory intervention – is being read as a simple, unambiguous, and easy-to-fix domain of economic creativity. As Jean Lave

13

and Paul Duguid ruefully observe, what started out as an observation on the social, complex, idiosyncratic, and contextual nature of learning and knowledge formation has ended up as a tool of analytical certitude and policy intervention: lists of factors to be ticked off, identikit tools to spot CoPs, and unambiguous steps to be taken by management.

On the other hand, the interest in CoPs is indicative of an important shift in thinking that recognizes that knowledge and creativity are born out of habituated practice (rather than competences mastered in isolation or bundles of codified knowledge unproblematically transmitted down the chain). This recognition is partly a rebuttal of old ways of thinking about knowledge, but also relates to a more general perception that capitalism – and discourses of competitive advantage – are becoming more dependent on mobilizations of knowledge, especially those embedded in the hidden and tacit qualities of situated practice. This dual aspect thus demands clarification of both the specificity of the term community of practice, and explanation of its use as a proxy for a more general shift in economic practice and thought. We address these two aspects of the paradox of community in turn, before addressing the organizational and spatial challenges posed by situated knowing.

1.2 Varieties of Situated Knowledge

There are many varieties of situated knowledge. They draw on different social, spatial, and organizational arrangements that are not reducible to the language of CoPs. For example, in a recent review of the literature on situated knowledge in varied work environments, we conclude that at least four distinctive types of knowledge 'community' should be acknowledged (Amin and Roberts 2008). There may be more types of situated knowledge and in forms that traverse the categories discussed below. A typical example is the world of big firms which seek to combine different types of situated knowledge, and for this, might be considered as a distinctive hybrid form held together by a particular mode of organization. However, with the focus held on the micro-practices of different working environments, the available evidence seems to suggest that the dynamics of craft-based (or task-based) knowing, professional knowing, high-creativity knowing, and virtual knowing differ considerably organizationally, socially, and spatially, with these differences influencing the nature of learning and innovation produced (see Table 1.2).

Table 1.2: Varieties of situated knowledge

Activity	Type of knowledge	Social interaction			Innovation	Organizational dynamics
		Proximity/nature of communication	Temporal aspects	Nature of social ties		
Craft-task-based (e.g. flute makers, artisans, insurance processors)	• Aesthetic, kinaesthetic, and embodied knowledge	• Knowledge transfer requires co-location – face-to-face communication, importance of demonstration	• Long-lived and apprenticeship-based • Developing sociocultural and institutional structures	• Interpersonal trust – mutuality through the performance of shared tasks	• Customized • Incremental	• Hierarchically managed • Open to new members
Professional (e.g. health care or education)	• Specialized expert knowledge acquired through prolonged periods of education and training • Declarative knowledge • Mind-matter and technologically embodied • Aesthetic and kinaesthetic dimensions	• Co-location required in the development of professional status for communication through demonstration. Not as important thereafter	• Long-lived and slow to change • Developing formal regulatory institutions	• Institutional trust based on professional standards of conduct	• Incremental or radical but strongly bound by institutional/professional rules • Radical innovation stimulated by contact with other communities	• Large hierarchically managed organizations or small peer-managed organizations • Institutional restrictions on the entry of new members

(*Continued*)

Table 1.2 (Continued)

Activity	Type of knowledge	Social interaction			Innovation	Organizational dynamics
		Proximity/nature of communication	Temporal aspects	Nature of social ties		
Expert or high creativity (e.g. scientists, researchers, performance artists)	• Specialized and expert knowledge, including standards and codes (including meta-codes) • Exist to extend knowledge base • Temporary creative coalitions; knowledge changing rapidly	• Spatial and/or relational proximity • Communication facilitated through a combination of face-to-face and distanciated contact	• Short-lived, drawing on institutional resources from a variety of expert/creative fields	• Trust-based on reputation and expertise • Weak social ties	• High energy • Radical innovation	• Group-/project-managed • Open to those with a reputation in the field • Management through intermediaries and boundary objects
Virtual (e.g. software developers, online groups, open-source communities)	• Codified and tacit from codified • Exploratory and exploitative	• Social interaction mediated through technology (face-to-screen) • Distanciated communication • Rich web-based anthropology	• Long- and short-lived • Developing through fast and asynchronous interaction	• Weak social ties • Reputational trust • Object orientation	• Incremental and radical	• Carefully managed by community moderators or technological sequences • Open, but self-regulating

Source: Amin and Roberts (2008).

The four types of knowledge work are characterized, for example, by distinct modes of social interaction. In task-craft-based communities, social interaction and knowledge exchange are located in practices of close interpersonal and physical proximity, as theorized by the original literature on CoPs. These are communities distinguished in the mediations of particular artefacts, tools, and work environments, kinaesthetic and aesthetic awareness acquired through the mastery of certain tasks in a shared division of labour, and the sociality of familiarity, talk, trust, and mutual support. At the opposite end of the spectrum, social interaction in virtual environments of creative engagement is mediated through various face-to-screen ethnographies, which, in turn, support practices of knowing that are much more reliant on distributed expertise and authority, light forms of sociality structured around joint endeavour rather than interpersonal familiarity, and a well-managed architecture of information management and conflict resolution (as demonstrated by Juan Mateos-Garcia and Edward Steinmueller with reference to large open-source communities in Chapter 10). In contrast, the knowledge practices of professional communities – health workers or teachers, for example – are mediated by institutional or professional loyalties, lengthy periods of training to master a given canon of thought and practice, and on-the-job social and material engagements similar to those in craft communities. Accordingly, relationality is the combination of workplace proximities as well as ties maintained at a distance through strong institutional and professional allegiances. In turn, expert and high-creativity communities, which are primarily concerned with creating new knowledge, have very different social arrangements, often structured around clearly defined and short-lived projects, underpinned by weak and multiple social ties, trust and loyalty based on professional and personal reputation, and an organizational architecture deliberately designed for contingent learning and reflexive deliberation (as shown by Harry Scarbrough and Jacky Swan in Chapter 6 on project-based innovation).

These variations of social practice have a direct bearing on the nature and centrality of knowledge and innovation in a grouping. For example, expert communities, which bring together highly specialized individuals explicitly to develop new knowledge, are deliberately organized to unlock frontier knowledge (as shown in Chapter 7 by Aurélie Delemarle and Phillipe Larédo relating to a group of scientists supported by the European Union (EU) to develop breakthrough innovations). The collaborative arrangements and dynamics that bring physicists, molecular biologists, and strategic policymakers together are designed to harness new creative energy with the help of agreed epistemic goals and structured projects (Haas 1992; Knorr-Cetina 1999). Social interaction is the servant of knowledge exploration. This is not the case with professional communities or task/craft communities such as flute makers, technicians, or insurance claims administrators, which are more concerned with the preservation of skills and professional integrity, along with incremental innovations that increase the utility and design of product or practice (Cook and Yanow 1993; Orr 1996). Learning and knowledge generation form part of a much wider set of social practices, often operating in tacit and non-explicit ways, and underpinned by social dynamics geared largely towards incremental change. While it would be wrong to portray such communities as simply reproducing existing knowledge, since the cultivation of quality and product 'elegance' lies at their heart, organizing for path-breaking creativity is not a central purpose.

Given these varieties of social conduct, organization, and creative outcome, it makes little sense to use the term 'community of practice' as a proxy for all types of situated knowledge (Brown and Duguid 1991). Such standardization contradicts the emphasis placed on fine-grain and context by the turn towards situated practice in explaining learning and knowledge formation – a turn that set out to show that economic creativity could not be treated in formulaic ways. At the very least, if current fashion continues, the word 'community' could be adjectively prefixed by words such as 'epistemic', 'professional', 'expert', 'craft', 'task', 'high-creativity', or 'virtual' to reveal the many ways of knowing by doing.

1.3 Community, Economy, and Creativity

Despite the variegated nature of situated practice, the general turn to community in interpreting economic creativity still needs to be explained. Why, in an age of big corporations, impersonal markets, organized learning, comprehensive regulation, global integration, and acquisitive self-interest, has an interest in community come to the fore? As already hinted, this interest is not reducible to nostalgia for another age of community-based economic organization, local industrial districts, craft cultures, and strong social ties (Sennett 1999). Instead, ideas of community are appearing in contemporary accounts of market behaviour, economic creativity, and capitalist reinvention, and on the basis of arguments that are more than wishful thinking. Practices of community, in various guises, are being situated at the very frontier of the market economy. The three opening chapters address different aspects of this conundrum.

First, new writing linking community to the market economy is beginning to question the assumption held by orthodox economic theories that organization by community is both counter-efficient and anachronistic. These theories, as Michael Storper summarizes in Chapter 2, associate community with rent-seeking behaviour, conservatism, and insider–outsider conflicts, all seen to frustrate free expression of preferences as well as market apprehension of individual choice. The outcome, it is claimed, is market distortion, reduced efficiency, and impeded uptake of growth opportunities – deficiencies that historically have been overcome by the replacement of governance by community with governance by impersonal institutions. This reading is in sharp contrast to the view held in socio-economic perspectives on the economy that communities can build trust, transactional capability, and associative skills, along with inter-mediating effectively between institutions and markets. Here, community is seen to support market efficiency and growth as a source of social capital.

Storper takes the case for community a step further by going to the heart of the emphasis in mainstream economic theory on individual agency and impersonal exchange. He does so by arguing firstly that interpersonal ties often lubricate impersonal markets by originating rules of exchange or by providing contact networks; secondly that communities can help individuals to discover their preferences by defining and making sense of situations in which agents find themselves; thirdly that communities can provide agency and voice in realizing preferences, since these are never fully transparent; and fourthly that communities can help individual agents to make more efficient choices than they might on their own by providing additional decision-making signals and filters.

Community, thus, along with other calculative intermediaries such as accounting conventions and economic theory itself (Callon 1998), can be seen as an active agent of market making and as a tool to help economic actors to negotiate their way. To this, we might add that, as an economic metaphor in its own right, community can act as a powerful signal of a particular kind of market economy, a proxy perhaps for the 'economy of qualities' (Callon et al. 2002), or for conventions of consumption and exchange that are not hedonistic or individualist (Boltanski and Thevénot 2006). 'Community' can define market behaviour, regardless of whether the 'rationality' of markets is distorted by the historical encumbrances of community, as mainstream economic theory would have. Indeed, as Deirdre McCloskey (2006) has argued, legitimacy for the idea of the market economy has depended historically on communitarian concepts such as sympathy, trust, and obligation to reconcile the individual and impersonal with the social and mutual, with both sides considered essential for market efficiency and general prosperity. In short, community is both consistent with market principles and formative as a signal of particular modes of market conduct.

This potentiality extends to economic creativity, as we have already seen, through practices of social interaction and collaboration acting as the spark of specific types of learning, knowledge formation, and innovation. Paul Duguid in Chapter 3 criticizes economic thinking that stresses codified knowledge or individual capability for failing to understand that tacit knowledge is the medium through which codified knowledge itself and individual expertise are activated and given practical meaning. Following Michael Polanyi, Duguid writes of the 'art of knowing', located in lived, material practices of doing, engaging, and communicating – practices that instantiate capabilities, experience, and learning through focused application to unlock creativity. This insight has become the baseline in sociological and ethnographic thinking on economic creativity, merging with exciting new thinking revealing the neurological, sensory, and embodied dimensions of perception and cognition. This work shows how affect shapes attitudes, moods, and creative propensities; how objects, bodies, brains, and digitally mediated machines form an unbroken chain of knowledge practice; and how the latter, in turn, weaves together embodied ability and the specifics of location (Lakoff and Johnson 1999; Amin and Cohendet 2004; Hayles 2006; Barsade and Gibson 2007; Ignatow 2007). It has unveiled a rich bricolage of human and non-human inputs which, in combination, and through situated practice, make knowing and its use for invention and innovation possible.

Duguid returns to the significance of community to this process. He makes two significant claims. First, he argues that community – shared practice with others – establishes a circular relationship between learning *about*, learning *how*, and learning *to be*. Community not only makes knowing come to the fore as a useful and tangible output, but it also puts the know-how of the individual and the group on display, along with ensuring that individuals learn to become knowledgeable partners. Community enriches the knowledge chain. Second, he argues that practices of community can be seen as a form of ethical inculcation, a willingness to share and contribute to joint venture even when the personal incentives for doing so are negligible. This is not a disposition that can be traced to altruism or expectation of future reward, but is the product of the practice itself of joint endeavour and engagement with others in a common project. Much of this operates at a precognitive level. Adenzato and Garbarini (2006, p. 755), for example, claim that in a shared functional space 'characterized by automatic, unconscious embodied simulation routines', a neurological response of 'resonance' is stimulated, which 'allows us to harmonize other people's actions with our own and to attune our own actions with those of other people, thereby establishing empathetic understanding between the observer and observed' (ibid.). Such 'being together in the world and understanding each other' (ibid.), we would argue, achieves more than facilitating understanding. It also opens new modes of interactive know-how through empathetic disposition towards both the known and the unknown.

Community acts as a mechanism of 'worlding', a keyword in Nigel Thrift's contribution (Chapter 4), which links the discourse of community to the discourse of knowledge capitalism. It has become commonplace to assume that ours is the age of competitive survival through the knowledge economy, based on producing and selling knowledge, renewing products and processes, unlocking creativity, upgrading skills and competences, exploiting intelligent machines and digital technologies, and commodifying thought itself. Those who can place themselves at the forefront of science, technology, and research; mobilize intelligence, creativity, and learning; infuse products with design and intelligence; and respond quickly to changing markets and new opportunities, are expected to reap the benefits of the knowledge economy. This is the repeated mantra of scholarly work on contemporary capitalism, as it is of practitioners and policymakers urging the business community, educational and research institutions, and society in general to change their ways. Even the most mundane of markets are urged to upgrade, track markets intelligently, and engage in symbolic manipulation. In this brave new world, the difference between knowing and not knowing, between invention and presumption, between creativity and the tried-and-tested, between reflexivity and reflex, is the difference between surviving or not in the economy. There is no middle way, even in the low-income countries, which are obliged in the medium to long term to prepare for the low-cost knowledge economy.

The discourse of community can be linked to this rhetoric of no escape from the imperatives of the knowledge economy – imperatives that need not work in favour of those with the highest knowledge, financial, or corporate endowments. It is a discourse of hope for the many rather than the few, allowing visualization of CoPs – between the small individual and the large organization – as new sites of competitive and innovative possibility drawing on situated practice to respond flexibly and lightly to the fast-changing global economy (Miyazaki 2006). It supports the idea that those who can work on the fine-grain of creativity based on social collaboration and interaction will also prosper, ensuring that the knowledge economy comes with distributed gains. It suggests that the promise of knowledge capitalism will not degenerate into a doom-laden story of evermore economic concentration and centralization, despite evidence to the contrary showing either how many a large organizations work CoPs to the bone and undermine their energy, or how markets continue to reward firms able to exploit transactional efficiency, corporate power, and technological or protected know-how. Between community and market/knowledge returns lies a raft of political and organizational intermediaries influencing allocation, as Lave acknowledges in the Epilogue.

It is not difficult to puncture the myth of community in the new knowledge economy, but less convincingly so if seen as a world-making exercise, as a way of making and sensing a new inhabitable map of economy and economic presence, as Thrift argues in his chapter. He sees the turn to CoPs as part and parcel of a broader sweep to re-engineer knowledge capitalism as the domain of systematic knowledge made tacit and then re-systematized through new projections and new methods that privilege being-in-togetherness. Thrift writes of how the corporate world has moved to a language of 'decisive moments', broken and unbroken connections, and semiotic construction of the economic environment, to be grasped through communities that simulate passion, desire, market direction, and invention; then mapped back onto the world as the pulse of economic worth. He argues, in turn, that the economic ontology being forced through these varied practices consists of new methods themselves mirroring the fast, intimate, affective, ethnographic, symbolic, and visual modes of apprehension of CoPs. Thus, thought itself, mirrored in the image of what is assumed to be practice, is operating on the world as a tool of categorization and intervention.

1.4 Organizing for Creativity

Integral to the move of the corporate world to 'decisive moments' has been a recognition of CoPs – and situated knowledge in general – as a mode of encouraging new learning and innovation. Private firms and public organizations are becoming increasingly interested in harnessing the creative energies of distributed sets of people united by common tasks, capabilities, and projects. A whole new language and practice of knowledge management, rolled out by business consultants, schools of management, iconic figures, publications, and manuals, has come to the fore with the promise of renewal through situated learning and knowing (Amin and Roberts 2007). As a consequence, the social and the communitarian – however defined – have returned to the heart of thinking on competitive advantage and capitalist creativity. This return forms part of a broader, and largely intuited sense that centralized command and control, hierarchy, rule-based reflex, reliance on technical and codified knowledge, no longer suffice in an economy marked by: shortened product, process, and technological cycles; increased interconnectivity and dependence between economic agents; heightened risk, uncertainty, and volatility in markets; intelligence, design, and anticipation inscribed in various domains of economic life; valuations themselves of economic worth that increasingly privilege knowledge and knowledgeability.

The search for new ways of harnessing distributed social intelligence to address – often unknowingly – these new challenges seems to have developed in two main directions. First, organizations are taking a fresh look at their internal resources, seeking ways to channel the creative energies of their employees and divisions in new ways (Amabile 1997, 1998; Woodman et al. 1993). This has brought an interesting range of sites into relief for intervention, including organizational climate, leadership style, organizational culture, resource and skills, and the structure and systems of an organization (Andriopoulos 2001). It is felt that the manipulation of such factors will help to cultivate creativity. So, for example, organizations are purposefully seeking to engineer informality, iterative purposefulness, and productive idleness, in order to unlock new social energies and improvisations by deliberately building in organizational slack and redundancy (Hatch 1999; Yanow 2001; Grabher 2004; Thompson 2005). After so many years of close corporate monitoring of employees and elaborate measures to eliminate idleness, autonomy, and sociality, this revaluation of independent social energy is widely perceived as a progressive development of equal benefit to employees and employers. Yet, it also comes with new risks. For example, as the social is nurtured in the workplace, work comes to dominate every aspect of the social, resulting in forms of premature employee burnout, all in the name of social autonomy; or, as authority becomes decentred, groups come to be terrified by the responsibility of self-management in a setting of performance-driven, goal-oriented, and inter-group rivalry with unclear and shifting rules of management and accountability (Stark 2007).

Second, organizations are identifying external knowledge opportunities through, for example, alliances and exchanges of various sorts with key competitors, small start-up companies, university spin-offs, consumer interest groups, professional associations, and social networks (including non-commercial hobby groups or e-forums such as YouTube or MySpace), actively in search of opportunities for corporate learning and access to knowledge diversity. Indeed, as Stark (2007) notes, continual search, diversity of evaluative principles, and rivalry between different knowledge domains are becoming the operative terms of knowledge production. The intensity of competition – normally a stimulant of self-preservation – is forcing firms and organizations to cross traditional ownership and functional boundaries to exploit the advantages of recombinant knowledge. This includes looking for ways in which social motivation for engaging in creative activity in non-commercial spheres, drawing on pleasure and intellectual stimulation, opportunities for creative self-expression, learning and sharing new insights, altruism, or reputation can be reconciled with the commercial imperative to harness creativity with tangible economic benefits.

In this quest for organization as a loosely held ecology of competing and complementary knowing worlds, the idea of organization by community has come increasingly into prominence as a management tool. Firms and non-commercial organizations are busily converting internal divisions and hierarchies into many job-specific or project-specific communities placed in more or less equal relationship with each other. They are also actively encouraging the CoPs and other domains of corporate organization to cultivate external links that enhance the possibility of new learning and new forms of creative discovery (see, for example, Wenger and Snyder 2000; Wenger et al. 2002; Saint-Onge and Wallace 2003). Recognizing, however, that a universe of CoPs can impede convergence and coherence, conflict with strategic and transactional imperatives (which might require more a hierarchical or certainly different mode of organization and governance), and become locked into embedded routines resistant to change, organizations are also looking for new ways of managing complex knowledge networks over which they only ever have partial and temporary authority. This includes exploring organizational repertoires that facilitate sharing, overlap, and inculcation into a common agenda (Wenger 1998), as well as developing agile tools of horizontal integration and network management including the use of boundary-spanning devices, project-based teams, asynchronous experiments, and effort to construct a spatial commons. These latter experiments, along with their achievements and limitations, are explored by the chapters in the second half of the book.

For example, Bart Nooteboom (Chapter 5) explains that bridging cognitive distance between CoPs is not straightforward, especially when the latter are formed explicitly to break free of established routines. He argues that cognitive distance tends to be small within and between communities engaged in path-dependent innovation, but larger within and between communities organized for exploratory innovation, dependent, as they are, upon dissonance, ambiguity, and creative tension between cognitive 'strangers'. Bridging cognitive distance, thus, cannot compromise cognitive variety, which partly explains why certain organizations have begun to look at boundary-spanning devices (e.g. spatial design or strategic meetings) and individuals (e.g. brokers and intermediaries) to facilitate interaction without disturbing the delicate balance between cognitive distance and cognitive proximity. He suggests that a richer analysis of exploitative and exploratory innovation requires the inclusion of a wider variety of learning groups both within and between organizations, including CoPs, epistemic communities, and professional communities. For it is the inter-organizational relationships between such groups that help to inhibit organizational myopia.

Project work is one form of boundary interaction emerging as an important tool of organizing for, and managing, diversity, based on temporary coalitions established explicitly to develop new knowledge by bringing together experts from different backgrounds to work on specific goals. The fruits of such interaction are expected to be imported back into the respective domains and spark a culture shift in organizational priorities in general. However, as Scarbrough and Swan note in Chapter 6, the greater the novelty of a project, the greater is the scope for learning. By taking a practice-based approach to projects, they shed light on the important connections and overlaps between projects and existing CoPs within and between organizations. These links are seen both as sources of learning and innovation based on recombinant knowledge and as a mode of organizational alignment. Projects can act as a catalyst for the development of new CoPs and can bring about radical breakthroughs in practice. Yet, the spread of such breakthroughs may be blocked by the embeddedness of existing practices. Consequently, as Scarbrough and Swan show, new knowledge arising from project work does not always ventilate through to different CoPs or the wider organizational environment.

In some arenas in which experimental knowledge is considered vital for survival and advancement, the cultivation of 'managed dissonance' and ambiguity is becoming part of the organizational repertoire (Stark 1999). Making such cultivation effective is by no means easy or guaranteed, sometimes because the full chain of connection between exploration and exploitation is poorly managed or cannot be managed, as Aurélie Delemarle and Philippe Larédo reveal in Chapter 7, describing an EU-organized venture to bring about breakthrough innovation in the scientific and technological arena of microchip design. They consider Asynchronous Circuit Design (ACiD), an inter-organizational epistemic community which did succeed in mobilizing difference and dissonance to produce breakthrough innovation, but was unable to secure its exploitation. Exploitation depended on specific public sector incentives to promote the widespread acceptance and uptake of the new standards, but this did not occur. The example demonstrates the significance of securing reach in broad terms, to include – in this case – regulatory changes that play a central role in supporting the chain of economic creativity from start to finish.

Experiments in spatial alignment are another way in which firms and organizations have begun to recombine cognitive variety, by exploiting both the offerings of geographical proximity and virtual means to gather and hold dispersed competence. The question of how the creative dissonance and 'buzz' at the core of learning and inventive social behaviour can be achieved in the absence of spatial proximity is addressed by Meric Gertler in Chapter 8. He argues that the interplay between dispersed CoPs and project teams can yield fruitful results if strong social affinities can be built at a distance. Such relational proximity can then bridge cognitive distance, ensuring that the 'buzz' of 'being there' necessary for creative engagement can be achieved through combinations of face-to-face and technologically mediated interaction. The capacity to bridge distance in this way allows organizations to recombine competences in new and varied ways, thereby expanding the creative resources from which new profit opportunities may be developed.

In Chapter 9 on knowledge generation in the creative industries of Montréal, Patrick Cohendet and Laurent Simon illustrate the challenges of organizing for dissonance in the context of a division of labour between communities, firms, and intermediaries in the same location. Noting the rich interconnections facilitating the circulation and combination of knowledge in a locally integrated but heterogeneous network, Cohendet and Simon argue that a distinctive mode of knowledge organization and management has evolved, involving considerable local interdependencies. They show how increasingly a core competence of knowledge-intensive firms is becoming that of developing creative slack through multi-project activities, delegating the building of creative capabilities to local actors in the city. This is a division of labour that allows speedy and flexible response to changing market and knowledge demands, but it is also one that reduces the ability of firms to rely on traditional mechanisms of authority and control, such as property rights or hierarchical tools of management, to secure guaranteed returns.

Whatever the managerial challenges associated with these varied examples of recombinance, alignment, translation, and spillover, it is clear that organizing for creativity demands a rethinking of the traditional models of organization based on hierarchy and transactional efficiency alone. It is widely recognized that such organization is ill-suited for the customized, flexible, and knowledge-intensive economy. Organizational slack and flexibility is required to exploit situated knowledge, and considerable two-way communication, horizontal and vertical, is needed to align dispersed and varied knowledge environments. Organization itself – in the form of inherited architectures, competing modes, and accepted norms – is getting in the way, even if the governance arrangements of situated practice are far from clearly understood.

David Stark (2007) has suggested 'heterarchy' as the metaphor for organization in the twenty-first century – a new logic of organizing characterized by minimal hierarchy and organizational heterogeneity, suited to harnessing and managing diversity in effective and flexible ways:

[H]eterarchy represents an organizational form of distributed intelligence in which units are laterally accountable according to diverse principles of evaluation. In contrast to the vertical authority of hierarchies, heterarchies are characterized by more cross-cutting network structures, reflecting the greater interdependencies of complex collaboration. They are heterarchical, moreover, because there is no hierarchical ordering of the competing evaluative principles. (p. 10)

According to Stark, organization by networks composed of autonomous units of competence and capability is dissolving boundaries external and internal to firms and organizations, in the process unlocking energy and inventiveness based on making assets out of ambiguity, distributed pragmatic reflexivity, and active rivalry between competing evaluative principles.

Management, in this context, is becoming the art of facilitating organizations that can reorganize themselves, according to Stark, looking for ways in which variety and ambiguity can be kept in play, developing tools of search and recognition quick to grasp emerging fruits of distributed exploration, constantly regrouping assets and redrawing boundaries, and negotiating the tension between cooperation and rivalry and between autonomy and control (see also Grabher and Ibert 2006). What this means on the ground is by no means clear, as firms and organizations come to consider their options, still tied to the expectation of increasing returns, easy exit when the chips are down, and the reflex to own or appropriate when new inventions yield dividends. If the condition of heterarchy is redefining the firm, as a resource base for experimentation and improvisation, as a broker of recombinance and dissonance, or as a manager of interdependencies and relational practices, what then remains of the will to own, control, accumulate, and maximize in capitalism? In a new world of increasing separation of ownership from organization, and transactional efficiency from economic inventiveness, few templates exist to guide firms on what to allocate internally and externally, how to manage relational interdependence, and how best to survive in the economy of values. The explorations of situated practice, managed ambiguity, ties that bridge but do not bind, and community mobilizers, can be seen as experimental lurches into an unknown that has yet to reveal its organizational hand in the way that hierarchy did in the twentieth century.

1.5 The Spaces of Situated Knowing

One of the major dilemmas of organization posed by the rise of distributed learning and knowing, crossing boundaries of various kinds, relates to space. In early work on CoPs, it was assumed that relational proximity and spatial proximity were one and the same. Learning and knowing by doing meant face-to-face contact and other forms of relational proximity facilitated by co-location. It is still largely assumed by practitioners that CoPs and other forms of situated practice privilege spatial proximity. Thus, firms and organizations plan for innovation through tight-knit work groups, assuming that the main challenge lies in joining up local know-how (as we have already seen), while regional actors trying to rebuild their local economies grasp the concept of CoPs as an opportunity to strengthen local ties to unlock tacit knowing, learning by doing, and social creativity.

Among researchers of situated practice, the discussion on space has moved on, notably in light of the rise of digital technologies facilitating relational proximity without spatial proximity. However, the debate continues to remain two-dimensional, polarized around a 'local versus global' dualism, with some pioneers such as Wenger (1998) recognizing that CoPs can be both locally based and distributed, and others such as Brown and Duguid (2000) arguing that the social life of information still requires a texture of co-presence to maximize knowledge returns. Similarly, in economic geography there has been a vigorous debate on the geography of tacit knowledge networks – with some insisting on the centrality of local embedding and others emphasizing relational ties in trans-local networks (see Amin and Cohendet 2004, for a summary). More recently, however, both sides have begun to acknowledge (as Gertler shows in Chapter 8) that situated practice comes in many spatial forms and intensities, involving entanglements of knowledge that cannot be reduced to the local/global choice (see also Lorenzen 2005; Boschma 2005).

Gertler also reveals the significance of grasping the active work that goes into sustaining relational proximity at various spatial scales and in varying spatial forms (including institutional, material, and logistic forces, in addition to those underpinning social interaction), instead of automatically assuming that given spatial configurations come with distinctive relational attributes. This is made amply evident by Mateos-Garcia and Steinmueller (Chapter 10), who show how open-source networks require specific tools such as technical complexity and careful network design to be effective, but also continual adjustment to manage the conflicts of open access. Sometimes such effort includes surprising inputs, such as far-located policy incentives, as Delemarle and Larédo show in Chapter 7 to reveal the hidden hand of a significant EU initiative. 'Being there' does not mean the same thing in different relational spaces, because each one draws of varied and specific inputs of situated practice.

One consequence, therefore, of this new spatial awareness has been an expanded understanding of the geography of situated knowing, now struggling towards naming different spaces, their texture, and their learning and innovation outcomes. This is an understanding showing how the varied spatial configurations of social practice come with specific properties, instead of flattening difference by claiming, for example, that spatial and relational proximity are equivalent and therefore substitutable. They patently are not. 'Being there' in relational ties is dependent upon an elaborate texture of organizational, technological, and informational intermediaries, which work in quite different ways to the intermediations of face, familiarity, and shared territory in ties dependent on spatial proximity. It is more than likely that these differences of communicative texture have a bearing not only on learning and knowledge practices, but also on outcomes. This said, it is also worth remembering that 'being there' is never reliant on single or nested spatial forms, but is a continuum of many spatial configurations of interactive practice, from face-to-face exchange to the exchange and interpretation of signs and talk across vast distances. Space is made through social practice, tracing a topography that not only exceeds but also thoroughly hybridizes the spaces we chose to define as cities and regions or corporate networks and virtual space. This is precisely why Scarbrough and Swan are able to confirm that the geography of project teams combines intense local proximity for short periods, with dispersal and distant connectivity. Similarly, as Cohendet and Simon show, in Montreal – a city full of intermediaries such as artists, musicians, research communities, specialist media, event organizers, and hospitality providers – active interaction with these intermediaries is an intrinsic component of the global knowledge chain of large creative firms located in the city.

To insist on a spatial ontology of knowledge that is set free from territorial reductionism is not to disregard the significance of urban, regional, and national space. Distributed knowledge networks that consist of transnational connections, satellite communications, and routine flows between places always intersect with territorially supplied inputs. We have learnt this from the research on learning regions, which insists on the centrality of local associational economies in the form of institutional support, inter-firm dependencies and local social capital, and we have learnt this from the research on tacit knowledge, which shows that situated practice is always dependent upon local ties, be they intense interactions between people or those between face and screen in an office buzzing with silent sociality. It is the combination of interactions in network space, corporate space, and regional space that defines the geography of situated knowledge.

The critical analytical and policy question – one which we are still far from fully understanding – is why in some places these combinations allow for increasingly local returns, while in others they benefit distant others. Does this have something to do with the strategic centrality of the CoPs in that location, for example, their place in a corporate knowledge hierarchy or their autonomy from corporate constraints, such that local ties can be freely explored? Does it have something to do with the weakness or peripheral nature of trans-local ties, forcing greater emphasis on 'being there' through local explorations? Does it have something to do with the presence of local intermediaries, as Cohendet and Simon seem to be suggesting, such that corporations come to locate 'higher-order' functions and knowledge tasks in these locations, deliberately to take advantage of a rich supply chain that also benefits many other local firms? These are the kinds of questions prompted – but only barely addressed – by the varied spatial tracings of situated knowledge in this book.

One final observation on space can be made. An important reason for not forcing situated knowledge into predefined spatial formations is the need to remain attentive to how the birth pains of the new knowledge economy might involve new modes of apprehending space. This is the central argument in Thrift's chapter. The turn to situated practice among researchers, practitioners, cartographers, and methodologists might be seen as a way of rolling out a different model of space in which environments 'animated' by situated practice come to be seen as necessary for economic organization as well as apprehending the knowledge economy. For Thrift, this coupling of new methods and new modes of interaction breaks sharply from a hitherto dominant mode of territorially based organization and interpretation of the world; a cartographic mode dictating the arrangement of inputs and measures of success. The new mode, instead, consists of working with 'inhabitable' maps drawing on many spontaneities of creative animation and sensing, and many spatial entities, including code, simulation, animated visualization, networks, affective communities, and virtual spaces. This proliferation of animated space and space that can be brought to life by situated practice of some shape can be seen as the engineering of new sites, measures, and disciplines of 'knowledge capitalism', a process of spatial opening to close down the old and the ill-fitting.

1.6 Conclusion

The discourse of community has returned to thinking about markets, economic creativity, organization, and space, centred on the idea of knowing and learning through situated practice. This development, we argue in this book, is both an opening and a closure. It is a closure if it loses sight of context, specificity, and legacy when invoked as a mantle for all seasons. Many types of knowledge practice not reducible to the language of community, indeed even to the language of situated practice, risk becoming understood as essentially the same. A new emphasis on the tacit and embedded, for example, risks displacing the salience of the codified and the disembedded, leaving us puzzled about what to make of the hard facts of science, technology, patents, and knowledge possessed and protected.

In turn, new forms of institutional and spatial organization – decentred, distributive, collaborative, non-hierarchical, flexible – being ushered in by a new economy of practice, are making older forms contained in territorial and corporate boundaries seem like anachronisms, somehow out of date and less powerful. Yet, the dynamics and returns of the knowledge economy still traceable to regulatory regimes; systems of innovation enshrined in the national educational, scientific, industrial, infrastructural, and policy environment; and the organized structures of research institutions, corporations, and industrial clusters continue to make themselves felt. The air of democracy and sociality suggested by the idea of situated practice is not one that flows freely.

On the other hand, the turn to community stands to radically alter thinking and practice relating to the knowledge economy. We can begin to understand why, as Storper argues, economic imperatives of many kinds and community need not be antagonists. We can begin to see the shape of a new stage of capitalism as well as some of its organizational and rhetorical foundations. We can anticipate how the language and measures of animated practice will come to frame calculation and classification. And we can glimpse at a new republic of organization and reward. In this regard, community – whatever its precisions and shades – can be taken as a keyword to grasp a new means by which every last drop of creative energy is put to economic use and competitive gain.

This is a paradoxical development, one that has to value situated autonomy and the energies of social interaction, but also put into place organizational forms that can harness and channel the creative outcomes, potentially killing off the goose that lays the golden egg. The world of situated practice liberates space and economy from many earlier moorings, but for how long before new fixtures of organization can re-establish the political economy of gain and pain, freedom and constrain, that capitalism depends on, remains to be seen.

References

Adenzato, M. and Garbarini, F. (2006). 'The *as if* in cognitive science, neuroscience and anthropology: a journey among robots, blacksmiths and neurons', *Theory and Psychology*, 16(6): 747–59.

Amabile, T. M. (1997). 'Motivating creativity in organizations: on doing what you love and loving what you do', *California Management Review*, 40(1): 39–58.

—— (1998). 'How to kill creativity', *Harvard Business Review*, 76(5): 77–87.

Amin, A. and Cohendet, P. (2004). *Architectures of Knowledge: Firms, Capabilities, and Communities*. Oxford: Oxford University Press.

—— and Roberts, J. (2007). 'Communities of practice? Varieties of situated learning', background paper prepared for the EU Network of Excellence, Dynamics of Institutions and Markets in Europe (DIME), available from: http://cops.dime-eu.org/files/active/0/Amin_Roberts.pdf

—— —— (2008). 'Knowing in action: beyond communities of practice', *Research Policy*, 37(2): 353–69.

Andriopoulos, C. (2001). 'Determinants of organisational creativity: A literature review', *Management Decision*, 39(10): 834–40.

Barsade, S. G. and Gibson, D. E. (2007). 'Why does affect matter in organizations?' *Academy of Management Perspectives*, February: 36–59.

Boltanski, L. and Thevénot, L. (2006). *On Justification: Economies of Worth*. Princeton, NJ: Princeton University Press.

Boschma R. A. (2005). 'Proximity and innovation: A critical assessment', *Regional Studies*, 39(1): 61–74.

Brown, J. S. and Duguid, P. (1991). 'Organizational learning and communities of practice: Towards a unified view of working, learning and innovation', *Organization Science*, 2: 40–57.

—— —— (2000). *The Social Life of Information*. Boston, MA: Harvard Business School Press.

Callon, M. (ed.) (1998). *The Laws of the Markets*. London: Blackwell.

—— Mèadel, C., and Rabeharisoa, A. (2002). 'The economy of qualities', *Economy and Society*, 31(2): 194–217.

Cook, S. and Yanow, D. (1993). 'Culture and organizational learning', *Journal of Management Inquiry*, 2(4): 373–90.

Grabher, G. (2004). 'Temporary architectures of learning: knowledge governance in project ecologies', *Organization Studies*, 25(9): 1491–514.

—— and Ibert, O. (2006). 'Bad company? The ambiguity of personal knowledge networks', *Journal of Economic Geography*, 6: 251–71.

Haas, P. (1992). 'Introduction: Epistemic communities and international policy coordination', *International Organization*, 46(1): 1–37.

Handley, K., Sturdy, A., Fincham, R., Clark, T. (2006). 'Within and beyond communities of practice: Making sense of learning through participation, identity and practice', *Journal of Management Studies*, 43(3): 641–53.

Hatch, M. J. (1999). 'Exploring the empty spaces of organizing: How improvisational jazz helps redescribe organizational structure', *Organization Studies*, 20(1): 75–100.

Hayles, N. K. (2006). 'Unfinished work: From cyborg to cognisphere', *Theory, Culture and Society*, 23(7–8): 159–66.

Ignatow, G. (2007). 'Theories of embodied knowledge: New directions for cultural and cognitive sociology?', *Journal for the Theory of Social Behaviour*, 37(2): 115–35.

Knorr-Cetina, K. (1999). *Epistemic Cultures: How the Sciences Make Sense*. Chicago, IL: Chicago University Press.

Lakoff, G. and Johnson, M. (1999). *Philosophy in the Flesh*. New York: Basic Books.

Lave, J. and Wenger, E. (1991). *Situated Learning: Legitimate Peripheral Articipation*. Cambridge: Cambridge University Press.

Lindkvist, L. (2005). 'Knowledge communities and knowledge collectivities: A typology of knowledge work in groups', *Journal of Management Studies*, 42(6): 1189–210.

Lorenzen, M. (2005). 'Introduction: Knowledge and geography', *Industry and Innovation*, 12(4): 399–407.

McCloskey, D. (2006). *The Bourgeois Virtues: Ethics for an Age of Commerce*. Chicago, IL: University of Chicago Press.

Miyazaki, H. (2006) 'Economy of dreams: Hope in global capitalism and its critiques *Cultural Anthropology*, 21(2): 147–72.

Mutch, A. (2003). 'Communities of practice and habitus: A critique', *Organization Studies*, 24(3): 383–401.

Orr, J. E. (1996). *Talking about Machines: An Ethnography of a Modern Job*. Ithaca, NY and London: IRL Press an imprint of Cornell University Press.

Roberts, J. (2006). 'Limits to communities of practice', *Journal of Management Studies*, 43(3): 623–39.

Saint-Onge, H. and Wallace, D. (2003). *Leveraging Communities of Practice for Strategic Advantage*. London and New York: Butterworth-Heinemann.

Sennett, R. (1999). *The Corrosion of Character: The Personal Consequences of Work in the New Capitalism*. New York and London: W.W. Norton.

Stark, D. (1999). 'Heterarchy: Distributing authority and organizing diversity', in J. H. Clippinger (ed.), *The Biology of Business: Decoding the Natural Laws of Enterprise*. London: Jossey-Bass, 153–79.

—— (2007). *For a Sociology of Worth*. Princeton, NJ: Princeton University Press, forthcoming.

Thompson, M. (2005). 'Structural and epistemic parameters in communities of practice', *Organization Science*, 16(2): 151–64.

Wenger, E. (2000). 'Communities of practice and social learning systems', *Organization*, 7(2): 225–46.

Wenger, E. C. (1998). *Communities of Practice: Learning, Meaning, and Identity*. Cambridge: Cambridge University Press.

—— and Snyder, W. M. (2000). 'Communities of practice: The organizational frontier', *Harvard Business Review*, 78(1): 139–45.

—— McDermott, R., and Snyder, W. M. (2002). *Cultivating Communities of Practice: A Guide to Managing Knowledge*. Boston, MA: Harvard Business School Press.

Woodman, R. W., Sawyer, J. E., and Griffin, R. W. (1993). 'Towards a theory of organizational creativity', *Academy of Management Review*, 18(2): 293–321.

Yanow, D. (2001). 'Learning in and from improvising: Lessons from theater for organizational learning', *Reflections*, 2(4): 58–65.

PART I

Community, Creativity, and Economy

2

Community and Economics[1]

Michael Storper

2.1 Should Community Have a Bad Name?

'Community' generally has a bad name in economics and allied social sciences. Since Mancur Olson, we associate groups – everything ranging from informal, traditional communities to organized groups – with a range of growth-limiting vices, including rent-seeking and blocking of change (Olson 1965). A second negative view of groups comes from several sources, including public choice theory, the economics of information, and contract theory. It provides a picture of the ways that collective life frustrates preference attainment: it is impossible to aggregate voices perfectly; leadership inevitably runs into principal–agent problems; and groups create insider–outsider dynamics, which in turn impede the factor mobility held to be the key to long-term economic growth.

The corollary of this negative, 'blocking' view of communities, is that much of economics and political economy is favourable to 'institutions'. This generally refers to broad rules of the game which, when appropriate, provide the order and stability in which markets can function. This facilitates the ongoing adjustments to the economy that make development possible. And, most importantly, institutions limit the damage that groups, or the 'players of the game' can do through things such as property rights, the rule of law, constraints on the executive, individual rights, and limits on monopoly power. Good institutions protect markets and individuals from the ravages of community, though there is immense debate about precisely which such rules/institutions do this optimally.[2]

In contrast, community has a rather good name in other quarters. The social capital literature argues that bonds between people, based on such things as trust, and underpinning social networks or associational life, have positive effects on social and economic development. Communities are held to encourage participation, generate forms of reciprocity that bind individuals to the wider society, and generally promote compromise and dampen conflict. Associational 'Putnam communities' are hence considered to be different from interest-based, rent-seeking 'Olson communities' (Olson 1965; Putnam 2000; Knack 2003). Overall, the mainstream economist's 'blocking' view of community stands in stark opposition to this theory of communities with effects of 'empowering and efficient exchange'.

A third view of community, developed in economic sociology, is more agnostic in outlook than either of the above. Actor-networks are, simply, unavoidable in many economic processes (Granovetter 1973, 1985).[3] The effects may be negative or positive, but in any case market exchange is underpinned by non-market group mechanisms. Some actor-networks are welded together through trust, interpersonal relationships, and reputations, all of which can substantially lower transaction costs and hence improve the efficiency of economic coordination, but some reinforce special interests and privileged access to resources.

One particular type of actor-network that has been the object of intense interest recently are 'communities of practice' (henceforth, CoPs), where the action shared in the network is some type of shared practice. One probable reason that there is so much interest in CoPs is that they correspond to so many important forms of modern organization that are not of the traditional community type. Many familiar organizations, such as firms, non-governmental organizations, and professional associations, are CoPs. CoPs are typically defined around the competences necessary for belonging to them, which allow members to engage in the routines of the community. One of the main concerns of analyses of CoPs is how competences and routines affect dynamic processes, or performance, of the organizations (such as firms) or systems (such as industries) to which they are relevant. One particular concern has to do with whether routines allow members or groups to improve their competences, such as through learning. Not all CoPs engage in, or facilitate, direct market exchange. Some of them may indeed do so, as when a professional actor-network establishes de facto standards for professional performance, and hence becomes an essential element of screening and signalling performance in labour or product markets. But some of them are well upstream of market processes, or are simply engaged in non-market activities, as in Putnam-type voluntary associations. CoPs are thus actor-network communities, but with some distinctive properties.

The 'blocking' view of the effects of communities on the economy has been most precisely formulated in relationship to the core concerns of economic theory, but the empowerment/exchange view has amassed a considerable literature in recent years.[4] A first task in considering community and economics is, then, to determine whether these two perspectives substantially cover the basic effects of community membership on the processes of preference determination and choice that are central to economics. Our response is that they do not, in four major ways that are detailed in Sections 2.2–2.5 below: (1) communities are often essential foundations of efficient exchange, and not just 'second-best' to markets; (2) communities can help individual economic agents discover their preferences; (3) communities can provide agency and voice in realizing preferences; and (4) communities can help certain types of efficient choice to emerge from a variety of preferences. Once we define these processes, we can then, in concert with the blockage and empowerment views of the effects of community, generate a more complete 'balance sheet' of the microeconomics of community and hence of the welfare effects of group life (Section 2.6).

Finally, we will consider the geographical aspects of community and economics. Traditionally, communities are identified with territories and, in a somewhat caricatured way, they are counterposed to a world of perfectly mobile factors. The story is much more complex than this today. Indeed, certain types of actor-networks and CoPs appear to be constructed more around links between practitioners, than links between geographically proximate agents. What are the differences between an economy structured (for better or for worse) by a society of territorially bound and differentiated groups versus one whose groups have no distinctive territorial roots? How does such a prospect relate to the core concerns of economic policies that promote factor mobility as their central objective (Section 2.7)?

In this chapter, we are interested principally in establishing the micro-foundations of communities or group life in the economy, and then aggregating up from there to broader possible effects of community on economic organization and performance. There is no question that groups and communities 'precede' individuals in time and over space; establishing micro-foundations is not the same as claiming that communities are instantaneously 'generated' by individual choices, as some caricatured views would hold. But the reverse does not hold either, that is, that individuals have no deliberative rationality and therefore are mere carriers of group routines and constraints imposed on them. Indeed, it is precisely the relationship between individual life and group life that gives rise to the most interesting insights into why communities exist and what they do.

2.2 Interaction: Interpersonal Relations and Impersonal Exchange

In the eleventh century, the Maghribi traders settled around the Mediterranean faced a problem. These descendants of Jews who had fled the Baghdad region in the tenth century had a close-knit community, but they needed distant agents for their commercial transactions, agents whom they could not monitor directly. Avner Greif (1993) shows that this community functioned according to the Merchants' Law, such that any agent who cheated would not be rehired by any member of the community for a long time, and the options available to such an agent were substantially reduced by such potential exclusion.

From the vantage point of economics, anything that minimizes transaction costs per unit of output is going to raise potential output. Such costs can be associated with information-gathering, as well as evaluation and determination of the reliability of information and possible moral hazards. Group membership can assist in all these dimensions of transacting, through reputation effects, signalling, and gate-keeping/filtering of participants. The production possibility frontier from a given stock of factors moves outward if, all other things being equal, there are increased possibilities for impersonal exchange and hence a deeper division of labour. Along these lines, Fukuyama (1996) argues that economies with greater generalized trust will more easily build large firms, extending the circle of exchange beyond what it could achieve through direct managerial control. But economically important trust can also operate at the level of communities such as the Maghribi traders. A more recent example is the way in which the world high-technology economy emanating from Silicon Valley has been extended to China, India, Taiwan, and Israel through the ethnic communities that Saxenian (2006) calls the 'new argonauts' – extensions of impersonal exchange that would not be able to take place without underlying communities. The bases of exchange in many areas of the economy are initially developed by CoPs, and as they are formalized, they then permit greater impersonal exchange to develop.

This issue is usually handled in economic analysis via comparative statics. Thus, Greif (1993) asks whether the Merchants' Law was a second-best solution in a world where spatially extended institutions that could guarantee exchange were effectively absent.[5] But in real sequences of economic development, it seems often that larger-scale institutions are ultimately forged from experiences that begin as community-based exchanges. Technological and organizational innovation almost invariably require this to be the case, because of their high levels of uncertainty. These activities then sometimes ultimately standardize their community-based exchange processes in the language of, and through the judicial power of, formal rules. But their origins in community-based processes should not be forgotten, because they facilitate the dynamics of economic development. To represent the process in the sole terms of comparative statics is to miss the way that exchange actually develops over time and space.

2.3 Discovery: Knowing What We Want

Does belonging to groups help or hinder an individual in achieving his or her preferences? There are several parts to this question: knowing what we want (the formulation of preferences), acting on what we want, and aggregate choice of what we want (making choices). Here we will take up the first of these. Looking into patterns of group membership and their effects on preference discovery would help us to take on a central question of welfare economics, that is the extent to which self-centred goals enhance welfare as opposed to goals defined by other influences, including social ties.

Until recently, economics eschewed the question of knowing what we want, preferring to assign it to subjectivity, the domain of psychology. Social choice theory claims that we cannot know the preferences of others and hence we cannot expect, in any meaningful way, to align our actions to achieve common goals (Robbins 1938; Arrow 1951, 1962). Public choice theory holds that merely being interested in what others want (except strategically) is likely to involve us in stifling our preferences, because it requires deference to others and to the – necessarily limited – goals we perceive as being jointly achievable.

There is wide agreement that social context and preferences are intimately related. Sociology stresses the role of socialization, and group experience is demonstrably very important in socialization, but says little about how socialization relates to the wide diversity of choices made by individuals in the same social groups (Alesina and George-Marios 2005; Alesina and Fuchs-Schundeln 2005; Bénabou and Tirole 2005).

Behavioural economics emphasizes *situations*, the idea that individual decisions are based on very local influences, rather than long-run well-being. Local stimuli trigger emotions, and these emotions influence decisions (Romer 2000). Ross and Nisbet (1991) argue that the central lesson of a large body of psychological research is the importance of situational factors in decision-making.[6] Prospect theory tells us that people put enormous weight on reference points that are local, arbitrary, and ephemeral (Kahneman and Tversky 1979). Mental accounting theory suggests that people make decisions and ignore events and consequences outside of a narrow, local domain (Thaler 1994). Hyperbolic discounters place extreme weight on the present, and cue-theory shows the large role of ephemeral situational forces (Laibson 2001). If these are the realities of decision-making, then the supply of situations is central to preference definition and choice.

Membership in communities, groups, or networks can be thought of as an important component of the supply of situations in which individuals find themselves. One obvious aspect of this is whether groups define situations that help their members to know what they want, and in a non-coercive way. If this is so, group membership can really be said to clarify things for their individual members, and not merely to inculcate group values in them, or to steer them toward short-term welfare-distorting values and preferences.[7]

For example, it might be simply that the supply of situations is a parameter for individual maximizing behaviour. If my neighbours are all members of a racist community, my payoffs to being racist will rise. If, on the other hand, there is an anti-racism group in the area, my payoffs to being not racist are altered. It could well be that joining the anti-racism group changes my perceptions of race by giving me information I would otherwise not have. A more subtle distinction, however, is that *interaction* within and between groups does not just provide me more information, it also provides me with *experiences* and *examples* that intersect with my own view of my self, and hence exercise an impact on how I define my preferences (Young and Durlauf 2001). This process of *discovery* is not considered in standard approaches to situations.

Another aspect of the supply of situations is their relationship to identity and, through this, the way we define our welfare goals (Akerlof and Kranton 2000). Sen (1985) distinguishes between self-centred welfare (involves no sympathy or antipathy toward others); self-welfare goals (maximizing may or may not involve attaching importance to the welfare of others); and self-goal choices (not restrained by the recognition of other people's pursuit of their goals). These three requirements – generally imposed jointly in economic models of choice – are in reality independent of one another. For example, one can violate self-centred welfare (someone else's misfortune affects our welfare), but this does not tell us whether or not their self-welfare goal will contain this criterion or not. There are obviously differences in subjectivity, as well as differences in situations, generating widely varying propensities for self-welfare goals to take into account the reality of others' lives.

In both the cases, where self-welfare goals conform to the standard definition, they do not take into account the welfare of others, and where they do take into account the welfare of others, an external reality may still be an instrument to understanding and defining these goals. We are speaking here not of membership as a simple sympathy device – sensitizing us to others' welfare and integrating it into our own welfare goals – but rather as an instrument of learning and understanding ourselves, and hence of defining our preferences, whether those preferences turn out to be strictly selfish or more generous. Sen (2002, p. 215) argues that 'we all have many identities that are ... depending on the context, crucial to our view of ourselves, and thus to the way we view our welfare, goals or behavioral obligations'. Dworkin (2002, p. 227) contends that a liberal community, one which allows individuals the autonomy to engage in self-discovery and, as we are suggesting here, helps them to do so, is not a 'superperson (which) embodies all the features and dimensions of a human life'. Community is an important source of resources for self-discovery, in this view, not a crushing, all-encompassing machine of total socialization. When it works in the way described here, it is precisely because community is partial, we can be members of many communities, and there are at least some possibilities of exit.

Note that this has nothing to do with using the social world as a device for defining one's preferences as those that are more achievable (more 'efficient' preferences); we return to this later. It simply holds that groups may help us know what we want, irrespective of whether we are likely to get it or not and that in addition we may want things that have to do with the welfare of others or with our joint welfare.[8] What we lack, however, are good theories about precisely when group membership obscures such self-welfare goals and when it clarifies them.

The notion that under some circumstances membership in groups helps actors to know what they want implies that larger-scale patterns of institutional development will differ according to the tissue of group life, because there will be different opportunities for 'principals' to learn what they want. Innovation, for example, can be 'pulled' by the demand of consumers for design, performance, and quality, which they only learn and sustain through communities (information acquisition, communication, identity), and then sustained economically through network externalities. Innovation can also be 'pushed' through producers' CoPs (norms, capacities, routines, gate-keeping). In this vein, one can think of fashion and design producers. Another example is technical communities such as the engineers that graduate from France's École des Mines or École Polytechnique, who give a strong imprint to the conception of infrastructure and the techniques used in building it in France, a strong innovation export of the French civil engineering industry. These preferences do not emerge spontaneously or individually. The core of the matter here is whether the standards for competences that are set up and used as gatekeepers to such producer CoPs really help in the work of discovery or whether they limit it. There is a circular interaction with the routines of producer communities, which require individuals to have competences and also, in some cases, are sources of imparting those skills to individuals or at least to screening for which individuals are good at them or not. There is not going to be an easy answer to this thorny question. It is difficult to imagine even the most revolutionary artist being able to carry out his or her revolution without the underlying skills that are learned through collective routines. But the conservative tendencies of many gatekeeping groups are also well known.

2.4 Getting What We Want: Agency and Voice

Any eventual contribution to economic efficiency in helping individuals to discover their preferences must be weighed against the costs of group membership in making choices. These are not just limited to the well-explored case of principal–agent dynamics, where there is a problem of aggregation of heterogeneous preferences. Even in the ideal case where no such agency problem exists, there are costs in defining the end collectively, and this would be true even where some kind of collective action or decision is needed for any individual to get what he or she wants. The most favourable combination would be big gains from community (collective action) as a means to reaching our ends, combined with small losses (costs) from group life in coordinating with others to define those ends, and small compromises on individual preferences.[9]

The canonical case from economics, where group membership stifles action by imposing big transaction costs on the realization of goals, or by stifling the pursuit of preferences through principal–agent dynamics, certainly covers an important set of real-world cases, especially at high levels of social aggregation (big groups, big institutions). But as we move down in scale, toward membership in smaller groups, there is less probability that they describe real welfare losses, and more that there are real gains. A key issue is how any economy affects the supply of such situations, notably through the way it structures the transaction costs of group membership. Such different supplies could generate huge variations, from one economy to another, in the aggregation of preferences and hence in their satisfaction. What types of preferences are these?

First, some outputs are indivisible and lumpy. They cannot be produced without aggregation of supply. Public goods like public transport fall into this category, as do virtually all consumption goods with strong network externalities. They can be detected through proxies (public opinion polls) or through organizations (lobbies). But the organizations only emerge in some cases, so an agent is needed.

Second, some preferences are obscure, even to those who hold them, until they get clarified through group membership and agency – as in discovery, discussed earlier. Groups translate them into understandable preferences and give them voice. Vague desires become realities through group process and access to others with similar desires and agents who assist them. Demands for public services or certain kinds of culturally specific goods do not emerge spontaneously from private preferences; nor do certain work methods, ethics, or standards of quality.

Third, some preferences are shameful or stigmatized when they remain strictly private. Many minority rights or tastes fall into this category. In the 1960s, when Black Power emerged as a cultural theme in America, it was shameful to affirm one's blackness in looks or behaviour. Until recently, a taste for pornography was shameful, as were many lifestyles considered 'atypical'. They are only initially voiced if they are transformed from fragmented individual desires to aggregates, and often it is the agents who see that this is occurring, who first break the taboo. They will possibly then emerge into the mainstream and at some later stage no longer need group mediation (the market for culturally specific goods and services can become mainstreamed in this way).

Fourth, some preferences are geographically or socially fragmented, so that their holders do not communicate. They become too marginal, within the boundaries of any effective market area, to be satisfied. On their own, they will probably not happen because the transaction costs will be too high. But if they correspond to 'strong bonds', such groups may sufficiently reduce such transaction costs or rank them high enough to bridge time and space, thereby overcoming aggregation costs and giving existence to these preferences.

One additional aspect of aggregation in these cases refers back to our analysis of discovery. Such preferences are likely to be discovered in smaller groups where preferences are strong and homogeneous, and risks are lower. If such preferences are widely but thinly distributed in the society, there is a double aggregation problem, of getting first to small-group discovery and then to aggregation to the larger scale. This has happened many times, when minority movements start out small and local and become big coalitions and ultimately become big social identity categories.

The supply of group or community membership opportunities that facilitate aggregation should depend on transaction costs in relation to the incentives and payoffs to supply and demand. Incentives correspond to the payoffs for group/community 'entrepreneurs' or leaders to supply membership opportunities, as well as for individuals to belong to them. This is also the response of mainstream economics to behavioural economics: even if people make situational choices, in the aggregate, situations are supplied according to rules that conform to rational culmination outcomes.[10] But this point has never been subject to any empirical proof, and commonsense holds that in every situation but a perfectly competitive market, the supply of situations is likely not to lead to culmination outcomes.

Historical institutionalists such as North (2005) go beyond this, allowing an independent role to cognitive frames and belief systems (see also Greif 1994). Political scientists draw our attention to agents that construct, and not merely reflect, interests (Jabko 2006). Moreover, there appear to be significant lags between changes in payoffs, specific types of belonging, and the beliefs and frames that lead people to bond with other people into groups. And if this is so, then beliefs and membership – that is, social interaction – could change the payoff matrix. I may believe something that leads me to be a member, and this ultimately enables me either to discover preferences or to realize preferences I could not have without being a member, or even that are different from what I expected to get by becoming a member. Certainly, religious groups, high-tech entrepreneurs, and certain CoPs fit this mould. The average non-expert cook does not become part of a culinary tradition expecting a payoff. However, when he or she joins, the collective payoffs may change as a result of increased network externalities, which in turn create feedbacks that change his or her individual payoffs, in ways that one cannot well estimate in advance. This is true of many sets of skills, as they first appear as new innovative inputs to the economy, before their ultimate effects – in terms of productivity and further qualitative dynamics and the possibility of satisfying preferences – can be estimated and codified. Interaction affects learning, and learning transforms agents.

Membership may also facilitate preference expression through the intrinsic value of being able to have a voice. Sen (2002, p. 159) argues for the fundamental relevance of the choice act itself. Behavioural economics has found that people are acutely sensitive to whether they have choice, and will often opt to make choices that affirm their rights to make choice as opposed to those that maximize their pecuniary interests. The possibility of choice responds to other criteria, such as 'fairness' or 'honour' or 'responsibility'. This is another layer to the definition of preferences. If choice means total independence from social constraint, then groups have no role in it; but if it means being able to express things that cannot be achieved individually, then group membership will have this intrinsic value for individuals.

To summarize, we could benefit from knowing more about the supply structure for membership that allows certain kinds of preferences to be expressed by reaching a minimum necessary aggregation threshold. If this is the case, then there should be a powerful incentive effect for the individuals whose preferences are made feasible in this way; however, we remain far away from being able to measure such an incentive effect. Associated with this, we would also need to know whether there are times when the 'right' agents are present, and others where the supply is distorted towards the 'wrong' agents, in terms of welfare. If non-distorting aggregation is weighted toward small groups or networks, are they likely to be parochial, and if so, do they 'turn around' and limit large-scale aggregation choices elsewhere by 'taking up the social choice space'? These are, to say the least, difficult but fascinating questions for research.

2.5 The Emergence of Choice

In many cases, no special coordination among actors is needed to ensure that the right large-scale aggregate choices are made (emergence of supply).

Individuals choose and in a world where markets are large, a diversity of outputs can be produced. Moreover, we can change our minds and be reasonably certain that most demands will find a supply, such that when individuals make mistakes they can reverse them. The overall configuration of outputs will be roughly 'right' in spite of the fact that individual choices do not need any special collective wisdom embodied in them. This is the standard case for markets and individuals.

Surowiecki (2004) argues that good, large-scale choices come about when certain conditions are satisfied, including diversity, independence, decentralization, and aggregation. He draws this from the economist's notion of the 'the wisdom of crowds'. The core of this wisdom, in standard models, is that even when many actors are situationally irrational or not fully informed (in the ways discussed in Section 2.4), their preferences will be randomly distributed. The remaining actors – as long as the four conditions hold – will therefore make appropriate aggregate choices. But there are two major objections to this view of things. First, as we pointed out in discussing the discovery of preferences, mere independence is unlikely to resolve all problems of situational behaviour. The entire faith of the wisdom of crowds theory has to rest on diversity, decentralization, and aggregation. But it follows that we know little about diversity and decentralization once we admit that discovery can be improved by group life. This will especially be the case of goods and services where sovereignty, low sunk costs, and perfect reversibility are not present.

If the 'wisdom' of unlinked individuals may be limited, is a 'crowd' structure the best way to link them? The standard usage of crowds seems to refer uniquely to the sovereign individual chooser, because then, so it goes, there will not be intractable principal–agent problems, impossibility dynamics, group think, social pressure, and impacted information. But in collective-choice processes, sovereign individuals will be less effective than something that is in-between small groups – such as families – or groups with 'strong' internal ties (such as ethnic minority diasporas), and large (internally anonymous) markets. In our terms, these are loosely structured communities, of which one version is the CoPs.

The reason they may help in choice processes is what Granovetter (1973) calls 'the strength of weak ties'. First, they have certain attributes which mimic the search features of markets and thus help in identifying good outcomes. These are internal cognitive diversity in search and reasoning behaviour; and independence and decentralization in expressing preferences and opinions on the part of members. In some cases, the information feedbacks on these search processes are better in groups than in open markets or crowds. 'Strong ties', by contrast, would not satisfy the need for diversity and independence. Second, membership may help in securing good decisions in those circumstances where markets might tend to fail. One of the strong points of highly decentralized, market-based decision-making is that it allows for trial and error. The mechanisms of trial are initiative, mimicry, and imitation. Information cascades provide for sequential imitation. But they also are fraught with many problems, notably hysteresis, herding, and overshooting. In many markets, this is not a long-term problem, because the failures that result are resolved *ex post*, although when they are macroeconomic or financial they can have hugely undesirable outcomes and become more difficult to absorb than we would like. That is why, for example, government regulatory authorities try to get financial markets to be more simultaneously – rather than sequentially – reactive, through immediacy and transparency.

There are two situations in which group membership can be helpful in avoiding the *ex post* 'fix it' solution, with its huge costs. One is that it can speed up the feedbacks, and hence enable corrections that weed out emerging bad-information cascades to be set into place before the system goes down the wrong path. Trust, norms and conventions, meta-information, and generally anything that facilitates more rapid and transparent exchange of information are consequences of weak ties. In cases where technological change involves high sunk costs or high costs of reversibility, such feedbacks can raise the probability of good choices. Another situation where membership helps is that sometimes bad choices are actually not very observable until it is too late and their consequences are hopelessly magnified. We do not have enough access to the consequences of the choices because the costs of obtaining them, or access to observing them, are too high. In this case, ties to the others who have made them, and the possibility, hence, of observing the consequences, makes the feedback work better. Many private electoral choices fall into this category.

Note that both these features can be combined in diversified expert communities, as for example in the health care field. Allowing these CoPs to carry out aggregation fulfils both these conditions, but ideally the communities should be weakly tied, so that diversity of opinion and competition of ideas is assured internally to the process of aggregation. Of course, nothing guarantees that these feedbacks are always going to lower the rate of bad choices. It might be that everyone involved in even these relatively large circles of feedback stands to gain from choices that are not so great, and so they perpetuate them because they will be big gainers, even if the overall consequences will be bad. So, the old questions of parochialism and rent-earning are present. Still, the larger the circles, the higher is the probability that they will be porous, and hence open to those who can see their wider consequences. This is certainly the tension in the financial derivatives industry, where large, loosely tied networks can hide certain bad decisions and information cascades, but where sometimes they are large enough for light to be shone on them by regulatory authorities before it is too late. Dispensing with networks altogether, however, is a utopia that would not work, so we are stuck with the problem of creating crowds whose 'wisdom' minimizes hysteresis and rent-seeking.

Even in situations where reversibility is not a problem, but extreme complexity is, communities help in guiding the complex system. Electoral behaviour is an obvious case: we vote on some issues that do not affect our lives directly, but do affect those of other people. We hold non-private values and we hold strong preferences for certain non-private consequences (Sen 2002). There is a lot of quibbling in social theory over whether, for example, I can care strongly about whether women should have the right to abortion even though I will very likely never have a private interest in access to abortion.[11] We might think that the right choice was made if we did not have ties to people who had been directly affected and could tell us that we voted for the wrong thing.

All in all, weak ties would seem to square the circle of ensuring diversity of inputs, independence, avoidance of groupthink on the input side, but allow better choice by facilitating aggregation.[12]

Membership – weak or strong – might also help in achieving the 'wisdom of crowds' in some conventional ways as well. For example, if many people can make choices that are in some way bad for them or for the society, but if the costs of making those choices are low, the chances are they will continue to make them. Thus, referring to an earlier example, it is easier to be racist if one has little contact with members of other groups, where there is low likelihood of having to act on one's views, and little ability to obtain first-hand information that could influence those views. Interacting with others may not cause us to stop hating them; but interacting in relatively intensive and structured ways can make it more costly to act on our preferences. Another example: we can allow others to choose poor-quality goods, thereby leaving a smaller market for high-quality goods, with the further indirect effect that those goods become an elitist and more-expensive output to have for ourselves (because it reduces economies of scale and network externalities), and the low-quality goods of others do not impinge on our environment. But group ties that raise community norms of quality could reverse these dynamics, making high-quality goods cheaper for all.

Finally, all these choice processes depend on the relationship between the organization of suppliers and consumers. In some markets, the producers have greater incentives to be organized than the buyers; one can think of political markets in this regard, so that the political parties and lobbies are more organized than the citizens. In government and services markets, unorganized consumers are at a disadvantage in influencing the choice menu and the overall evolution of choice. Where producers are organized as CoPs that promote learning and skill acquisition and efficiency-enhancing standards of quality, the choice set for consumers will be altered in a potentially welfare-enhancing direction. By contrast, if group structure, for whatever reason, creates situations that are prone to distorting decisions through short-term and short-sighted imitative reasoning, hyperbolic discounting, and so on, and if the penalties to such group think are relatively low, or if they have endogenous effects that raise pay-offs over time by drawing in others, then groups may indeed be capable of reducing welfare.

2.6 The Welfare Effects of Community

The potential benefits of group life to economic actors are generally underestimated, especially in the four areas discussed above, which together can be called 'coordination and preferences'. These are underestimated both by the mainstream 'blockage' school of thought, and the alternative 'empowerment/exchange' view. A simple way to summarize this case is as follows:

WELFARE OUTCOMES OF COMMUNITY =
Σ {INTERACTION/PREFERENCES/CHOICE} +
{EMPOWERMENT/EXCHANGE} - {BLOCKAGE}
where:

INTERACTION/PREFERENCES/CHOICE = increased impersonal exchange/productivity + discovery/incentive + increased agency/incentive + emergent choice/productivity

EMPOWERMENT/EXCHANGE = social capital + trust + lower transaction costs + better verification of qualities of partners + low-cost sanctions

BLOCKAGE = higher transaction costs, coordination difficulties + principal–agent costs + parochialism + rent-extraction

This is a very wide palette of possible effects. We are a long way from having methods that would allow us to go upward from actors to groups for particular cases, not to mention for the overall 'group structure' of a whole economy. But achieving the latter would immeasurably brighten the light that economic sociology sheds on economic development, while achieving the former would allow us to think more accurately about the potential effects of policies that support certain types of communities, such as the contemporary attraction to CoPs in innovation policies. A few points can be made about such an assessment.

2.6.1 *Club goods and the problem of bundling*

Groups are by nature providers of club goods and services and this is true whether the group is interest-based (Olson groups), associational (Putnam groups), or actor-network, including CoPs. In order to get the benefits of being in the club, members must accept the interactions that underpin them.[13] All such interactions may have intended goals and impose costs, that we accept, to reach them; but they may also have unintended costs and consequences for members. In other words, one of the main reasons that people may engage in group 'blocking' behaviour is not because they want to do so, but because it is the price to pay for what they perceive to be the benefits of group membership. I did not join the CoPs of university professors in order to block change; but such CoPs may in fact block a lot of change. This is just as true of non-interest-based groups (non-Olson), groups as of lobbies and other sorts of rent-seekers. Moreover, the consequences of such bundling may make these consequences unclear to the chooser or so difficult to calculate that decisions about group membership and about the rules of group membership for others will be clouded in obscurity.

CoPs are a particularly complex case of bundling of effects. Actor-networks provide connections to individuals (hence empower them), but they also exclude those who are not members of the network and who may have 'competences' to join. The door is then open to the construction of institutionalized power by central actors in the network. If the network occupies a strategic position in some economic process (e.g. making large-scale choices of infrastructures with huge sunk costs), its role in making choices may fall short of the optimal weak ties process alluded to earlier. Such actor-networks may come to display serious principal–agent problems and Olson-type characteristics. The same may be said of the routines of a community of practice.

2.6.2 *Positive as well as negative externalities*

But things may also work in the other direction. There may very well be positive externalities of group membership, that is, that accrue to people who are not members of the group. Putnam (2000) claims that strong associational life leads to better politics and even to better economic growth, and backs the claim up with some rudimentary statistical correlations; but he does not formalize the reasoning behind this intuition.

Think about the standard elements of the Romer (1990) growth model: rivalry and excludability are the key determinants of whether some factor of production (in his case, knowledge, in our case group life) can generate a growth-enhancing increasing return. In the case of knowledge, this takes the form of an economy-wide knowledge externality, because knowledge is ultimately non-rivalrous and, in the long term, not excludable.

Interaction is excludable, as in the case of the Maghribi traders. But it is non-rival, in that its basic pattern does not get 'used up'. The conventions or norms that lead to it do not wear down through use. The impersonal exchange to which it gives rise may be an increasing function of the initial limited interaction, however, in that people learn about exchange and they may in turn be in a position to widen their exchanges, if not with the initial group, then with others, spreading out into other domains. All depends on how the tendency to rent-seek and keep a narrow circle intersects with the desire and opportunity to learn and possibly expand one's earnings in other spheres.

Discovery is intrinsically non-rival. It may be excludable if it requires a high level of community-based understanding and context to make or understand the discovery. But, here again, we know little about the extent to which discoveries that can only be made within communities can be shared with non-members and in turn help the latter to define their own preferences in ways they would otherwise not be able to do.

Voice is a club service, with some non-rival characteristics. It can become a rival service if my voice cannot be used by you in any way because you lack legitimacy or scale by virtue of my existence. It can be excludable or not, depending on membership structure. This makes it complicated from a welfare standpoint; we tend to think of it as a combat of different interests, each seeking to crowd out the other, but this is not at all clear, as Sen (2002) has illustrated in his analysis of the problem of social choice.

The emergence of choice through weak ties is a rival and excludable service, once the choices are made, and especially if they involve large sunk costs or irreversibilities, as in the infrastructure example used above.

But if the choices are made in the way we have claimed above, with the enhancing effects of group participation, then the non-rivalrous and excludable character is only apparent, not real. What kind of group structure would be necessary to navigate the shoals between COPS that have strongly positive effects in guiding large-scale choice and those that do the opposite?

2.6.3 *The supply of situations*

The impulse to create groups is strong across all societies and yet the actual empirical contours of group life – type and level – are quite different from one place and time to another. There are many possible reasons for these differences, including everything from different preference structures to different costs of coordination (scale and diversity). Some of the difference is likely to come simply from the incentives, costs, and pay-offs to group membership. And this in turn will be shaped by the overarching rules within which groups are established and interact: in a word, higher-level societal 'institutions'.

We have argued elsewhere at length that research on institutions suffers from a split between those interested in societal-level rules, and those who concentrate on communities or groups (Storper 2005; Rodriguez-Pose and Storper 2006). All economies are shaped by both, and indeed, it is their interactions that determine the economic effects of each. For example, if the empowerment theories of groups are correct, then communities may lower transaction costs and make economic exchange wider and more efficient; but the extent to which they do this and avoid rent-seeking in so doing, depends on the broader rules of market interaction to which they are subject. Likewise, an economy with few intermediate group levels may suffer excessive bureaucratic costs, and problems of confidence and preference revelation and voice, even if its rules are strong. Rent-seeking groups will be free to go all the way when there are inexistent or weak possibilities for entry of competing groups; and they will be strongly tempered when institutions ensure the possibility of competition, exit by group members, and mobility to other groups. Institutions, in the sense of rules of engagement, thus shape the supply of situations, which in turn shapes at least some of the balance between negative and positive effects of communities. No examination of whether, for example, reinforcement of CoPs in the knowledge economy would enhance economic welfare or not, can be complete without weighing how the broader rules context affects all the dimensions of group life examined above.

Institutions influence the supply of opportunities for agents to form groups as well. One is reminded of the antagonism to CoPs (*corporations*) during the French revolution, and the institutional (constitutional and political) project to destroy their influence. The hostility to these CoPs was engendered by their perceived Olson qualities. The fact that such a powerful project only partially succeeded (Rosenvallon 2004) is testimony to the power of the impulse to form such communities. But the institutions unleashed on the *corporations* profoundly altered the quantity and morphology of such CoPs in modern France, as well as their internal functioning, their relationship to the economy, and the economic benefits and costs they generate. A key question in understanding different levels of innovation in today's world is: why are there different levels and types of innovation CoPs? Any answer must involve a consideration of the institutional rules that affect the opportunities for such groups to function. Taiwanese engineer associations in Silicon Valley are supported by access to venture capital, itself initially a CoPs which probably responded to both financial and associational incentives. But it is difficult to imagine an association of Taiwanese engineers in France, even if venture capital levels were to increase in that country. That is because the institutional forces that affect the supply of opportunities to form groups often have sources that are not apparent to the naked eye and far away from 'innovation institutions' in the narrow sense.

In any case, a balanced analysis of communities requires that we consider how society (rules and institutions) and community (groups) interact. It cannot content itself with analysing the internal workings of communities or even the interactions between communities.

2.7 Are Communities Still Useful to the Economy? The Economic Geography of Communities

Nothing is more characteristic of economic policy thinking today than the notion that factor mobility is essential to growth and development, and that this requirement is intensifying with the acceleration of technological change and global market integration. 'Factor mobility' applies to technologies, sectors, firms, and – of course – places, and each of these may involve labour, capital, natural resource, and knowledge inputs. The benefits of mobility are both static (specialization) and dynamic (pushing or moving toward the technological frontier). Even from this standard perspective, however, it is admitted that the costs of mobility are borne unequally by different strata of the labour force (McCulloch and Yellen 1977).

In contrast to this perspective, there is a less coherent, but persistent, set of doubts about factor mobility, many of which come from the 'empowerment and exchange' theories of community, noted above. To the extent that communities are built around long-term processes of creating norms, conventions, reputation effects, and mutual commitment, the factor mobility can be a problem for these forms of social life. Suburbanization – a form of daily factor mobility – is cited by Putnam (2000) as a principal cause of declining associational life in the USA. This is a long-term worry in the sociological literature, from Durkheim's 'anomie' to the recent communitarians and social capital theorists. Loss of community, for them, can generate loss of meaning and identity, and for individuals it can generate a loss of social networks, leading to anxiety, depression, and disengagement from the non-market exchanges that generate a large part of the services essential to the functioning of society, politics, and economy (Sandel 1996; Sennett 1999; Putnam 2000). It can also lead to loss of the networks that determine economic position through access to exchange (Granovetter 1973).[14]

Critical views of factor mobility sometimes take extreme forms, clothing themselves in nostalgic and romantic views of group life, and often themselves misrepresent communities as unchanging, stable environments. Moreover, at least some group life reconstructs itself in the face of mobility – from nation-states to CoPs to neighbourhood associations, and so it is wrong to associate communities uniquely with tradition; but we do not have tools for evaluating whether loss of community has transitory effects on individuals, and whether the gains from change outweigh the losses for such individuals. Thus, when naïve and caricatured visions of community are put aside, there is certainly room for a debate about the benefits and costs of factor mobility in relationship to the spatial and temporal bases of community life. Whole cultures have been effectively destroyed by mobility, and though this process is as old as human civilization, it is very probably accelerating and taking new forms (Lear 2007).

In addition, in direct contrast to the Olson view that groups block change, an extensive case-study literature on local economic development (Becattini 1990; Florida 1995; Cooke and Morgan 1998; Farrell and Knight 2003) demonstrates that under some circumstances, community life creates capacities to redeploy economic resources very successfully. Unfortunately, these claims have had little direct confrontation with the standard view, because of the different methods used, generally involving little or no formalization and even less testing with large-scale comparative evidence.[15]

Still, this is a potent question, because so much policy today is motivated by the desire to increase such mobility in the face of the twin pressures of globalization and technological change, as for example in the Lisbon Agenda of the European Union (EU 2004).

2.7.1 *Communities and global integration*

The starting point for thinking about this is to realize that most groups are territorialized. There are some groups that are not exclusively anchored to a particular territory (city, neighbourhood, country, region, continent), including such CoPs as international networks of professionals. But even in the latter case, there are often 'local CoPs in global CoPs networks', an intricate multi-scalar geometry of relations. In any given territory, a complex matrix of groups shapes the local economic environment. The consequence is that such group life, combined with formal institutions, influences the outputs and productivity levels of each economy, through the particular mix of coordination/preference, empowerment/exchange, and the blockage effects it generates.

In addition to promoting labour mobility, another dimension of the European Commission's official position on European integration is that it should reconcile exchange with diversity: a 'Europe of regions' (EU 2004). This specifically refers to the promotion of durable collective differences between the European economies, preserving their specificities, based on the assumption that this will benefit Europe as a whole. Economic theory is more sceptical. On the one hand, generating fluid factor mobility presupposes a certain institutional harmony and levelling between places; on the other, given different factor endowments, each region should discover the efficiency-based specialization that expresses its comparative advantage. Diversity based on standard comparative advantage generates a territorial mosaic of specializations that allow economies to function efficiently; most importantly, they change over time in concert with the new possibilities for combining inputs into outputs.

European policymakers are Janus-faced when dealing with this subject, some emphasizing the diversity that comes from comparative advantage, while others refer to collective or institutionalized diversity. They rarely tell the public that the two sources of diversity are radically different and that their policies pull in two different directions. American federalists and public choice theorists like to think that they square the circle by emphasizing certain forms of harmonization and free trade, while allowing different territories to make their own, locally appropriate institutional choices in many areas, but as we shall see, this is not entirely valid.

There are potentially positive effects of institutionalized diversity; the coordination/preferences and empowerment effects lie at the heart of the economic development of a territory or nation that is favourably endowed with them. But the net effect will always depend on the blockage effects that are present as well, in the form of organized interest groups, political coalitions, state structures, and rent-seeking through development policies.

Is the collective diversity of something akin to a 'Europe of regions' likely to enhance welfare and development? Assume that the differential distribution of communities leads to an array of territorially specific specializations in output, in addition to those generated by comparative advantage. These specializations reflect the effects of interaction/choice, blockage, and empowerment/exchange *within* different territories on what and how they produce. There is an analogy here to the production of culturally specific goods and services by different places.

In a multiregional world economy, it is difficult to say whether this is greater variety than would be obtained under the condition of institutional/community homogeneity and free trade; this is because the 'diversity between' places it generates might be at the price of 'diversity within'. Collective life could enforce more homogeneity within, even as it preserves diversity between places. A fair guess is that the diversity is different in the two cases, where the diversity generated by differences in institutions/communities between territories is slower to change than strictly efficiency-based diversity. Output and consumption inside territories probably changes faster when it is the result of comparative advantage, because institutions – including communities – are slower to change than markets. Data on economic convergence for Europe suggest that it has institutionalized/community diversity, because significant growth rate differentials between regions are persistent, with unaligned economic cycles. In the USA, by contrast, the states are simply at different points in the same economic cycle, suggesting that their pattern of specialization and diversity is more tipped toward comparative advantage.

Each type of diversity – comparative advantage, or institutionally generated – has its price. Indeed, something like a Europe of Regions or a world of culturally/institutionally differentiated territories trading with each other will generate winners and losers from the different types of diversity they generate. The literature on cultural diversity and globalization has developed analytical models of this type of question (Cowen 2004; Janeba 2004; Rauch and Trindade 2005). Thus, if the world is very diverse under autarky, and trade leads to the breakdown of collective structures and more imitation of the dominant goods/services pattern – which happens when costless trade and communication exist – then trade might be inferior to autarky by reducing diversity. A reduction in diversity could also come about if there are economies of scale in production and Hotelling (duopoly) behaviour induces producers to cater to the 'middle of the market', rather than its edges. At a high level, this can lead to 'cultural destruction'. Moreover, consumers of imported 'cultural' goods tend to gain, while consumers of exported goods will lose. If the latter are greater than the former, there is potential overall welfare loss.

The process of imitation between places will be affected by network externalities in consumption, possibly accentuating convergence towards the extremes or towards the dominant taste. In a more dynamic perspective, if tastes are partly endogenous to learning and imitation (discovery, agency), what starts out as a realignment of production and consumption patterns can result in realignment of the situations in which people learn and discover for the next round of production and consumption.

If what we have said about community is valid, then two points follow. First, insofar as differences in output and consumption result not from institutional 'barriers' but from interaction, discovery, voice, choice, and empowerment/exchange, the value of a world of different regions rises because the output and consumption diversity it contains reflects 'real' preferences, and not second-best ('we are old fashioned because we don't know any better or can't have anything better'); and correspondingly, if integration reduces this diversity, it is likely that the post-integration equilibrium will reduce both intra- and inter-territorial welfare.

For homogeneous goods, integration probably increases welfare, whereas for strongly heterogeneous or specialized goods based on community values, and especially those with consumption externalities, the effects of integration could be more mixed (McElreath et al. 2003; Rauch and Trindade 2005). Theory and policy have a real interest in understanding these dynamics and in getting the right post-integration equilibrium. Though the 'Europe of Regions' is mostly just a politically correct moniker, there is a serious issue behind it when it comes to diversity of production and consumption, just as there is at a world scale in the negotiation of trade rules.

2.7.2 Institutions, diversity, and innovation

Douglass North argues that European success in development 'was the dynamic consequences of the competition among fragmented political bodies that resulted in an especially creative environment' (North 2005, p. 138). More recent literature on the size of nations emphasizes the internal gains from appropriately sized units, which achieve the right trade-offs between minimizing heterogeneity of preferences and reducing coordination costs and getting the benefits of scale (Alesina and Spolaore 2006). Taken together, they suggest that development is facilitated by internal coherence at some scale, but that diversity and exchange among units let many ideas emerge and then competition and exchange will select and refine them.

This is different from the view that we could extrapolate from standard theory, since it suggests collective diversity 'between', and not just individual factor mobility and diversity 'within', as key to development. One of the biggest puzzles of historical development is why the fragmented European states managed to develop so much virtuous, competitive exchange in the late Medieval and early Renaissance periods, instead of allowing their internal collective structures to block it, as they had for centuries previously.

A world of diverse communities appears to maximize its potential contributions to development only when there are well-enforced societal rules of exchange and openness, effectively placing groups in fair (i.e. non-violent) competition with one another, while not destroying the virtuous aspects of their diversity. Historically, this has occurred in the presence of certain kinds of state structures and political regimes, on the one hand, and outward-looking 'bridging agents', on the other. A good example is what Saxenian (2006) terms the 'new Argonauts', the mobile agents from local high-tech communities that bind Silicon Valley to Israel, Taiwan, and China. Without strong community structures, the wider processes of impersonal exchange and specialization that spread development geographically would be weaker, and so would innovation within the world high-tech economy as a whole. Oddly enough, the most 'globalized' of systems, the international high-technology production and innovation system, is really a composite of intricate, territorially rooted, community structures. But without institutions – trade rules, intellectual property rights, inter-group competition, enforceable legal rights generally, international organizational practices and 'translating' agents – none of this would be possible, because there would be no way to get from interpersonal exchange to impersonal exchange, with its intricate divisions of labour and specialization.

Communities of practice appear at all geographical scales in this process. They may take the form of relatively localized actor-networks, as well as constituting the structure of the agents that enable different territorial nodes to relate to each other to form the global innovation economy. Sometimes these CoPs overlap with other forms of community, as in ethnic networks or interest-based professional categories who engage in persistent rent-seeking and lobbying. Certain individuals may belong to both local CoPs and global CoPs, and indeed they may even belong to more than one local CoPs, as in Saxenian's cases of Taiwanese and Indian engineers.

Given that blockage tendencies exist in all communities, the rules of engagement, and not just the internal functioning of communities, are essential to economic outcomes. Moreover, if history is any guide, pluralism is important to limiting the rent-seeking blockage effects of communities and maximizing their innovative potential. The open question for research is the scale at which such pluralism must operate: 'within' or 'between' territories, and at what scale of territory, as well as how less territorialized networks can be subjected to the beneficial effects of pluralism and competition. These types of distributed actor-networks, if big and powerful enough, may have 'lock-in' and Hotelling effects that tend to limit such competition and increase welfare losses.

2.7.3 Scale and diversity: is community an illusion?

In one sense, these questions of diversity within and diversity between are just side effects of the scale of the units of observation. For example, as we reduce the scale of territorial units that we analyse, there are strong chances that they will become institutionally more internally cohesive and homogeneous and hence that economic diversity and institutional competition is obtained through exchange with other places. As scale gets bigger, there will be more internal diversity. Research on community – as on institutions in general – is extremely sensitive to the territorial scale of units of observation and great prudence therefore must be used in going forward.

At the same time, the irregular scale of units of observation is unavoidably real. Such things as legal boundaries, custom, and culture, express the functioning of real communities reflecting the varying territorial scales of real, accumulated practices and social bonds. So it would be naïve for the researcher to claim that if we had homogeneous units of observation, the issue would disappear. For example, the Europe of Regions is a set of fairly small units, with rather high levels of collective organization 'within' and a lot of exchange between. The USA, in spite of its federalist system of government, is socially and economically more a case of big regions with a lot of factor mobility, so that the diversity of production methods and consumption styles is found more 'within', reproduced from place to place, than from a diversity between places, with a certain homogeneity at the large scale.

This means that if policy hopes to enhance development, it must account for starting points. In the Europe of Regions, it involves insuring that the process of exchange, or bridging, between regions is strong and dynamic, and that regions do not become closed off, stagnant, rent-seeking community structures. In a system such as the USA, exchange and mobility are strong, but sometimes this comes at the price of the strength of community structures in situ, weakening their internal coherence (or 'bonding'). In Europe, widening of bridges between coherent communities might be needed in order to get scale and exchange; in the USA, a deepening of bonds within them in order to get more efficient coordination.[16] Neither public choice theory nor social capital theory allows policymakers to appreciate this difference.

As noted above, there appear to be some communities that have a very strong global structure. They are not entirely 'de-territorialized', of course; even in the case of high-technology networks, there are strong local nodes: Silicon Valley, Taipei, Bangalore, Ireland, Israel. But an interesting question presents itself: with their further globalization, could there emerge world monopolies in certain types of community functions? Could these networks enforce parochialism and rent-seeking and limit competition and innovation? One could argue that a certain global plutocracy already does some of this, especially with the weakening national identities of the top world elite. In any case, understanding the ways that such widely dispersed networks contribute to the economic process along the lines suggested in this chapter, is likely to be a key question for institutionalist economics and economic sociology in the decades to come.

Merely asking these kinds of questions suggests how far the more policy-oriented branches of institutionalist economics are from being able to help us with knowing what, if anything, to do about groups and communities. In practical terms, many economies have needed a strong dose of rent-destroying openness, so that up until now, the existing tool kit has been useful. But in many areas of the world, we are asking more and more questions about how to keep the 'good' side of community while throwing out the 'bad' – from the Europe of Regions to the problem of 'exit' in the USA, to the 'need for social underpinnings of development' in emerging countries. A reintegration of the question of community into economics thus deserves its place on this agenda.

2.8 Conclusion

Community has a bad name in economics because it is partly deserved. But there are vast other aspects of community that complicate the picture. Economics has tended to be neglectful about posing questions about these other aspects as empirical phenomena, while the contributions of sociologists, economic historians, and students of local and regional economic development have awakened us to them. But paradoxically, economic reasoning is a good way to think about the nature of these aspects in a coherent theoretical framework that integrates both negative and positive contributions of group life to the economic process, and that is what we have endeavoured to do in this chapter. In addition to attempting a more complete picture of the welfare effects of community, we have noted that in any real situation of economic development, several other aspects of context are likely to be critical to how communities contribute to economics: the broader societal institutions that define the supply of situations for forming communities; their rules of engagement with markets, especially through competition and exit; and the geographical arrangements of communities, which determine the relationship between coordination effected within communities and competition between ideas and agents between communities. Research on these topics admittedly faces formidable methodological obstacles, but the agenda offers very exciting possibilities for the study of groups to contribute broad insights into the relationship between economy and society.

References

Akerlof, G. E. and Kranton, R. E. (2000). 'Economics and identity', *Quarterly Journal of Economics*, 115: 715–53.
Alesina, A. and Spolaore, E. (2006). *The Size of Nations*. Cambridge, MA: MIT Press.
——and Fuchs-Schundeln, N. (2005). 'Goodbye Lenin (or not?): The effect of communism on people's preferences', NBER Working Paper (www.nber.org/papers/w11700).

Alesina, A. and La Ferrara, E. (2005). 'Preferences for redistribution in the land of opportunities', *Journal of Public Economics*, 89: 897–931.

—— and George-Marios, A. (2005). 'Fairness and redistribution', *American Economic Review*, 95(4): 960–80.

Arrow, K. J. (1951). *Social Choice and Individual Values*. New York: Wiley.

—— J. (1962). 'The economic implications of learning by doing', *Review of Economic Studies*, 29: 155–73.

Becattini, G. (1990). 'The Marshallian industrial district as a social-economic notion', in F. Pyke, G. Becattini, and W. Sengenberger (eds.), *Industrial Districts and Inter-firm Cooperation in Italy*. Geneva: International Labour Office.

Bénabou, R. and Tirole, J. (2005). *Belief in a Just World and Redistributive Policies*, mimeo. Princeton, NJ: Princeton University.

Bowles, S. (1998). 'Endogenous preferences: The cultural consequences of markets and other economic institutions', *Journal of Economic Literature*, 36: 75–111.

—— and Gintis, H. (2002). 'Social capital and community governance', *Economic Journal*, 112: 419–36.

—— —— (2003). 'Persistent parochialism: Trust and exclusion in ethnic networks', Working Paper. Santa Fe, NM: Santa Fe Institute.

Cooke, P., and Morgan, K. (1998). *The Associational Economy: Firms, Regions and Innovation*. Oxford: Oxford University Press.

Corneo, G. and Gruner, H. P. (2002). 'Individual preferences for political redistribution', *Journal of Public Economics*, 83: 83–107.

Cowen, T. (2004). *Creative Destruction: How Globalization is Changing the World's Cultures*. Princeton, NJ: Princeton University Press.

Della Vigna, S. and Malmendier, U. (2002). 'Contract design and self-control', mimeo.

Dworkin, R. (2002). *Sovereign Virtue: The Theory and Practice of Equality*. Cambridge, MA: Harvard University Press.

European Union (EU) (2004). 'Exploiting Europe's territorial diversity for sustainable economic growth,' Ministerial Conference, Rotterdam, 29 November.

Farole, T., Rodriguez-Pose, A., and Storper, M. (2007a). 'Human geography and the institutions that underlie economic growth: A multi-disciplinary literature review'. London School of Economics, manuscript under review.

—— —— —— (2007b). 'The institutional determinants of economic growth: A cross-country empirical investigation'. London School of Economics, manuscript under review.

Farrell, H. and Knight, J. (2003). 'Trust, institutions and institutional change: Industrial districts and the social capital hypothesis', *Politics and Society*, 31(4): 537–66.

Florida, R. (1995). 'Toward the learning region', *Futures*, 27(5): 527–36.

Fukuyama, F. (1996). *Trust: The Social Virtues and the Creation of Prosperity*. New York: The Free Press.

Glaeser, E. L. (2004). *Psychology and the Market*, Discussion Paper 2023. Cambridge, MA: Harvard Institute of Economic Research.

Granovetter, M. (1973). 'The strength of weak ties', *American Journal of Sociology*, 78: 1360–80.

—— (1985). 'Economic action and social structure: The problem of embeddedness', *American Journal of Sociology*, 91: 481–510.

Greif, A. (1993). 'Contract enforceability and economic institutions in early trade: Evidence on the Maghribi traders', *American Economic Review*, 83: 525–48.

—— (1994). 'Cultural beliefs and the organization of society: An historical and theoretical reflection on collectivist and individualist societies', *Journal of Political Economy*, 102(5): 912–50.

Jabko, N. (2006). *Playing the Market: A Political Strategy for Uniting Europe*. Ithaca, NY: Cornell University Press.

Janeba, E. (2004). *International Trade and Cultural Identity*, working paper, (www.nber.org/papers/w10426). Cambridge, MA: NBER.

Kahneman, D. and Tversky, A. (1979). 'Prospect theory: An analysis of decision under risk', *Econometrica*, 47: 263–91.

Knack, S. (2003). 'Groups, growth and trust: Cross-country evidence on the Olson and Putnam hypotheses', *Public Choice*, 117(3–4): 341–55.

Laibson, D. (2001). 'A cue theory of consumption', *Quarterly Journal of Economics*, 66(1): 81–120.

Lear, J. (2007). *Radical Hope: Ethics in the Face of Cultural Devastation*. Cambridge, MA: Harvard University Press.

McCulloch, R. and Yellen, J. (1977). 'Factor mobility, regional development, and the distribution of income', *Journal of Political Economy*, 85 (1): 79–96.

McElreath, R., Boyd, R., and Richerson, P. (2003). 'Shared norms and the evolution of ethnic markers', *Current Anthropology*, 44 (1): 122–9.

North, D. (2005). *Understanding the Process of Economic Change*. Princeton, NJ: Princeton University Press.

Olson, M. (1965). *The Logic of Collective Action: Public Goods and the Theory of Groups*. Cambridge, MA: Harvard University Press.

Putnam, R. (2000). *Bowling Alone: The Collapse and Revival of American Community*. New York: Simon & Schuster.

Rauch, J. E. and Trindade, V. (2005). 'Neckties in the tropics: A model of international trade and cultural diversity', working paper, (www.nber.org/papers/w11890). Cambridge, MA: NBER.

Robbins, L. (1938). 'Interpersonal comparisons of utility: A comment', *Economic Journal*, 48(192): 635–41.

Rodriguez-Pose, A. and Storper, M. (2006). 'Better rules or stronger communities? On the social foundations of the institutional change and its economic effects', *Economic Geography*, 82 (1): 1–25.

Romer, P. M. (1990). 'Endogenous technological change', *Journal of Political Economy*, 98(5): S1071–102.

Romer, P. M. (2000). 'Thinking and feeling', *American Economic Review*, 90(2): 439–43.

Rosenvallon, P. (2004). *Le modèle politique français*. Paris: Editions du Seuil.

Ross, L. and Nisbet, R. (1991). *The Person and the Situation*. Philadelphia, PA: Temple University Press.

Sandel, M. (1996). *Democracy's Discontent: America in Search of a Public Philosophy*. Cambridge, MA: Harvard/Belknap.

Saxenian, A. (2006). *The New Argonauts*. Cambridge, MA: Harvard University Press.

Sen, A. (1985). 'Goals, commitment and identity', *Journal of Law, Economics and Organization*, 1: 2 (Reprinted in *Rationality and Freedom*, 2002, Harvard University Press).

—— (2002). *Rationality and Freedom*. Cambridge and London: Harvard University Press.

Sennett, R. (1999). *The Corrosion of Character*. New York: W.W. Norton.

Storper, M. (2005). 'Society, community and economic development', *Studies in Comparative International Development*, 39(4): 30–57.

Surowiecki, J. (2004). *The Wisdom of Crowds*. New York: Doubleday.

Thaler, R. (1994). *The Winner's Curse*. Princeton, NJ: Princeton University Press.

Young, H. P. and Durlauf, S. (2001). *Social Dynamics*. Washington, DC: Brookings Institution.

Notes

1. Previous version presented at DIME Durham Conference on 'Communities of Practice', October 2006. I thank the participants at that conference for their comments. Tom Farole gave the paper a close reading and many valuable suggestions.
2. This question is dealt with in more detail in Section 2.7.2 of this chapter.
3. In addition, any examination of the question of community has to try to distance itself from its highly charged political meanings. In the Anglo-Saxon political world, community conjures up images of 'natural' social bonds, the mobilization of underprivileged groups, and the healing of the wounds of a highly fragmented society through the involvement of community-based organizations and other NGOs in the political process. International organizations have come to embrace these 'communities' for the work they supposedly do in implementing development programmes. In other regions, such as social democratic Europe, 'community' tends to be viewed with suspicion, as a form of particularism, weakening the pursuit of the common social good.
4. For an extensive review of both these literatures, see Farole et al. (2007a).

5. There is a general debate about this question of whether such forms can be optimal or just second-best (Bowles and Gintis 2002, 2003).

6. I owe this review of situationalism to Glaeser (2004).

7. There is some literature on the degree of endogeneity of preferences and the role of situations: Bowles (1998); Corneo and Gruner (2002); Alesina and Fuchs-Schundlen (2005); Alesina and LaFerrara (2005); Alesina and George-Marios (2005); Bénabou and Tirole (2005).

8. For example, certain things are only achievable as network externalities in production or consumption.

9. This case is rarely considered in public choice theory, because the latter assumes that any group with big pay-offs to membership will then conflict with other groups' desires and possibly extract rents from its position. But – as we shall argue in Section 2.5 – if these cases approach 'social choice', there is little risk of these losses outweighing the gains.

10. As noted, behavioural economics shows that, in certain kinds of situations, people will make choices that bear little resemblance to standard rationality (that which achieves 'culmination outcomes') (Glaeser 2004, p. 8, after Della Vigna and Malmendier 2002). But it says little about how such situations are supplied. Group life supplies some situations. What are they, in relationship to choice?

11. Dworkin (2002) and other philosophers take up the possibility that our 'comprehensive consequentialist preferences' could be illiberal, that is wanting to deny someone else rights and freedoms, or to impose a morally homogenous vision on a heterogeneous world. In any case, Dworkin also points out that none of the positive benefits of community as a form of coordination require moral homogeneity within the group; it simply requires that the weak ties be useful in allowing us to make choices we want over certain kinds of private and comprehensive outcomes. The questions of whether that involves illiberal behaviour on the part of the group, or illiberal outcomes, are important, but beyond the scope of this chapter.

12. This might not be limited to cases where we do not feel the impacts directly. We could unwittingly make choices that have an indirect, but unpleasant impact on us, but not be able to connect the dot of our choice to this outcome. This is certainly the case with things such as traffic. Only by comparing experiences with others might we be able to draw the lines between the dots.

13. This can include involuntary communities, such as those imposed by exclusion or discrimination: once 'forced' into the club, if we want what it can provide us (even as an undesired second-best), we must accept its interactions (Young and Durlauf 2001).

14. There are viewpoints from other disciplines, such as neuroscience and evolutionary biology that can make other claims about the benefits and even the

necessity of group life to human survival, to human identity and to human happiness, but they are beyond the scope of this chapter.

15. For a review of some of the evidence, see Farole et al. (2007*a*). For statistical testing of some of these issues, see Farole et al. (2007*b*).

16. For more detailed analyses of the question of bonding and bridging in relationship to economic development, see Storper (2005) and Rodriguez-Pose and Storper (2006).

3

'The Art of Knowing': Social and Tacit Dimensions of Knowledge and the Limits of the Community of Practice

Paul Duguid

In the 15 years since its appearance, Lave and Wenger's (1990, 1991) notion of 'community of practice' (hereafter, CoP) has developed a remarkably wide following. Its appeal owes a good deal to the seductive character of *community*, aptly described as a 'warmly persuasive word' (Williams 1976, p. 66). As Østerlund and Carlile (2005) note, most citations of Lave and Wenger have focused on community and ignored practice. Yet it is practice that makes the CoP, the social locus in which a practice is sustained and reproduced overtime, a distinct type of community.[1] Practice is thus critical to CoP analysis. We should not, however, lose sight of the community. The CoP is inherently and irreducibly a social endeavour.

Inevitably, claims about its inherently social character put CoP theory at odds with individualist approaches to knowledge, found most noticeably in economics, where ideas of something irreducibly social are generally viewed with distaste. Von Hayek (1988) regards *social* as a 'weasel' word. Von Mises (1962) suggests that any dissent from economists' methodological individualism 'implies that the behavior of men is directed by mysterious forces that defy analysis and description' (p. 17). Yet the force of von Mises' argument is itself a little mysterious. There is no logical reason why the rejection of methodological individualism entails mystical forces – though it may entail disagreements with economists. Other economists (Cowan et al. 2000) have detected more mysticism in discussions of 'tacit knowledge'. In an attempt to locate much of the importance of the CoP in the tacit knowledge shared among its members, this article thus advances its case primarily in contrast to economistic claims for the theoretical sufficiency in accounts of human practice of explicit knowledge of individuals. The article accepts that both notions – the CoP and the tacit – have been deployed with a fair amount of mysticism. But it argues that both, nonetheless, have residual analytical usefulness and raise important issues about learning that are overlooked by standard economic explanations. Thus, the article hopes to show how and where CoP theory can illuminate, while economics perhaps cannot, what Polanyi (1966) calls 'the art of knowing'.

It begins by exploring the tendency within economics to align knowledge with information. It then examines the argument of Cowan et al. (2000) in some detail, questioning their confident substitution of the tacit with the explicit. Having argued that the tacit deserves a place in discussions of knowledge, the article then explores this concept in the context of communities and networks of practice. Finally, it concludes that the features of CoP theory that make it insightful both limit the areas where it can be useful and restrict its compatibility with other theoretical viewpoints.

3.1 Knowledge and Economists

Ideas of the 'information' or 'knowledge' economy have drawn many economists towards epistemological issues. Early pioneers such as von Hayek (1937, 1945), Machlup (1962), and Arrow (1969) are no longer alone. One way knowledge has been made economically manageable has been to reduce it to information. This move burrows through awkward aspects of knowledge in search of some sort of fundamental particle that is economically tractable.[2] Cognitive science and computer science have made parallel moves, concluding that human knowledge and machine information are ultimately one.[3] Perhaps the most confident account of the economic demystification of knowledge comes from Simon, a computer scientist and economist:

All the aspects of knowledge – its creation, its storage, its retrieval, its treatment as property, its role in the functioning of societies and organization – can be (and have been) analyzed with the tools of economics. Knowledge has a price and a cost of production; there are markets for knowledge, with their supply and demand curves, and marginal rates of substitution between one form of knowledge and another. (Simon 1999, quoted in Ancori et al. 2000, p. 256n)

If Simon is right, innovation, learning, and knowledge diffusion are no more problematic than the production and distribution of widgets. With the right incentives, knowledge will be produced, articulated, and shared without problem. All that remains is a little work for political economists.

Some economists remain less confident, finding awkward puzzles in the way people deploy knowledge and, to the exasperation of Cowan et al. (2000), continuing to invoke the notion of tacit knowledge. Implicitly asking how can we exchange something that we cannot articulate and may not even know we possess; tacit arguments fit uneasily within Simon's paradigm. Cowan et al. attempt to mop up this recalcitrant rearguard and end, at least for economists, this alliance with an economically problematic notion. They believe that the stakes are high: 'The concept of the inextricable tacitness of human knowledge forms the basis of arguments... against... every construction of rational decision processes as the foundation for modeling and explaining the actions of individual human agents' (p. 218).[4] If the tacit survives as analytically defensible, not only Simon's models of knowledge but also all economic models of human action might be at risk.[5]

3.1.1 *The sceptical economists*

Cowan et al. (2000) dub their critique 'the skeptical economists [hereafter, SE] guide to "tacit knowledge"' (p. 213). They motivate their discussion around a paradox in arguments for government-subsidized research. On the one hand, they say, subsidy-seekers argue that because markets deal poorly with public goods like information, government intervention is necessary. Yet when it is claimed that some nations will freeride on the research subvention of others, the same people (according to the SE) argue that tacitness makes innovative knowledge 'sticky' and so prevents free riding. Knowledge, the SE argue, cannot be both so 'leaky' that markets fail, and yet so 'sticky' that free riding fails. The source of this incoherence, they claim, lies in this quasi-mystical notion of tacitness. Champions of the tacit are guilty, the SE argue, of concluding that what they cannot see must be inherently invisible. While a group of experienced colleagues may, in Polanyi's (1966) famous phrase, 'know more than [they] can say', it does not follow what is left unsaid is fundamentally unsayable. Knowledge workers may lack incentives to overcome the 'substantial marginal cost' of codification, but there is no ontological barrier between tacit and explicit.[6]

Scrutiny of this argument is difficult because the SE do not examine any economists who actually fall foul of this paradox. An earlier version of the essay (Cowan et al. 1999) pins blame on an odd Anglo-French group – Harry Collins, Michel Callon, and Bruno Latour – and the three make a residual but barely explained appearance in the later paper. Not only do these three antagonists sit uneasily together, but none is an economist, and none is known for this argument. Another candidate might be the conservative scientist Kealey (Cowan et al. 2000, p. 224, n. 12), who does oppose government-subsidized R&D. He has already suffered a withering critique at the hands of one of the SE (David 1997). Curiously, neither Kealey's spurious argument nor David's damning dismissal turn on the tacit. Furthermore, Kealey too – as David (1997) makes abundantly clear – is not an economist. In the absence of named protagonists, the SE target has many of the characteristics of a straw man.

There are reasons to doubt the force of the SE argument. First, while inveighing against the idea of unarticulable knowledge, the SE dismiss it from their argument as 'not very interesting' (p. 230) and instead discuss articulable knowledge and the conditions of its codification. Thus, they beg the central question they purport to raise.

Second, while they report Polanyi talking of a tacit *dimension* to knowledge (p. 249, emphasis added), they fail to treat it as dimension putting tacit and explicit on a continuum ('Our focus has been maintained on ... the dimension along which codification appeared at one extremum and tacitness occupied the other'; p. 249). Two dimensions and two ends of a continuum are, of course, distinct. Polanyi was arguing that the tacit is not reducible to the explicit. The SE are determined that it should be, hence, their translation of dimension into continuum.[7]

Third, while lamenting that the tacit has come loose from 'epistemological moorings' (p. 213), the SE themselves duck philosophical questions. For instance, they characterize Polanyi's epistemological argument as primarily a theory of perception. Equally, the SE allude to Ryle's (1949) famous distinction between knowing *how* and knowing *that*, but do not bother to consult Ryle himself.[8] Ryle, like Polanyi, argues that the two aspects of knowing are complementary, knowing *how* helps to make knowing *that* actionable. They are not, however, substitutable: Accumulation of know *that* does not lead to knowing *how*. Know *that*, we acquire in the form of explicit, codified information. By contrast, 'we learn *how*', Ryle argues, 'by practice' (1949, p. 41).

The idea that knowing *that* does not produce *knowing how* is important. Oakeshott (1967) talks of

... the tacit or implicit component of knowledge, the ingredient which is not merely unspecified in propositions, but which is unspecifiable in propositions. It is the component of knowledge which does not appear in the form of rules and which, therefore, cannot be resolved into information or itemized in the manner characteristic of information. (p. 167)

Such arguments highlight the philosophically problematic recursiveness implicit in the idea that knowledge can be transferred through codification. Codification cannot explain how we come to read new codes. If all we have is the explicit, then a new codebook must either explain itself or require another codebook to do the explaining. The argument is thus trapped between circularity (with codebooks explaining themselves) and an infinite regress (with codebooks explaining codebooks). Such explanations must, as Wittgenstein (1958) argues, 'come to an end somewhere' (p. 3e).[9] Ryle points to another, irreducible kind of knowledge or activity that gets us started, that shows us *how* and gives us, in Oakeshott's terms, the necessary 'judgment' to put rules into effect.[10] Indeed, a chain of epistemological arguments stretching back to Socrates and the *Meno* suggests that codified knowledge, the explicit dimension, rests on an uncodifiable substrate that tells us how to use the code. In Aristotle's words:

While it is easy to know that honey, wine, hellebore, cautery, and the use of the knife are so, to know how, to whom, and when these should be applied with a view to producing health, is no less an achievement than that of being a physician. (Aristotle 1908, Book V, part 9)

Explicit knowledge, from this viewpoint, is not a self-sufficient base, but a dependent superstructure. 'Into every act of knowing', Polanyi claims, 'there enters a tacit ... contribution' (1958).

Thus, while knowledge may include codified content, to be used it requires the disposition to apply it, which cannot itself, without risk of recursion, be propositional. As Fodor (1968) puts it, knowledge involves not simply (indeed not even necessarily) knowing how the thing is done, but knowing how to do it, and the two are quite distinct. Explaining a joke is quite different from telling a joke. They may both play a part in the world of humour, but they are not equivalent or substitutable.

3.1.2 *Tacit appeal*

In their eagerness to dismiss the tacit, the SE portray it as little more than a fad brought into economics by Nelson and Winter (1982) and rapidly blown out of proportion:

A notion that took its origins in the psychology of visual perception and human motor skills has been wonderfully transmuted, first from an efficient mode of mental storage of knowledge into a putative epistemological category (having to do with the nature of knowledge itself), from there into a phenomenon of inarticulable inter-organizational relationships and finally to the keys to corporate, and perhaps national, competitive advantage! (p. 223)

Rooting Polanyi in the 'psychology of visual perception' ignores his struggle to understand scientific invention, though this is close to the SEs heart. (Polanyi was, of course, himself a gifted chemist.) It also overlooks the immediate appeal of his idea in diverse fields, including linguistics (Chomsky 1965), physics (Ziman 1967), philosophy (Fodor 1968), political science (Oakeshott 1967), the sociology of economics (Coats 1967), and economics (Richardson 1972); the last coming well before Nelson and Winter.[11] All appear to have recognized that Polanyi addressed an absence not so much to do with the stock of knowledge within their field as with the acquisition and appropriate use of that knowledge. Indeed, this multidisciplinary eagerness reflects less the emergence of a new fad than the dwindling of an old one – the time-honoured faith, identified with the enlightenment but going back much further, in explicit, codified knowledge. This faith gave rise to a long pursuit of such things as the universal library and the complete instruction manual.[12] Championing the explicit to the exclusion of the tacit may threaten to take us back, not forward.

3.2 A Little Learning

Learning throws light on the importance of the tacit for dealing with codified knowledge. It is impossible to specify and hence codify *all* the knowledge involved in even the most elementary practice (as Fodor (1968) points out, this would take us down to the level of firing neurons and beyond). Were it possible, it seems unlikely to be helpful. A brief list of all that is involved in tying a shoelace would overwhelm a learner. Despite the SE faith in explication, in instruction as in design there is great value in economy in the sense of leaving as much as possible unsaid (Kreiner 2001;

Brown and Duguid 1996). But in considering codification, quantity is not the only issue. Quality matters as well, for it is not clear that codified knowledge is equivalent to the tacit knowledge it comes from. The codification of knowledge may be less a matter of translation (though translation itself is rarely innocent) than transformation, whereby the codified no longer serves the purpose of the tacit it replaces.[13] Uncodified knowledge provides background context and warrants for assessing the codified. Background no longer works as background when it is foregrounded.

In learning situations, for example, it is not simply what a mentor or teacher can say, but also what he or she implicitly displays about the particular art, craft, or discipline. As a thought experiment, consider those enormously lucrative textbooks that in one 'new' edition after another introduce economics students to the discipline. Curiously, their authors often continue teaching, many times prescribing the very textbook into which they have distilled their codified knowledge. If texts can contain the requisite knowledge, as the SE suggest, then this is surely an odd situation. It might be argued that these teachers deliberately keep some of their knowledge uncodified to give them a double stream of income, one from writing and another from teaching. That situation, economics suggests, would surely act as an incentive for rivals to codify the missing knowledge in an alternative textbook that would find a ready market. Students armed with the complete knowledge in codified form would not have to pay the fees of the expensive universities where the star professors teach – or go to class at all. Yet economists continue to write and teach. One star economist (McCloskey 1985) suggests why:

Economics is ... a matter of feeling the applicability of arguments, of seeing analogies ... of knowing when to reason verbally and when mathematically, and of what implicit characterization of the world is most useful for correct economics. ... Problem-solving in economics is the tacit knowledge of the sort Polanyi described. (p. 178)[14]

Indeed, the failings of many teachers can probably be attributed less to their lack of explicit knowledge of a discipline than to their inability to exhibit the underlying practice successfully. For all their disciplinary wisdom, teachers are usually unaware of quite what, from their students' perspective, is on display and of the 'stolen knowledge' (Brown and Duguid 1995) their students carry away.

The idea that 'knowledge people reveal in action complements what they reveal in precepts' is again an old one. It penetrates the false dichotomy that opens the *Meno*: 'Can you tell me, Socrates, whether virtue is acquired by teaching or by practice?' (Plato 1953). It also helps explain the power of apprenticeship and why apprenticeship is not merely the preferred method of 'manual' trades, but also of the higher reaches of academic disciplines. Polanyi noticed this about his own discipline:

The large amounts of time spent by students of chemistry, biology and medicine in their practical courses shows how greatly these sciences rely on the transmission of skills and connoisseurship from master to apprentice. It offers an impressive demonstration of the extent to which the art of knowing has remained unspecifiable at the very heart of science. (Polanyi 1958, p. 55)

Hayek reports something very similar about his discipline:

We need to remember only how much we have to learn in any occupation after we have completed our theoretical training, how big a part of our working life we spend learning particular jobs. . . . Even economists who regard themselves as definitely above the crude materialist fallacies . . . commit the same mistake . . . toward the acquisition of such practical knowledge . . . the reproach of irrationality. (von Hayek 1945, p. 522)

But the political scientist Oakeshott perhaps best sums up the process:

And if you were to ask me the circumstances in which patience, accuracy, economy, elegance and style first dawned upon me, [they came from] a Sergeant gymnastics instructor. . . not on account of anything he ever said, but because he was a man of patience, accuracy, economy, elegance, and style. (Oakeshott 1967, p. 176)

Oakeshott reflects Ryle's (1949) argument that to do something patiently, accurately, economically, elegantly, or stylishly does not involve two processes – an act and a 'mental' monitoring – each of which can be specified in a set of rules. (In organizational literature, Weick et al. (1999) notion of 'mindfulness' echoes Ryle's insight.[15]) Further, Oakeshott emphasizes that transferring knowledge, particularly to newcomers, involves more than transferring codified knowledge. Declarative statements are always underconstrained – usefully so, if our argument holds that voluminous explicit information is more likely to increase uncertainty than reduce it. Suffering from problems of self-referentiality, no text is able to determine the principles of its own interpretation; or, to put it another way, all are open to multiple interpretations. Approaching a text as sincere or ironic yields two diametrically opposed interpretations of its meaning (a problem that famously landed Daniel Defoe in the stocks). A tacit understanding of the ground rules for interpretation thus plays a role in grounding a particular interpretation of a text – a facet of interpretation that originates outside the text to be interpreted.

3.3 Interpretive Communities

Which interpretation is seen as appropriate depends not on the text, but on the nature of the community making the interpretation (Fish 1994). As Arrow (1974) and Leonard and Sensiper (1998) point out, the same knowledge is used in quite different ways in different occupational communities, much as the Bible finds radically different interpretations among different sects. Consequently, as teachers induct students into their discipline, they spend a great deal of time showing students how to read, for this is not simply a matter of learning to decode a text in the abstract, but of learning to decode from the perspective of that discipline (which is why we should not be too hard on those economists who teach from their textbooks).[16] The knowing *how* involved, CoP theory suggests, is the product of communities of practice.

3.3.1 *The community of practice*

Talk of learning, apprenticeship, and communities helps to bring the discussion back to the CoP. This, as noted, was introduced as a theory of learning, drawing much of its evidence from studies of apprenticeship (Lave and Wenger 1991). Within a CoP, knowledge is instantiated dynamically in what Giddens (1984) calls knowledgeability, including 'all the things which actors know tacitly about how to "go on" in the context of social life without being able to give them direct discursive expression' (p. xxiii). Membership in the CoP offers form and context as well as content to aspiring practitioners, who need to not just acquire the explicit knowledge of the community but also the identity of a community member.[17]

Thus, learning in the sense of becoming a practitioner – which includes acquiring not only codebooks, but also the ability to decode them appropriately – can usefully be thought of as learning *to be* and contrasted to what Bruner (1996) calls 'learning *about*'.[18] The former requires knowing *how*, the art of practice, much of which lies tacit in a CoP. Learning *about* only requires the accumulation of knowing *that*, which confers the ability to talk a good game, but not necessarily to play one. Transforming knowing *how* into knowing *that*, the tacit into its nearest explicit equivalent, is likely to transform learning from learning *to be* into learning *about*. The CoP's knowledge, in tacit or explicit form, may be distributed across the collective and their shared artefacts rather than held by, or divisible among, individuals (Hutchins 1995). Within the CoP the knowing *how* of the community, not merely of an individual, is on display.

3.3.2 *Networks of practice*

Because tacit knowledge is displayed or exemplified, not transmitted, in most circumstances a CoP is likely to involve face-to-face interaction.[19] Of course, not all practice is local. In many areas, the practice is shared widely among practitioners, most of whom will never come into contact with one another. The *network* of practice (NoP) designates the collective of all practitioners of a particular practice. For example, Knorr Cetina's (1999) 'epistemic culture' of high-energy physicists constitutes a global NoP that has within it multiple local CoPs. Though practice is not coordinated within a NoP as it is in a CoP, common practices and common tools allow distant members to exchange global know *that* and to re-embed it (Giddens 1990) in effective, coherent ways through the mediation of their locally acquired knowing *how*.[20] Consequently, where practice precedes it, explicit knowledge may appear to have global reach (or to be 'leaky'). Where it does not, the same knowledge may appear remarkably parochial (or to be 'sticky').

The central distinction between the CoP and the NoP turns on the control and coordination of the reproduction of a group and its practice. Newcomers enter the network through a local community. You become an economist by entering an economics department in Chicago, or Berkeley, or Columbia – a route that may mark you for life, in part because the tacit knowledge of the local community profoundly shapes your identity and its trajectory.

3.4 Epistemic and Ethical Dimensions of Practice

Economistic explanations of knowledge diffusion focus on the codification of knowledge (Cohendet and Steinmueller 2000), access to information (Mokyr 2002), reduction of transaction costs (Williamson 1981), and specification and protection of private interests (Coase 1988; North 1981). The practice perspective modifies these assumptions along two distinct dimensions. On the one hand, there are difficulties around what knowledge people *can* meaningfully share. Such involuntary barriers to sharing might be thought of as epistemic entailments of practice. On the other, there are also difficulties concerning what people *will* share – not everything has its price. Local communities and even disaggregated NoPs may simply not want to share, or they may want to hide what they know. These voluntary constraints on sharing can be thought of as the ethical entailments of practice. These entailments distinguish the 'can/cannot' of knowledge flow from the 'will/would not'. The tacit dimension of a practice's knowledge – knowing *how*'s shaping of propriety, rather than know *that*'s suitability as property – profoundly affects these entailments. Knowledge, that is, may stick or flow for epistemic and ethical rather than just economic reasons.

3.4.1 *Epistemic entailments: can/cannot*

Divisions of labour lead to von Hayek's (1945) divisions of knowledge, which create distinct epistemic cultures. Within such cultures, explicit knowledge can travel and remain actionable; between, it usually cannot without difficulty. Economists generally acknowledge epistemic barriers between large cultural groups, between, for example, Europe and Asia. They seem less willing to consider them on a smaller scale, yet barriers seem to occur at the level of the CoP. Within CoPs or NoPs the potential for flow is high. Shared knowing *how*, produced by shared practice, creates the possibility of productive sharing of knowing *that*. But when the practice and knowing *how* of two communities are different, epistemic barriers develop and productively sharing knowing *that* becomes much more challenging – even when the different practices lie together within an organization (Bechky 2003; Carlile 2002).[21] Explication or codification does not solve the problem.[22]

3.4.2 *Ethical commitments: will/would not*

Arguments like Simon's (described earlier) or Teece's (1986) about 'regimes of appropriation' assume that financial incentives will prevent those who have competitive knowledge from sharing it with those outside the regime. Yet people will sometimes share what self-interest predicts they hold secret, and conversely will not share, despite encouragements, when it expects them to reveal. Whether they will or would not share may be determined by the ethical considerations reflecting a community's standards of propriety.

The idea that practice develops community standards that rise above self-interest is an old one. Marx and Engels (1978) argued that those among whom labour is divided develop a 'communal interest' (p. 53). Durkheim (1960) argues that 'the division of labor becomes a predomin- ant source of social solidarity at the same time it becomes the foundation of the moral order' (p. 333). More recently, MacIntyre (1981) has argued that 'the self has to find its moral identity in and through its membership of communities' (p. 205).[23] Thompson (1971), following Marx, suggests that such social groups will resist, in the name of their moral interests, appeals to their economic interests.[24] In all, if we want to understand individuals' capacities and motives for sharing knowledge, we need to look not just at the knowledge, but at the communities in which their knowing *how* was shaped.

3.5 Conclusion: Paradox Resolved?

Though the route has been a long one, we might now be in a position to resolve the paradox that motivated the SE critique without needing to reject the tacit all together. To understand the distribution of knowledge, we should not look at knowledge à la Simon, as if it were a widget whose production and consumption could be modelled without reference to producers or consumers. Knowing *that*, as explicit, codified propositions, probably can be modelled this way. But it cannot usefully be isolated from the knowing *how* that makes it actionable.

For the SE, economic arguments about knowledge appear incoherent when, on the one hand, protagonists claim that knowledge causes markets to fail because it is a public good, yet on the other, the same protagonists apparently maintain that knowledge production merits subsidy and resists free riders because knowledge is not a public good. In short, knowledge appears to be both 'leaky' (Liebeskind 1996) and 'sticky' (von Hippel 1994). The argument, however, focuses on knowledge independent of knowers and the situation in which knowledge is used. It is different knowers and their knowing *how* that turn the same knowledge from sticky to leaky. The ability to read gives any competent users of a language access to knowledge codified in that language. But access to that explicit know- ledge does not confer the ability to put it into appropriate use. Tacit knowledge, which confers that ability, is, by contrast with the explicit and codified, remarkably sticky.

Knowledge paradoxes arise, then, by confusing the dimensions of know- ledge or by assuming that we can substitute one for the other without problems. Nowhere, perhaps, is this more evident than in the endless problems of 'best practice' diffusion. On the one hand, theorists of 'best practice' put their finger on the essential point: Practice is critical. On the other, they regularly attempt to move a best practice from one community to another by codifying and circulating the explicit knowledge. What, of course, is truly critical is the knowing *how* embedded in the practice and wrapped around with ethical and epistemic commitments. Without these – and these are admittedly very hard to transfer – the explicit is worth relatively little. Many have tried to imitate the form of Toyota's production methods; few have managed to replicate the quality of its practice.

Codification is remarkably powerful, but its power is only released through the corresponding knowing *how*, which explains how we get to know and learn to do. Because it is not so economically tractable, the SE try to dismiss this knowing *how* as readily substitutable by the more compliant knowing *that*. The argument leads them, this essay argues, to attend to what people can say but to overlook what they can do; to be able to describe what people know, but not account for how they come to know; to be able in theory to quantify a person's knowledge, but not to assess its quality. In making their case, the SE have mapped a very important part of the terrain of knowledge (see Cowan et al. 2000, fig. 2), but not all. In particular, they have failed to show how we get access to the terrain and what we can do when we get there.

This argument attempts to reveal limits in some economist's accounts of knowledge. At the same time, it exposes limits to CoP analysis, which has occasionally been stretched well beyond its capacity. By emphasizing how CoP theory differs from more individualist social sciences, the argument also intimates limits to the theory's compatibility. To recap, the argument proposes a theory of knowledge acquisition rooted not in the epistemological stocks of individual heads, but in the flow of practice within communities. Communities, it holds, have emergent properties that, while they are no doubt the outcome of individual actions, amount to more than the sum of those actions and more than the amortization of transaction costs. If this is right, then CoP theories may not fit well with approaches to work and knowledge that, at least on the surface, appear congenial.

For example, Cohen and Prusak (2001) highlight similarities between CoP and social capital theories. Social capital (SC) theories draw attention to networks of individuals that help to embed economic interactions in social relations (Polanyi 1957; Granovetter 1973, 1985). Through social exchanges, people build webs of trust (Fukuyama 1995; Putnam 1993, 2000), obligation, reputation, expectations, and norms (Coleman 1988). In these webs, SC theory suggests, people are willing and able to share knowledge and coordinate action. Most CoP theorists would go along with these claims, but some would pause at the word 'able'. That is, CoP analysis accepts the importance of social capital networks to understanding why people will and will not share. But it makes a distinction between people's willingness to share and their ability to share, suggesting that people have to engage in similar or shared practices to be able to share knowledge about those practices. Thus, where SC theory points to unseen links, CoP theory points to unseen boundaries – boundaries shaped by practice – that divide knowledge networks from one another. These boundaries may prevent communication despite all the obligations of good will and social capital that connect them or, indeed, all the incentives of financial capital that may entice them. Indeed, while advancing the *social*, a good deal of SC theory has nonetheless remained fairly close to its roots in economics (residual in that word *capital*).[25] This has a couple of implications. First, SC theorists' focus on 'rational actors' (Coleman 1988) portrays social groups as little more than 'combinations' of individuals (Nahapiet and Ghoshal 1996). So while SC analysis encompasses a broad array of social groups, including such things as firms, bowling leagues, housing organizations, and families, the CoP perspective, by contrast, limits itself to communities and networks where practice is coordinated or at least shared. Second, while some SC theorists, again like economists, view the sharing of knowledge as little more than the exchange of 'information that facilitates action' (Coleman 1988, p. 104) between individuals, and as primarily determined by ties, strong or weak, and goodwill, CoP theory suggests the challenge of communication is more complex. Social capital focuses primarily on the circulation of knowledge promoted by what is here called the ethical commitment of the people involved. But, from the point of view of CoP theory, it overlooks the corresponding epistemic commitment. If that too is not shared – as it is among CoPs and NoPs, but not necessarily among SC networks – then in the end no amount of bowling together will bring about shared, actionable knowledge.

These distinctions are not made to vaunt the superiority or even hegemony of CoP theories over rivals. CoP theory, as has already been suggested, only addresses certain topics involving quite special types of community and networks. Social capital is much broader and economics, of course, broader still. Indeed, this essay deliberately seeks to restrict the application of CoP theory, pointing instead to other theories that are less limited and more adaptable. It is hoped, however, that the edges of CoP theory thus narrowed will provide a sharper analytical tool that can tell us more about the 'art of knowing'.

References

Ancori, B., Bureth, A., and Cohendet, P. (2000). 'The economics of knowledge: The debate about codification and tacit knowledge', *Industrial and Corporate Change*, 9(2): 255–87.

Argyris, C. and Schön, D. (1978). *Organizational Learning: A Theory of Action Perspective*. Reading, MA: Addison-Wesley.

Aristotle. (1908). *The Nicomachean Ethics*, trans. W. Ross. Oxford: Clarendon Press (http://www.ilt.columbia.edu/publications/Projects/digitexts/aristotle/nicomach ean_ethics/book05.html accessed March 10, 2004).

Arrow, K. J. (1969). 'Classificatory notes on the production and transmission of technological knowledge', *American Economic Review*, 59(2): 29–35.

—— (1974). *The Limits of Organization*. New York: W.W. Norton.

Bechky, B. A. (2003). 'Sharing meaning across occupational communities: The transformation of understanding on a production floor', *Organization Science*, 14(3): 312–30.

Bollier, D. (2004). 'Who owns the sky? Reviving the commons', *In These Times*, 29 March (http://www.inthesetimes.com/comments.php?id=631_O_1_O_C accessed February 18, 2005).

Brown, J. and Duguid, P. (1995). 'Stolen knowledge', *Educational Technology*, 33(3): 10–15.

—— —— (1996). 'Keeping it simple', in T. Winograd (ed.), *Exploring Software Design*. Menlo Park, CA: Addison-Wesley, pp. 129–45.

—— —— (2000). *The Social Life of Information*. Boston, MA: Cambridge University Press.

—— —— (2001). 'Knowledge and organization: A social-practice perspective', *Organization Science*, 12(2): 198–213.

Bruner, J. (1996). *The Culture of Education*. Cambridge, MA: Harvard University Press.

Carlile, P. R. (2002). 'A pragmatic view of knowledge and boundaries: Boundary objects in new product development', *Organization Science*, 13(4): 442–55.

Chomsky, N. (1965). *Aspects of the Theory of Syntax*. Cambridge, MA: MIT Press.

Coase, R. H. (1988). *The Firm, the Market, and the Law*. Chicago, IL: University of Chicago Press.

Coats, A. W. (1967). 'Sociological aspects of British economic thought (ca. 1880–1930)', *Journal of Political Economy*, 75: 706–29.

Cohen, D. and Prusak, L. (2001). *In Good Company: How Social Capital makes Organizations Work*. Boston, MA: Harvard Business School Press.

Cohendet, P. and Steinmueller, W. E. (2000). 'The codification of knowledge: A conceptual and empirical exploration', *Industrial and Corporate Change*, 92(2): 195–209.

Coleman, J. S. (1988). 'Social capital and the creation of human capital', *American Journal of Sociology*, 94: 95–120.

Cowan, R., David, P. A., and Foray, D. (1999). 'The explicit economics of knowledge codification and tacitness,' paper prepared for the EC TSER 3rd TPIK Workshop, Strasbourg (http://econpapers.hhs.se/paper/wopstanec/99027.htm accessed 10 March 2004).

——————— (2000). 'The explicit economics of knowledge codification and tacitness', *Industrial and Corporate Change*, 9(2): 211–53.

David, P. A. (1997). 'From market magic to calypso science policy: Review of Terence Kealey', *The Economic Laws of Scientific Research: Research Policy*, 26(2): 229–55.

Davis, N. Z. (1975). 'Printing and the people', in *Society and Culture in Early Modern France*. Stanford, CA: Stanford University Press, pp. 189–226.

Durkheim, E. (1960). *The Division of Labor in Society*, trans. G. Simpson. Glencoe, IL: Free Press.

Fish, S. (1994). *Is There a Text in This Class? The Authority of Interpretive Communities*. Cambridge, MA: Harvard University Press.

Floridi, L. (1999). *Philosophy and Computing: An Introduction*. London: Routledge.

Fodor, J. (1968). 'The appeal to tacit knowledge in psychological explanation', *Journal of Philosophy*, 65(20): 627–40.

Fukuyama, F. (1995). *Trust: The Social Virtues and the Creation of Prosperity*. New York: Free Press.

Giddens, A. (1984). *The Constitution of Society: Outline of the Theory of Structuration*. Berkeley, CA: California University Press.

—— (1990). *The Consequences of Modernity: The Raymond Fred West Memorial Lectures*. Stanford, CA: Stanford University Press.

Granovetter, M. (1973). 'The strength of weak ties', *American Journal of Sociology*, 78(6): 1360–80.

—— (1985). 'Economic action and social structure: The problem of embeddedness', *American Journal of Sociology*, 91(3): 481–510.

Grey, H. C. (2002). 'The political implications of information theory, digital divide, culture and human-computer interface design and the revolution in military affairs', paper presented at the SSRC Summer Institute, Information Technology and Social Research: Setting the Agenda, Columbia University, New York.

Hutchins, E. (1995). *Cognition in the Wild*. Cambridge, MA: MIT Press.

Knorr Cetina, K. (1999). *Epistemic Cultures: How the Sciences Make Knowledge*. Cambridge, MA: Harvard University Press.

Kogut, B. and Zander, U. (1996). 'What do firms do? Coordination, identity, & learning', *Organization Science*, 7(5): 502–18.

Kreiner, K. (2001). *The Ambiguity of Sharing: Knowledge Management in the Context of New Product Development*, IOA Working Paper. Copenhagen: Copenhagen Business School.

Lave, J. and Wenger, E. (1990). *Situated Learning: Legitimate Peripheral Participation*, IRL Report IRL90–0013, February. Palo Alto, CA: Institute for Research on Learning.

———— (1991). *Situated Learning: Legitimate Peripheral Participation*. New York: Cambridge University Press.

Leonard, D. and Sensiper, S. (1998). 'The role of tacit knowledge in group innovation', *California Management Review*, 40(3): 112–32.

Liebeskind, J. P. (1996). 'Knowledge, strategy, and the theory of the firm', *Strategic Management Journal*, 17: 93–107.

Machlup, F. (1962). *The Production and Distribution of Knowledge in the United States*. Princeton, NJ: Princeton University Press.

MacIntyre, A. (1981). *After Virtue: A Study in Moral Theory*. Notre Dame, IN: University of Notre Dame Press.

Marx, K. and Engels, F. (1978). *The German Ideology: Part One*. New York: International.

McCloskey, D. N. (1985). *The Rhetoric of Economics*. Madison, WI: University of Wisconsin Press.

Mokyr, J. (2002). *The Gifts of Athena: Historical Origins of the Knowledge Economy*. Princeton, NJ: Princeton University Press.

Moxon, J. (1693). *Mechanick Exercises, or The Doctrine of Handy-Works*. London: Printed and sold by J. Moxon.

Nahapiet, J. and Ghoshal, S. (1996). 'Social capital, intellectual capital, and the organizational advantage', *Academy of Management Review*, 23(2): 242–68.

Nelson, R. and Winter, S. G. (1982). *An Evolutionary Theory of Economic Change*. Cambridge, MA: Belknap, Harvard University Press.

Nonaka, I. (1994). 'A dynamic theory of organizational knowledge creation', *Organization Science*, 5(1): 14–37.

Nonaka, I. and Takeuchi, H. (1995). *The Knowledge-Creating Company: How Japanese Companies Create the Dynamics of Innovation*. New York: Oxford University Press.

North, D. C. (1981). *Structure and Change in Economic History*. New York: W.W. Norton.

Oakeshott, M. (1967). 'Learning and teaching', in R. S. Peters (ed.), *The Concept of Education*. London: Routledge & Kegan Paul, pp. 156–77.

O'Donnell, J. (1998). *Avatars of the Word: From Papyrus to Cyberspace*. Cambridge, MA: Harvard University Press.

Orlikowski, W. J. (1992). 'The duality of technology: Rethinking the concept of technology in organization', *Organization Science*, 3(3): 398–427.

Orlikowski, W. J. (2002). 'Knowing in practice: Enacting a collective capability in distributed organizing', *Organization Science*, 13(3): 249–73.

Østerlund, C. and Carlile, P. (2005). 'Relations in practice: Sorting through practice theories on knowledge sharing in complex organizations', *Information Society*, 21(2): 91–107.

Plato (1953). *Dialogues*, trans. B. Jowett. Oxford: Clarendon Press (http://classics. mit.edu/Plato/meno.html accessed March 10, 2004).

Polanyi, K. (1957). *The Great Transformation: The Political and Economic Origins of Our Time*. New York: Bacon.

Polanyi, M. (1944). 'Patent reform', *Review of Economic Studies*, Summer, 2: 61–76.

——(1958). *Personal Knowledge*. London: Routledge & Kegan Paul.

——(1966). *The Tacit Dimension*. Garden City, NY: Doubleday.

Putnam, R. D. (1993). *Making Democracy Work: Civic Traditions in Modern Italy*. Princeton, NJ: Princeton University Press.

——(2000). *Bowling Alone: The Collapse and Revival of American Community*. New York: Simon & Schuster.

Richardson, G. B. (1972). 'The organisation of industry', *The Economics Journal*, 82(327): 883–96.

Ryle, G. (1949). *The Concept of Mind*. London: Hutchinson.

Shannon, C. and Weaver, W. (1964). *The Mathematical Theory of Communication*. Urbana, IL: University of Illinois Press.

Simon, H. A. (1999). 'The many shapes of knowledge', *Revue d'Economie Industrielle*, 88: 23–39.

Star, S. L. and Greisemer, J. R. (1989). 'Institutional ecology, "translations" and boundary objects: Amateurs and professionals in Berkeley's Museum of Vertebrate Zoology, 1907–39', *Social Studies of Science*, 19: 387–420.

Steinmueller, W. E. (2000). 'Will new information and communication technologies improve the "codification" of knowledge?', *Industrial and Corporate Change*, 9(2): 361–76.

Teece, D. J. (1986). 'Profiting from technological innovation: Implications for integration, collaboration, licensing, and public policy', *Research Policy*, 15: 285–305.

Thompson, E. P. (1971). 'The moral economy of the English crowd in the eighteenth century', *Past and Present*, 50: 76–136.

Tuomi, I. (2000). 'Data is more than knowledge: Implications of the reversed knowledge hierarchy for knowledge management and organizational memory', *Journal of Management Information Systems*, 16(3): 103–18.

von Hayek, F. A. (1937). 'Economics and knowledge', *Economica*, 4(13): 33–54.

——(1945). 'The use of knowledge in society', *American Economic Review*, 35: 519–30.

——(1988). *The Fatal Conceit: The Errors of Socialism*. Chicago, IL: University of Chicago Press.

von Hippel, E. (1994). 'Sticky information and the locus of problem solving: Implications for innovation', *Management Science*, 40(4): 429–39.

von Mises, L. (1962). *The Ultimate Foundation of Economic Science: An Essay on Method*. Princeton, NJ: Van Nostrand.

Weick, K. E., Sutcliffe, K. M., and Obstfeld, D. (1999). 'Organizing for high reliability: Processes of collective mindfulness', *Research in Organizational Behavior*, 21: 81–123.

Williams, R. (1976). *Keywords: A Vocabulary of Culture and Society*. New York: Oxford University Press.

Winter, S. G. (1987). 'Knowledge and competence as strategic assets', in D. Teece (ed.), *The Competitive Challenge: Strategies for Industrial Renewal*. Cambridge, MA: Ballinger, pp. 159–84.

Wittgenstein, L. (1958). *Philosophical Investigations*, trans. G. E. M. Anscombe. Oxford: Basil Blackwell and Mott.

Ziman, J. M. (1967). *Public Knowledge: An Essay Concerning the Social Dimension of Science*. Cambridge: Cambridge University Press.

Notes

1. It is this sustenance and reproduction of practice through the opposing demands of continuity and displacement that gives CoPs their interdependent tension and dynamism. Nonetheless, the notion has repeatedly been applied to transient, cross-functional teams and miscellaneous work groups. See, for example, Nonaka (1994).

2. Hables Grey (2002) portrays information as a fundamental particle. The commonplace notion that there is an ascendancy from data through information to knowledge appears regularly in the economics literature (Ancori et al. 2000). Tuomi (2000) exposes flaws in the argument.

3. Shannon and Weaver (1964) note that the technical sense of communication is indifferent to meaning. The technical notion suggests that information reduces uncertainty; many who have to deal with the 'tsunami of information' in the current 'flux' (Steinmueller 2000, p. 373) understandably assume the opposite. Applying the technical notion to human practice assumes that humans are Turing machines, a complex claim that needs to be argued rather than assumed (Floridi 1999).

4. Page numbers refer to Cowan et al. (2000) unless otherwise noted.

5. While this article does attempt to defend the tacit from this attack, I am more sceptical than the SE and do not hold that such a defence threatens the foundations of economics.

6. The paradox – though not its political implications – is suggested in Winter (1987) and addressed directly in Brown and Duguid (2000, 2001). Intriguingly, Polanyi, the indirect target of the SE, was very interested in the political issues. See Polanyi (1944).

7. The economic historian Mokyr (2002) clearly recognizes the dimensional, irreducible character of tacit knowledge ('Tacit knowledge and formal or verbal knowledge should not be thought of as substitutes but as complements', p. 73).

8. Ryle is often misread, perhaps most egregiously by Nonaka (1994) and Nonaka and Takeuchi (1995).

9. See also Wittgenstein (1958, pp. 19e, 29e, and 40e).

10. The SE concede that 'Successfully reading the code . . . may involve prior acquisition of considerable specialized knowledge (quite possibly including knowledge not written down anywhere)' (p. 225). They give no explanation, however, of how such acquisition occurs. See also p. 232, notes 18 and 233.

11. Richardson (1972), who discussed the terrain between market and hierarchy early and with insight, notes, 'Technology cannot always be transferred simply by selling the right to use a process. It is rarely reducible to mere information to be passed on but consists also of experience and skills. In terms of Professor Ryle's celebrated distinction, much of it is 'knowledge how' rather than 'knowledge that' (p. 895).

12. Diderot and D'Alembert's encyclopaedia is the cynosure of enlightenment codification, but such things as Moxon's (1693) 'exercises' offer earlier examples. See also Davis (1975). For early belief in a universal library and its rebirth in the digital age, see O'Donnell (1998). Philosophically, logical positivism perhaps marked the end of this confidence in the exclusive character of explicit knowledge, though clearly it lives on in economics.

13. The multiple terms Nonaka (1994) uses to try to encompass the process of translation hint at some of the problems inherent in the notion. As well as translating and transforming, these include *externalizing, converting, interacting, interchanging, articulating, merging, shifting, entangling, resolving, transferring, harmonizing,* and *crystallizing.*

14. Endorsing Ryle's notion that these things come with practice, McCloskey ends by admonishing students with a very old joke situated insightfully for a new domain: 'How do you get to the Council of Economic Advisors? . . . Practice, practice' (McCloskey 1985, p. 178).

15. Ryle's argument raises some questions about Argyris and Schön's (1978) notion of 'second loop learning'. See also Giddens's (1984) Rylean discussion of reflexive monitoring, which concludes, 'Understanding is not a mental process accompanying the solving of a puzzle. . . . It is simply being able to apply the formula in the right context' (p. 20). Polanyi, it needs to be noted, did not agree with Ryle on this point. See Polanyi (1958, p. 372).

16. David's (1997) critique of Kealey, for example, rightly scolds Kealey, a biochemist, for failing to read economics literature as an economist would.

17. While 'identity' can seem unpleasantly 'soft' and far distant from hard-headed economic analysis, its importance is stressed in Kogut and Zander's (1996) influential essay.

18. Compare Aristotle's comment, cited earlier, that knowing when and how to apply treatment is 'no less an achievement than that of *being* a physician' [emphasis added].

19. See Giddens (1984) and in particular his use of Garfinkel's theory of 'facework'. See also Orlikowski (1992, 2002). (Orlikowski has been centrally instrumental in introducing Giddens's work to organizational studies and this article is particularly indebted to her.)

20. The looseness of coordination within an NoP allows for innovation through epistemic speciation.

21. Alternative means to bring two different communities into alignment though not necessarily understanding include routines (Nelson and Winter 1982), boundary objects (Star and Greisemer 1989), and the price mechanism (von Hayek 1945).

22. Whitehead's joke about *Principia Mathematica* – he claimed to understand every word but not one of the sentences – suggests the limits of codification.

23. As both are cited in this article, it should be noted that Giddens rejects MacIntyre's view of moral order.

24. Thompson shows how, across the eighteenth century, English people used the moral economy to defend their customary rights from the market economy. 'Open source' software offers intriguing modern parallels (Bollier 2004).

25. Coleman (1988) is quite explicit. His aim is 'to import the economist's principle of rational action for use in the analysis of social systems proper... the concept of social capital is a tool to aid in this' (p. 97).

4

Re-animating the Place of Thought: Transformations of Spatial and Temporal Description in the Twenty-First Century

Nigel Thrift

4.1 Communities of Practice

My take on the issue of communities of practice may initially appear to be an oblique one, founded in the generalities of social theory and without a sufficient footing in empirical work. So I will begin this chapter by explaining my interest in the pursuit of the idea of communities of practice and how it has transmuted into something rather different: a symptomatic reading of why this approach, and others like it, have become current and popular.

My interest in communities of practice arose from four different but related projects. One such project has been a long-standing interest in theories of situated practice, which, in my case, has transmuted into a project called non-representational theory, concerned with trying to outline a different style of doing politics which has at its heart transformations of space that bring with them transformations of thought (Thrift 1996, 2005b, 2007). The second project has been my interest in the history of management knowledge; in this history, communities of practice figure as one in a series of means of refreshing management practice, as so-called management fads (Thrift 2005b). The idea of communities of practice, understood as a means of producing distributions of enthusiasm, has proved to be a more or less effective shuttle in this milieu, just like any other management fad,[1] not least because it proves very difficult to disentangle the notion from many other such notions equally working themselves out across organizations in locally specific forms. The third project has been a history of clock time in England that I have been writing with a colleague for the last few years (Glennie and Thrift 2008), in which the concept of communities of practice was used *in extenso* as a means of approaching the sheer heterogeneity of use of clock time (clock time as used by astronomers and astrologists, for example, as opposed to clock time as used by seafarers) – with mixed results. The concept worked well for relatively small and well-drawn communities like those already mentioned but produced mixed results for any other kind of community. In particular, the most interesting thing – how novel practices of clock time travelled, or did not travel, between communities of practice and became general – proved to be no more illuminated by this notion than by many others.

The final project – and the one I want to concentrate on in this chapter – is my work on the way in which increasingly we are able to see a different model of space being rolled out by various agencies, one in which tacit embodied knowledge is being assisted and augmented through the design of *animated environments* that allow continual rehearsal and feedback, so allowing all manner of passionate interests to bubble up. In other words the redesign of interaction that has taken place over the last twenty years (Moggridge 2006) has allowed all manner of communities of practice to be founded and thrive in a way that would have been very difficult before.

As I will show, the background to the redesign of these environments is the circulation of a repertoire of ideas-cum-methods-cum-constructed realities like communities of practice that are understood *as attempts to produce rapid presence and authenticity by building instant ways of life* calling on theories and, more particularly, *methods* drawn especially, although not exclusively, from the social sciences (Thrift 2004a, 2005a, 2006). In other words, the concept of communities of practice is part and parcel of a more general impulse to construct quick-fire, 'instant'[2] communities by drawing on bodies of understanding which allow these communities to both be founded and have grip, in particular by making systematic knowledge tacit through the various means of systematizing tacit knowledge that can now be found and applied[3]: What seems certain is that it is impossible to understand the circulation of concepts like communities of practice without attending to how the spatial environment has been redesigned so that these concepts can simultaneously become affects and percepts as part of a more general project of the construction of a different kind of place; what I will call '*worlding*', *a word that stands for re-truthing the world*. These new practices of worlding, of what might be called realization, form the backbone of this chapter.

'Worlding' has a phenomenological ring to it and that is both right and wrong. Phenomenology has usually been associated with the authenticity of ongoing and concernful being. But worlding is about *constructing* that authenticity, often just for a few brief moments, usually with the aim of making a commercial return. There are two main theorists of worlding – Maurizio Lazzarato and Peter Sloterdijk – and I want to start this chapter by addressing their work, work which concerns making being *explicit* and therefore able to be operated on. In a sense, this chapter is about the hard work put in by business to 'explicitation' (Latour 2007) through concept practices like 'community of practice' and the dividends that it has paid in terms of constructing series of realities – new kinds of inhabitation – in which business forms a foregrounded background. In particular, I will outline how a new kind of spatial 'atmosphere' is being created which allows different kinds of subjects, objects, and worlds to be thrown together through the construction of what I will call the 'inhabitable map'. In effect, what I will be trying to outline is the beginnings of a fundamental transformation in the description of objects and communities, akin to that which occurred in the eighteenth century (Wall 2006) which constitutes a shift in what we know and what we want to know, enabled by how we know, one occasioned, exactly as in the eighteenth century, by a set of uncannily similar major cultural changes

... experientially, [by] technologically new ways of seeing and appreciating objects in the ordinary world through the popular prostheses of microscope, telescope, and empirical analysis; economically, [by] the expansion of consumer culture in the increasing presence and awareness of things on the market, in the house, and in daily life; epistemologically, [by] the changing attitudes toward the general and the particular, the universal and the individual; and, narratively, [by] the perception and representation of domestic space. (Wall 2006, p. 2)

In the second part of the chapter, I will then move on to how business has practised the art and science of explicitation. I will argue that this process involves drawing on methods drawn mainly from the social sciences, though often in heavily mediated forms involving the cultural circuit of capital. I will want to outline the qualities of the sweep of a new generation of research methods that are now being applied to space and place.

I will argue that the proliferation of these research methods, as marked by seemingly endless compendia and book series[4] is itself part of the process of worlding that I want to examine.[5] In particular, I will argue that these methods are making places into what I will call dynamic laboratories, animated environments which constitute laboratories in the field (combining the qualities of both) and which are simultaneously engines that allow the production of truths. Animated environments produce linked sites of permanent learning by redefining the situatedness of place, taking the laboratory – understood as a generic 'placeless' place (the 'laboratory') in which systematic knowledge is generated – out into the field. Landscape and labscape merge, so to speak (Kohler 2002), producing a new kind of authenticity in which the field is used in a laboratory-like way. It is this latter quasi-didactic project, in which formal and tacit knowledge is merged as a result of a redefinition of space and place, that I particularly want to concentrate on in this chapter. Whilst we should not be surprised by this development – it has been a feature of Western societies since at least the industrial revolution, as access to knowledge of either kind has become increasingly easy to achieve – what is interesting now is the sheer scale of the development, and the way it is producing a makeover of Western thought at several levels, a makeover which can be thought of as a kind of reanimation. This project requires a redefinition of place, what place is, and what it does: place is caused to move and respond. Moves afoot in the various methodological camps to produce greater attention to place and to values like recursivity, reflexivity, and participation cannot be seen as simply emancipatory. In part, they are also an element of and driven by a more general zeitgeist of the *generalized survey and interrogation* of subjects and objects and the construction of flow spaces that will allow that interrogation to, quite literally, take place.

Of course, what exactly all this might mean for us – do these developments signify the emergence of a new kind of digitalized Palladian landscape[6] or the construction of a new outer circle of Hell? – is still opaque. In the third part of the chapter, I will top the discussion off by turning to these political questions, since they are not just about how these instant environments are able to attain grip on our lives but also about how these environments are becoming our lives so that grip has itself become an inadequate term because it implies one thing operating on another rather than a melding of the two – or the creation of a third term. In turn, I will suggest that what is needed politically is a project of what Peter Sloterdijk calls 'ventilation' or 'air-conditioning' in which spaces are loosened up so that they provide resources for political thinking and responsiveness.

However, I will also point to the need to temper the rhetoric that currently circulates about the abundance of knowledge produced by new forms of community of practice by showing how whole shadow worlds of knowledge exist which are unable to be accessed by the general population.

4.2 New Worlds and New Worldings

To understand the practices of worlding, I will begin by drawing on the work of two of its most eminent theorists, namely Maurizio Lazzaratto and Peter Sloterdijk. What these two authors have tried to do, and what they have in common, is their desire to show how modern business has moved on from a focus on producing objects to a focus on producing phenomenal worlds which must inevitably be spaces, howsoever constructed, if they are to have grip. Thus, as Lazzarato points out, the business enterprise does not create its object but the world within which the object exists. As a corollary, the business enterprise does not create its subjects (as happened in the older disciplinary regimens) but the world within which the subject exists.

The company produces a world. In its logic, the service or the product, just as the consumer or the worker, must correspond to this world; and this world in its turn has to be inscribed in the souls and bodies of consumers and workers. This inscription takes place through techniques that are no longer exclusively disciplinary. Within contemporary capitalism the company does not exist outside the producers or consumers who express it. Its world, its objectivity, its reality, merges with the relationships enterprises, workers and consumers have with each other. Thus the company, like God in the philosophy of Leibniz, seeks to construct a correspondence, an interlacing, a chiasm between the monad (consumer and worker) and the world (the company). The expression and effectuation of the world and the subjectivities included in there, that is, the creation and realization of the sensible (desires, beliefs, intelligence) precedes economic production. The economic war currently played out on a planetary scale is indeed an 'aesthetic war'. . . . (Lazzarato 2004, p. 188)

In this world of worlds, the corporate aim is to produce, most particularly, what might be called *decisive moments* of semiosis which can be played in to. However, Lazzarato does not provide much detail on how these worlds are produced, apart from some rather emblematic references to brands and such like.

Yet the process of producing temporary unities which exceed all delineable qualities while still loosely implying them has a deeply engrained cultural history. A good example is provided by the decisive moment. This cultural technology was, in large part, an invention of Renaissance paint-ers trying to depict major turning points in history. They would build up scenes in great detail in which the disposition of every person and object counted as a part of a moment straining towards realization. The motif was subsequently taken up by photographers, and especially photojournalists. Famously, for Henri Cartier-Bresson, the decisive moment (the title of his exhibit at the Louvre, the first photographic show ever to be so honoured) was the instant when a shutter click can suspend an everyday event within the eye and heart of the beholder producing a confluence of observer and observed. It is the 'simultaneous recognition, in a fraction of a second, of the significance of an event as well as the precise organization of forms which gives that event its proper expression' (Cartier-Bresson 1952). Then, the decisive moment is still very much a mainstay of modern drama. Whole productions have been built around articulating the power of one moment, as in Deborah Warner's ability to focus the whole of *Titus Andro-nicus* on the moment where the raped Lavinia comes on stage, having had her hands chopped off and her tongue cut out. Her uncle, coming across this wreck of a woman, seemingly incomprehensibly bids her good day and asks her where her husband is. The moment is often cut from the play by directors as impossibly discordant but Warner made it into a triumph, the key being, as she put it 'doing the right thing at the right time'. Finally, and most obviously, there is film. Cinema can be understood as a series of practical meditations on summoning up decisive moments: 'truth 24 times a second', as Godard (cited in Mulvey 2005, p. 15) once put it. Cinema is able to produce not just speed, but delay and deferral – preserv-ing the moment at which the image is first registered in a kind of extended present of redefined significance.

Note one other thing about this history of the decisive moment. In each case, these moments have to be revealed by new mechanical *methods* that can reorder and transform the raw material of passing time and spatial difference – from different painting materials through the lightweight and mobile 35 mm camera through particular means of lighting and moving to slow motion and stop frame and the possibilities of digital special effects. In each case too, as has been pointed out many times, they involve a reworking of the relation between the observer and the observed, moving from a tableau-like relationship to one in which the observer attends differently through a sustained attentiveness which is also a 'suspension of perception' (Crary 1999). This sustained attentiveness is, of course, the mainstay of and precondition for the production of decisive moments.

In practice, the production of decisive moments means the production of spaces that are able to produce and represent decisive moments of all kinds: everyday life becomes a cavalcade of semiotically charged and rapidly changing moments which can be used for profit, realized through more and more carefully designed spaces, designed to elicit particular responses, designed to unleash speculation and creativity, and designed to amplify what counts as the object. That these decisive moments are increasingly produced through conscious spatial design can be seen in the proliferation of work on making space into a conscious asset in generating creativity (as at the workplace), and the voluminous work on generating experience economies.

This is where Peter Sloterdijk's work becomes relevant to my argument. In his *Sphären* trilogy, Sloterdijk takes Heidegger on dwelling as a root point of reference but then spatializes his thinking by posing the question of being as the question of being together: 'one is never alone only with oneself, but also with other people, with things and circumstances; thus beyond oneself and in an environment' (Sloterdijk 1998).[7] 'Being-a-pair' or a couple precedes all encounters.[8] In other words, Sphären is concerned with the dynamic of spaces of coexistence, spaces which are commonly overlooked, for the simple reason that 'human existence . . . is anchored in an insurmountable spatiality' (Sloterdijk 2005, p. 229).

Continuing on with this spatial problematic, Sloterdijk is concerned with how distances intercalate and produce different kinds of being-to-getherness. Sloterdijk identifies three waves of globalization, each with its corollary of new forms of 'artificial' construct. The first wave is the meta-physical globalization of Greek cosmology, the second wave is the nautical globalization since the fifteenth century, and the third wave is now upon us. Whereas the first wave created an esoteric geometricism and the sec-ond wave created an exoteric cosmopolitanism, the third wave of rapid communication is producing, through the work of 'joining the nervous systems of inhabitants in a coherent space' (Sloterdijk 2005, p. 226), a global provincialism of 'connected isolations', of microclimates in which 'communicative relations are replaced by the inter-autistic and mimetic relations, a world that is constructed "polyspherically and interidioti-cally"' (Funcke 2005). A certain kind of being-togetherness is thereby threatened. Thus

At the centre of the third volume is an immunological theory of architecture, because I maintain that houses are built immune systems. I thus provide on the one hand an interpretation of modern habitat, and on the other a new view of the mass container. But when I highlight the apartment and the sports stadium as the most important architectural innovations of the modern, it isn't out of art- or cultural-historical interest. Instead my aim is to give a new account of the history of atmospheres, and in my view, the apartment and the sports stadium are important primarily as atmospheric installations. They play a central role in the development of abundance, which defines the open secret of the modern. (Funcke 2005)

For Sloterdijk, in other words, the modern world has become bubble/ foam, a series of consumerist monads cut off from each other and constantly, even manically, inventing new responses – decisive moments that in truth decide little at all and make us immune to many forms of shared understanding and human flourishing.

Whatever the case (and I think that this vision is far too bleak, ignoring, for example, the growth of consumer communities of practice that show a considerable verve which cannot easily be encompassed by the system), the point is that space and time are themselves becoming not so much wrappings around the objects of consumption as integral elements in the generation of an individualized mass consumption which revolves around more than the simple commodity: the object is but a part of a larger ensemble, a world which is perhaps best understood as a semiotically enhanced atmosphere which allows individualized relationships to thrive (Wheeler 2006). This is a world perfused with signs sent and read because each environmental niche is always also a semiotic niche. Space and time are no longer something external but a key moment in the design of these myriad semiotically enhanced worlds and this requires a recursive envelope which can transmit sensation as much as information. Thus place mark 2 is both deeper than what came before in that it is loaded up with all manner of signs, and shallower in that it depends on the control (or, rather modulation) of the sensation and the information it imparts. But what is clear is that these places are meant to be more responsive – thinking spaces of a kind. They are semiotic machines which are crucial elements of a new world-modelling system, machines that produce worlds by constructing organizations of half-intuited marks and tokens that suppress some details and highlight others. These organizations function, in other words, as a kind of electrical infrastructure of attention, producing associated commonplaces.

How might we understand the spatial practices of 'worlding'? Neither Lazzarato nor Sloterdijk provide much sense of how space is changing to provide the new accommodation that will allow these practices to thrive. For example, Sloterdijk tends to work with historical archetypes like the glasshouse or latterly the stadium in order to understand the different ways that space can be curated. But the use of these archetypes can often produce spurious metaphorical understandings. So I want to take a different tack. I want to suggest that what we are living through is the time of the production of new locational machinery (Conley 2007), and specifically the production of what I will call the *inhabitable map*. In other words, this is a time in which space itself becomes a means of conveying information and communication – actual qualities loaded with affective as well as cognitive value – with the goal of *approximating the rhythm of thought*, rather than simply a material template through which information and communication must be conveyed.

We might call this permanent state of restlessness a kind of 'emotive realism' (Thrailkill 2006), in that the inhabitable map is able to reach out to the feeling body and, quite literally, incorporate it by producing complex interactions achieved through a complex of devices which redescribe the surface and texture of space. The combined effect of these devices has been to produce worlds which not only respond to, but also initiate action, both because they themselves are, however crudely, able to generate affects because they exist in and across sensory registers which make it easier to nestle in the affective realm. In turn, these worlds have a new feeling for thought and a corresponding taste for new kinds of knowledge (Wood 2005).

In this new form of nervous system, space has been transformed in three ways. First, it conveys a cultural understanding of space which relies on a transformative approximation of position rather than absolute geometric coordinates, what I have called elsewhere 'movement-space' (Thrift 2005a).[9] Second, it becomes a communicative mass of quantitative and qualitative *signs*. The environment becomes utterly semiotic.[10] Third, it no longer needs to be overcome. Rather it needs to be designed, prototyped, and rolled out, rather like a semiotic carpet: it is not so much that place is altered on paper or screen and then the vision is built, as that space becomes equated with the act of drawing itself and the kernel of thinking that such a practice makes possible (Turk 2006).

Increasingly, therefore, space is not enclosed in the same way. It is no longer an ensemble of contiguous communities which transmit to each other. Rather it is becoming a spatialized matrix of becoming, a continuously unfolding field, a surface for making provocations which, though calculated in all kinds of ways, can have open outcomes. It is making the move from a means of providing enclosure and material consistency, to the spatialization of different moments in a matrix: the one immutable is mutability so that 'objects' become constantly provisional and therefore able to be linked to passions in a continuous process. It has become a spatialization of time absolutely consistent with the idea that space has become 'a science of nature in the making' (De Beistegui 2004). Thus, even architecture, which arguably has the most invested in the enclosure world-view, is experimenting with surface animation, interactive environments, interconnected spaces, and even fused spaces. Some architects have talked about the death of place, about space becoming 'a matter of making strategic decisions and experiencing moments at remote and asynchronically related sites' (Bouman 2005: 21), about site as always a set of sites constantly embroidering one another (Spiller 2002). The information structure and the physical structure would become as one in this convergence[11] culture (Jenkins 2006). But it might be more correct to say that what was a mundane background has now been able to reach such a concentration of intensity that it is becoming a foreground. If I were looking for an analogy, it would be in the way that in the history of painting what was formerly understood as background, something understood as the cheap stuff, to be inserted by assistants, is foregrounded as landscape painting. The necessary but incidental side panels take to centre stage.

I do not want to go too far. Inevitably this discourse is something of an exaggeration.[12] It constitutes an implied space (Wall 2006), a space of potential. For the driver stuck in a traffic jam, it will seem an absurd goal (but even these drivers increasingly drive cars which have become part of a vast informational space; Thrift 2004b). For many of the world's poorest people, for example, it will seem nothing but a bitter mockery of their straitjacketed lives (although even they very often have mobile phones). The discourse is an ambition, but it is not without any kind of reality. Thus, it is an ambition backed up by vast resources. It is an ambition which already has some bite and will, I believe, have far more, given the vast number of socio-spatial experiments currently taking place, ranging all the way from the vast number of attempts to create more intelligent spaces, through all the experiments in social networking currently taking place to truly experimental adventures in architecture, performance, and art which are both attempts to represent the new reality and interventions in producing it.

In turn, I want to argue that this production of the inhabitable map must be seen as part of a much wider tendency which is the mass production of communities of practice achieved by producing communities in which knowledge formation becomes a continuous practice woven into the spatial fabric. The ambition is certainly clear – to produce a process of knowledge formation which is simultaneously more systematic and, in the ease with which new knowledge is able to be stimulated by novel practices of intersubjective cooperation, functions effectively in the tacit realm.

This tendency is being manifested in two main ways in business at present, each of which is linked to the other by their attention to *the generation of passionate interests*, these interests being understood in the classical Tardean way as the root of economic psychology and of the generation of markets and organizations (Latour and Lépinay 2007): value is wrested from tacit desires and beliefs combined in a 'psychological'[13] vector. One is through the institution of communities of innovation in business. In pursuit of knowledge and innovation, these communities try to achieve a number of things. First, they attempt to stimulate passions, vitality if you like. Second, they attempt to allow the world to speak: the organization no longer acts as a boundary. They take an 'external approach' (Ancona and Bresman 2007), if you like, generating many extensive ties to those without the organization – ties which are useful both because there is a need to hear customers and explore their enthusiasms, and because knowledge needs to be continually gathered in from outside the organization, although now that the organization has been lowered into the flow of practice, outside is no longer an adequate description of where the organization's boundaries end. Third, they attempt to produce what might be called extreme execution. That is, they attempt to speed up the whole process of producing a product through the rapid production of teams able to be adapted to the project at hand. Numerous businesses are trying to set up communities in which passions can be more skilfully generated, in which the world is allowed to speak more forcefully to them, and in which the product can become a process swiftly completed. I have described this process in detail elsewhere (Thrift 2006).

The other way is through the institution of a 'flock and flow' (McCracken 2006) consumer economy and it is this development that I will concentrate upon in the remainder of this section, and with good reason. It is, I think, unarguable that an important historical process has been taking place since, in, or around, the 1970s and that is the hastening of a process of 'mass' individualization and idiosyncratic volatility in the consumer economy which supports and is supported by a new form of psychological individuality and self-determination (Zuboff and Maxmin 2002). The desire to be understood and treated as an individual is now more or less constantly expressed, in particular through the medium of a reinvented consumption which can satisfy three values: sanctuary from the pressures of the working world, various forms of giving voice to self-expression, and social connection.[14]

In the standard enterprise logic of managerial capitalism, people must adapt to the terms and conditions of consumption set by gatekeeper producers. But the real essence of the individuation of consumption is an inversion of that logic. It requires the agents of commerce to operate in individual space. There they form a relationship with the individual.... (Zuboff and Maxmin 2002: 171 and 172)

That is the real import of current managerial buzzwords like long tail, co-creation, and the like (Thrift 2006). And it requires that enterprises know much more about their customers and strive to enter into an individual-ized and dynamic relationship with them. It requires, in other words, nearly continuous survey and interrogation of people who are much more likely to think of themselves as qualified players who enterprises must resonate with. Indeed, they might be thought of as the latest episode in a history of survey, a point I will return to.

But there is more to it than this. For the new kinds of active and reflexive space that have been forged from the abundant knowledge landscape enabled by the consequences of modern technological developments also allow consumers to fashion large numbers of collaborative and often highly participative consumer communities, so producing a vast new realm of collective intelligence and innovation based around the intensification of passionate interests (Chesbrough 2006; Chesbrough et al. 2006; Thrift 2006). These consumer communities can be mainstream or quirky but they are rarely dull: if they were, participants would simply exit them.[15] Leadbeater (2006) and other luminaries argue that the gener-ation of so many new communities is the consequence of the ability to be organized without drawing on much in the way of formal organization. Equally, the generation of so many new communities is interpreted as the rise of spontaneous authority in which innovation and creativity become mass activities carried out through blurred and voluntary divisions of labour, rather than being the preserve of elites carried out through struc-tured and involuntary divisions of labour.[16] Undoubtedly, as I have pointed out elsewhere, this can all be overdone, but equally it points to significant changes – consumers do not want just more choice but more say, consumers do not want just passive consumption but also active intervention in products and services, consumers do not just want operating instructions but also want to be the operating instructions, and so on. Increasingly, in other words, consumers are attempting to make their own worlds.[17]

4.3 The Rise of Place-Based Research Methods Communities

As I have pointed out, the practices of worlding require a different form of production of space, one which involves a process of constant recursive survey and interrogation which is internal to the practices of community formation and which simultaneously involves the production of spaces. But it is worth asking how these practices have come about and why. To do this I want to turn to what may seem an unlikely source: academe itself. For I want to argue that the academy has been no passive bystander in the production of these new worlds but an active participant.

It has often been argued that space and place were rediscovered in academe because of the strong theoretical push of the so-called spatial turn that has tracked across most of the social sciences and humanities. Certainly, it has, I think, become clear that the old categorical ways of thinking which simply aggregated populations up into general classes which were distributed across space in varying proportions are no longer adequate. In part, this is because these categorical ways of thinking are echoes of a bygone form of discipline which is now being superseded by much more individualized forms of discipline which take in many more variables in characterizing character (e.g. increasingly, various indicators of biological well-being). These individualized forms of discipline which arise out of a mixture of technique, changes in the nature of commodity production (Zuboff and Maxmin 2002), and shifts in the mode of subjectivity, have highlighted the importance of place understood as more than context in that they make it much easier to see its operation once individuals become more than the sum of their parts and can be understood as moments of individuation, moments of intensity which are parts of more general movements of becoming (Toscano 2006). Place can then no longer be seen as an incidental correlate but must be understood as a crucial element in human flourishing. Place is in us all. Quite literally.[18]

Whilst this theoretical recasting has clearly been important, its impact has perhaps been overstated. To begin with, it is important to note the more general empirical recasting of the world which has brought place to the fore. In particular the sheer mobility of the contemporary world, signalled by phenomena like the rise of logistical knowledge and the prominence of migration, which mean that places have become coupled together and that one place is always shadowed by others, coupled with a more and more complex spatial environment (as indexed by, for example, the rise of so-called super-diverse places; Vertovec 2005), buttressed by a general increase in a place awareness (as indexed by, for example, the sheer number of publications on places, let alone the expansion of environmental concern)[19] has surely been as important.

But there is a further potent agent that needs to be taken into account. That is the application of different *methods* of survey of space and place by many and various methodological communities operating inside and outside academe. It is the proliferation and profusion of these place-based or place-sensitive methods that I most particularly want to examine. In a sense, I want to argue that the boys (and girls) in the back room have been as responsible for the production of descriptions of the modern world as any theorist.

Over time, or so I will argue, the application of these methods has begun to produce a new kind of placeness which is a vital part of the constitution of the inhabitable map. This placeness is just as complex and variegated as what went before, but it constitutes a new kind of landscape which is replete with its own forms of experience which approximate the world that these methodological communities are trying to form as their methodological fictions take up residence in reality. Once, in other words, we finally get away from the idea that methods are not just reports back from some found and uncorrupted reality of what is there but are themselves parts of the development of new theres, we can start to see the full richness of this new prospect.

Gieryn (2006) has noted that there are many ways in which researchers can build methodological relationships to place and to the people in them, and that these have varied over time. Thus, the Chicago School of Urban Studies – arguably the first modern school of place-based research – deployed three main 'shuttles' in order to demonstrate that it was constructing a 'truth spot' which guaranteed both the knowledge it was producing and Chicago as a laboratory within which knowledge could be produced and guaranteed, namely 'found and made', 'here and anywhere', and 'immersed and detached'. These shuttles constituted oscillations which also constituted means of authority. Thus, 'found and made' described the oscillation between the city as found in a natural state and the city as a laboratory specimen; 'here and anywhere' described the city as a singular location and yet as having a general story to tell; while 'immersed and detached' described the way in which the researcher is positioned as both immersed in the city (and thus as open to surprise, emotion, vulnerability, and empathy) and yet also able to distance himself or herself from its circumstances when necessary. As I shall point out, the nature of these shuttles is changing. The city is now naturally a laboratory, continually being put to the question. Its inhabitants are in a state of perpetual survey and assume that this is a part of life. Because of the high degree of all but instant linkage between locations and people occasioned by the media, each part of the city is likely to contain traces of itself: it is naturally both singular and general. And the city has been the object of myriad self-conscious exercises in place-making which have forever muddied a distinction between observer and observed (Sheringham 2006), not only in the guise of travellers' tales but also in the form of the kinds of orientations that can be adopted, whether these are faux-realist or lost but with style (as in that strand of work that stretches from the earliest situationist experiments to the latest artistic commentaries which mix method technology and place in unholy ways). Indeed, with the rise of the Internet, this kind of observation is – to an extent at least – being democratized, with myriad observers constantly reporting back on places.

What I want to do first in this section is to briefly survey the shifting landscape of social science methods, understood as a series of technologies for not only understanding the world but also operating on it. In doing this, I want to show how the shuttles that guarantee knowledge of truth and place now assume quite different relationships between 'home' and 'field' than was current at the time of the Chicago School, producing a quite different form of inquiry which presupposes a world of places and communities which has not existed in the same form before. This does not seem to me to be about the old and hackneyed divisions between qualitative and quantitative methods, or synchronic and diachronic approaches, or other such oft-remarked-upon contrasts, important though these may still be to their proponents. Nor is this a matter of the undoubted differences in research cultures, given that these are often extreme, between different bands of social researchers.[20] Rather, I want to show that this shift is a part and parcel of a more general change in the character of methodological study whose ambitions are only now becoming clear. These ambitions are concerned with producing inhabitable maps which will continuously report on themselves as they evolve. In other words, both data and research methods increasingly work at levels which allow place to have a say.

These changes in the character of methods depend on a dialectic between data and methods. Most importantly, data has expanded its reach both quantitatively and qualitatively and this expansion arises out of a convoluted and sometimes unpredictable interaction between data and methods; new methods generate new data and vice versa. Thus, first of all, there is the sheer *amount* of data that is now available to be operated on, whether this is quantitative or qualitative in nature which is, simultaneously, redefining what is counted as primary or secondary information (as in the growing vogue for 'netnography' which uses blogs and personal web sites freely available on the Web, or interventions into various discussion groups or Web communities as means of creating various kinds of listening posts). The sheer amount of data available on places has been particularly pushed by the growth of the commercial domain, with some of these data now entering the public domain (as in the case of some Experian data; see Webber 2007). Second, datasets have also become more *complex*, containing more information which can be related in more and different ways. These datasets often arising out of the ability to use various government and other data in ways which heretofore would have been difficult. A good example is provided by the use by economists and geographers of schools and health service data to consider issues like segregation or the outcomes of particular government policies (e.g. Burgess et al. 2005). Third, datasets often involve much more complex orientations to time. Thus, more comprehensive longitudinal datasets have arisen around the world, datasets which have often become multinational (as, for example, in work on time use or world values or labour-force involvement). These datasets are a continuous investment, often mutating slightly with each pass as new questions are added. In them, data are either continuously collected or are linked over time. Fourth, the rise of new kinds of methods is leading to an extension of the sensory registers that are worked in. For example, most commonly, visual methods of all kinds have proliferated, often in line with technological advance. For example, the ubiquity of cameras has allowed visual research methods to be extended in all kinds of ways: allowing respondents to use small disposables, camera phones, small video cameras, and so on. But, increasingly, other registers are also being invoked. Thus, sound, taste, touch, and various kinaesthetic information (like gait) are now being sought, often taking a leaf out of work done in the humanities, as a means of capturing forms of experience like emotion which constitute primary forms of data in modern life. As one dancer put it, 'feelings are facts' and the challenge has become how to represent them as data. Fifth, the parallel turn to material culture has produced a wide variety of datasets which did not exist before or were simply not considered to be operable data. Thus, not only has a host of consumer data become available but museums and galleries can now be viewed as sources of social science insight. Sixth, datasets increasingly contain place-bound information as more than simply an illustration of variation. More and more datasets either systematically build in place or start from it. And finally, most methods are no longer, if they ever were, just the preserve of academic researchers. To the extent that this has ever been true, it is quite clear that research methods now exist in a web of use which stretches from academe and government through to business and civil society. There are thriving methods communities in areas like market research and political consultancy, for example.[21] To summarize, new methodological ambitions have become possible because what counts as data has changed, not least because new hybrid classes of objects can be created out of these ambitions such as objects that were heretofore regarded as impermanent and/or highly localized – for example, goods for sale, in transit or in storage, vehicles on the road, events, discarded items, pollution, weather – and also because it is more and more possible to obtain data on 'individuals'. Knowledge of these things expressed as methods and data both redefines what counts as objects and individuals and by making them visible alters their relationship to us.

These changes in data are both driven and being driven by technological change. Thus, the ability to record and transcribe has been speeded up by all kinds of technological aids. Similarly, the ability to permanently archive data cheaply and in a form that it can be easily reused is at least in sight. Importantly, these changes do not only produce more speed and memory, they also extend analytical range. Thus, calculations that would have heretofore been impossible become attainable. Again, it becomes possible to use simulation as more than a tool as an instrument in its own right. And increasing store and speed also allows text, pictures, and other image information to be presented and analysed in ways not before dreamt of, and to be integrated with each other. The result is a plethora of possibilities, many of which are only beginning to be explored as the social sciences begin to intersect with performance. For example, it seems clear that, so far as grid computing is concerned, one of its main uses will turn out to be the construction of vast archives of text and visual data of the kind currently used predominantly in the humanities to exactly consider place-based phenomena like landscape and site.

As I have pointed out, the generation of new data has proceeded in lockstep with the invention of new methods. There is no space here to review each and every new area of social methodology: all that needs to be said is that they are multiple and multiplying. Rather, I want to suggest that most new methods – from the new work in ethnomethodology to recent advances in sequence analysis – share some common aspirations. If we were to describe these ambitions, rather than their rougher and readier reality, I think we would have to pull out five main characteristics. First, these methods are reactive. That is, they are no longer understood as an end point but are cross-sections of a continuing process, pulled out to infinity. They can be repeated, though often with alterations. Second, they are historical, in the sense that they acknowledge path dependence and emergence. They are tracks over time, rather than fixed point analyses. Third, they are increasingly technologically driven by software. Software can be used to order and analyse ethnographic transcription, to understand turn-taking and the patterns of conversation, to focus on the key moments in focus groups, or to zero in on where visual attention is being directed, as well as to run laboratory tests or make multilevel modelling or methods imported from genetic sequencing into something even unskilled researchers can grapple with. Fourth, they can be used to maintain and repair data. Thus, new techniques have made it easier to utilize particular kinds of data that heretofore would have been opaque to analysis, brush up data that would have been too incomplete to use, link data that are of different types, use data that would have been thought not to constitute a proper sample, and so on. And, finally, they acknowledge complexity. That does not mean that the methods can always describe the vagaries of that state, but it does mean that they understand that the world is complex and cannot be reduced. Instead the ambition is to understand emergent patterns, playing to the idea of a generative social science (Epstein 2006).

There is also a much more relaxed approach to what these methods are achieving. The wave of critiques of positivism in the 1960s and 1970s, the postmodern critiques of the 1970s and 1980s, the ethnographic absolutisms of the 1980s and 1990s, have, or so it seems to me, dissolved into something more forgiving. There is a general emphasis on rigour but not at the expense of a narrow sectionalism. There is a general emphasis on sophistication, but not at the expense of appropriateness. Though methodological approaches do still clearly differ, still there are also much greater commonalities. For example, economists are no longer ashamed to be caught mining extensive datasets. Anthropologists are willing to countenance redefining ethnography so that it can include objects that cannot answer back, and need to be approached at an angle, as in various para-ethnographic excursions. Sociologists and geographers have become interested in the insights that can be gleaned from work in performance.

In other words, the world is increasingly recognized to be a dappled one (Cartwright 1999). This is not an age for truth fanatics, even though the dividing lines between methodological communities of practice are often still well defended. Worlding demands a host of different skills.

The renewed interest in place does not just emerge, then, from place suddenly getting its just desserts. It also emerges from a change in how methods themselves are being thought of, the result of theoretical changes in how methods are conceived of (Abbott 2001) which make place easier to understand, the rise of new and speedier technologies and a slow but sure redefinition of what counts as truth, resulting from the methodological history of the last forty years.

But the general tendency towards considering place as a vital part of data and method has also clearly been boosted in four ways. First, there is intensive mapping on a scale never before seen. Thus Cosgrove (2005: 149) points out that

[Large North American cities] are some of the most intensively mapped spaces in the history and geography of the planet: every square metre is geo-coded by government and private or commercial agencies for purposes ranging from environmental protection, public health, and safety, efficient transportation and transportation to property insurance, marketing, political persuasion and religious evangelism. Maps have played a critical role in shaping their physical spaces and land uses, and continue to control the daily lives of citizens through zoning ordinances, zip codes, and the myriad territorial regulations that shape urban daily life.

These kinds of developments have only been underlined by the advent of mass satellite surveillance over the last five years which makes the city visible and, of course, provides a powerful new source of data and methods as well a means of isolating more detail than was ever possible before.

Second, the rise of geodemographics and geographical information systems more generally, has fostered a generic series of spatial technologies which are also means of social analysis. Socio-spatial analysis has become a norm, backed up by all kinds of spatial statistics that have been developed since the 1960s which have been at the very least sensitive to the problems of space and place (e.g. the ecological fallacy, scale, and autocorrelation) and which, more recently, have been developed, at least in part, with the contextual properties of space in mind (e.g. multilevel modelling, geographical regression). Thus, geodemographics and geographical information systems do not just describe a world. Through the categorizations and modes of search that they have produced, they are beginning to become a means by which the world is constructed. As Burrows and Gane (2006) argue, geodemographic classifications are not just representational grids, they are means by which people increasingly sort themselves.[22] Thus, an increasingly automated agency produces all kinds of other forms of agency which do not just follow but provide the means to construct and activate addresses. Third, properties that are often considered place-like, for example, materiality, emotion, and the like have become easier to capture and represent as all manner of new spatial metrics have been invented. Fourth, at the same time, place itself has been changing its character. It is a cliché which still holds some truth that places are increasingly about movement and many modern technologies of data-gathering have been formulated precisely to track a world of fast-moving people and objects which depict place as a network of relations rather than a set of fixed points. This generalized logistical model has increasingly become apparent in all corners of everyday life: it is how (quite literally) things turn up (think only of the growing availability of satellite navigation systems, GPS receiver, and the like, often incarnated in devices as simple as a mobile phone or PDA). Further, as various forms of tagging, name recognition, and sequence analysis become increasingly effective (see, for example, Thrift 2004*a* on RFIDs) so what hoves into view is a world in which everything can be tracked. Indeed, recent papers on tracking mobile phone users may become simply the beginning of a major shift in social science methodology as it becomes possible to track and record individuals in something approximating real time. Further, these systems of mass movement are now generating their own effects. For example, supply chains can suffer from amplification in which what is detected as a variation is amplified further down the supply chain, thereby producing larger and larger errors. Similarly, in-car navigation systems are now producing flocking effects wherein as cars using satellite navigation systems take congestion avoidance action so they produce alternative centres of congestion.

In turn, a series of important methodological developments have occurred as all these developments have bedded in. In particular, the emphasis on properties of emergence means that these methods can increasingly be seen as buzzing, lively tools, rather than solitary research interventions, and these are tools for building worlds – a point to which I will return in some detail. Thus, methods like microsimulation and agent-based modelling, understood as part of a more general attempt to produce a generative social science (Epstein 2006), are attempts to demonstrate alternate worlds and emergent effects as well as simply tools for tracking policy. Similarly, the emphasis that place drives on methods that are able to cope with many co-varying factors simultaneously becomes important as a means of isolating more and more detail. Next, these methods are increasingly interactive, that is they are part of a process of constant revisiting. Increasingly, this means more than simply an ambition to produce repetition, through repeat surveys or certain other forms of recursivity. Rather, one of the goals is increasingly to involve respondents in the process of research. That has, of course, been a favourite meditation of ethnography, which has often discussed the role of respondents and the exact responsibilities of researchers towards them. It is central to much work that involves devices like focus groups. It has blossomed in studies of vulnerable people. It is a cardinal point of feminist research methods. It has become a main-stay of the burgeoning experimental apparatus of psychology and behav-ioural economics which is now moving out into other disciplines. And it is, of course, the preserve of a mushrooming ethics industry. But, increas-ingly it also means the deployment of deliberative approaches, such as the use of citizen juries. It might even mean the vagaries of participatory research, in which the respondents take a hand in dictating what the research problems are, and may even take a part in the research process themselves, thus completing the circle and underling my point that we can all be researchers now.[23] Then, places are allowed to become performa-tive. Performative approaches, in which a toolbox largely derived from the humanities is deployed, are becoming increasingly important as a means of acting out events, as a means of research in their own right. By acting out,[24] it is possible to produce understandings that are not easily achieved in any other way. Importantly, much of the force of this research comes exactly from trying to understand the exact force of space in producing events. In turn, this research is part of a burgeoning effort intent on creating more interactive spaces which spans subjects as different as infor-mation technology (and especially the study and creation of interfaces), architecture (Bullivant 2005), performance art, installation and site-based art, and film. And finally places are no longer seen as simply about people: they are also seen about all manner of other things, from objects through non-human life to the grip of the contours of the land (architects), in multiple combinations. This ability comes in particular from the ability to apprehend and map objects that were formerly regarded as intangibles, such as markets[25] or emotions or equations so as to be able, for example, to produce 'archaeologies of the present' in which methods originally applied in archaeology which are purely about the object domain are transferred into the contemporary moment (Büchli and Lucas 2001;

Jacobs 2006). These new forms of representations of objects are becoming a crucial element of what objects are, representations which, in effect, are forming an air traffic control system for objects (Sterling 2005), one which challenges extant representational technology.[26]

Let us now come back to Gieryn's three shuttles in the light of all these developments. What we can see is that place has been relocated, re-placed if you like by methods communities of practice. Thus, the first shuttle, back and forth between found and made, is much more difficult to deploy. The idea of a city as a laboratory understood as a strict scientific analogue was always a difficult one to deploy. Now it has become impossible. Rather, a more general experimental and performative turn has become apparent in which places become *dynamic laboratories* without a stable point of reference. Then, the shuttle back and forth between here and anywhere has transmuted as many different stories have become possible about just one place and as places have become linked in ways which mean that stories about one place are always and automatically about other places or chains of places. Finally, the shuttle back and forth between immersed and detached has become more and more complex. By some accounts a state of detachment is simply impossible. In any case the myriad accounts of reflexivity have destabilized the idea that detachment is a necessary goal.

To summarize, place is being re-described through a battery of data, technologies, and methods in the latest chapter in a history of survey and interrogation. In turn, new kinds of citizens are being revealed, who are a part of a world of mass individual logic that these spatially attuned technologies and methods have done much to bring about.[27] Indeed, it could be argued that 'corporate managers, popular experts, media figures, and ordinary citizens speak in a social scientific language that has become virtually indistinguishable from... culture at large' (Igo 2006: 289). To repeat my message once more, these technologies and methods are not just representational, they are formative.

4.4 Conclusions: The Inhabitable Map and Its Perils

In this chapter, I have tried to weave together the communities of practice literature and some contemporary thinking on space, showing how each implies the other, concentrating especially on how they both imply the development of *new sensings that allow new practices of worlding*, rather than simply knowledge formation, as the literature on communities of practice would often have it. In particular, I have returned – again and again – to the question of the kind of space that is now becoming prevalent and how we might describe it, showing how it is a part of processes of worlding that are becoming extensive and that reach right into academe. Many of the developments presaged by what I have called the inhabitable map are likely to be positive, providing, for example, new kinds of political ventilation. However, such a vision of worlding also has its downside, and this does not just arise from privacy issues, important as those undoubtedly are. Rather they arise from two other reservations.

One is the more insidious process of control that will be possible. If all objects are going to be able to be tagged, thus producing a vast ecology of things bent towards individualized consumption, so, at the same time, they can be tracked and modulated. This vision of a future of spontaneous authority is undoubtedly akin to the society of control that luminaries like Deleuze and Haraway sketched in the 1980s, a society in which an enhanced cybernetics held sway allowing the continual redefinition of the problem and solution in real time (or something close to it) in line with events. But, as Haraway (2006) herself has argued recently, this enhanced level of responsiveness no longer seems quite the right description of how things are. Rather, as I have expounded, the goal now is not so much to track objects as to create whole worlds in which tracking is simply a part of the infrastructure of what objects are and how they relate. In other words, right at the heart of 'experience' will be cookies that do not so much tag every move as become what defines movement itself (Thrift 2005a). Worlds are being intensified, *cook-ied* up, if you like.

The analogy is an apt one, I think. For it suggests a leap as great as that which occurred when cooking was invented, a technique of altering the environment that allowed food to be primed and intensified in such a way as to produce a new external organ. Subsequently, the body itself began to evolve, as energy could be used for activities other than digestion. Similarly, the battery of methods coupled with new technologies now available is beginning to produce a new kind of sensory organ. In previous papers, I have likened this organ to a hand. Perhaps what is being extended is exactly our sense of touch – and objects' sense of touch too (Classen 2005). It is possible to feel knowledge, to taste it, in new ways (Wood 2005).

The second reservation provides an even more serious caveat. It may seem as though I have depicted a movement towards an age of abundant knowledge and an almost unlimited collective intelligence.[28] But that is wrong. There are limits. The worlding I have depicted is an umwelt like any other in that it has systematic biases to seeing only certain things. Other things simply do not appear at all. Thus, Galison (2004) points to a classified universe which may be as large as the unclassified one and which puts paeans of praise to the liberatory possibilities of open access in perspective. In the United States, for example

In 2001 there were thirty three million classification actions; assuming (with the experts) there are roughly 10 pages per action, that would mean roughly 330 million pages were classified last year (about three times as many pages are now being classified as declassified). So the U.S. added a net 250 million classified pages last year. By comparison, the entire system of Harvard libraries – over a hundred of them – added about 220,000 volumes last year (about 60 million pages, a number not far from the acquisition rate at other comparably massive universal depositories such as the Library of Congress, the British Museum, or the New York Public Library). Contemplate these numbers: about five times as many pages are being added to the classified universe than are being brought to the storehouses of human learning, including all the books and journals on any subject in any language collected in the largest repositories in the planet. (Galison 2004: 230)

This secret universe cannot be allowed to persist. It can only warp a process of worlding that is warped enough already. If we are going to inhabit maps, rather than simply use them as aids to orientation, we need to be sure that the maps include the whole landscape.

References

Abbott, A. (2001). *Time Matters: On Theory and Method*. Chicago, IL: University of Chicago Press.

Ancona, D. and Bresman, H. (2007). *X-Teams: How to Build Teams that Lead, Innovate, and Succeed*. Boston, MA: Harvard Business School Press.

Bouman, O. (2005). 'Architecture, liquid, gas', *Architectural Design*, 75(1): 14–22.

Büchli, V. A. and Lucas, G. (2001). *Archaeologies of the Contemporary Past*. London and New York: Routledge.

Bullivant, L. (ed.) (2005). 'Special issue on 4D space: Interactive architecture', *Architectural Design*, 75(1).

Burgess, S., Johnston, R., and Wilson, D. (2005). 'England's multi-ethnic educational system? A classification of secondary schools', *Environment and Planning A*, 37: 45–62.

Burrows, R., Gane, N. (2006). 'Geodemographics, software and class', *Sociology*, 40: 793–812.

Calhoun, C. (ed.) (2007). *Sociology in America: A History*. Chicago, IL: Chicago University Press.

Cartier-Bresson, H. (1952). *The Decisive Moment*. New York: Simon & Schuster.

Cartwright, N. (1999). *The Dappled World: A Study of the Boundaries of Science*. Cambridge: Cambridge University Press.

Chesbrough, H. (2006). *Open Business Models: How to Thrive in the New Innovation Landscape*. Boston, MA: Harvard Business School Press.

—— Vanhaverbeke, W., and West, J. (eds.) (2006) *Open Innovation: Researching a New Paradigm*. Oxford: Oxford University Press.

Classen, C. (ed.) (2005). *The Book of Touch*. Oxford: Berg.

Conley, T. (2007). *Cartographic Cinema*. Minneapolis, MN: University of Minnesota Press.

Cosgrove, D. (2005). 'Carto-City', in J. Abrams and P. Hall (eds.), *Else/Where: Mapping New Cartographies of Networks and Territories*. Minneapolis, MN: University of Minnesota Press.

Crary, J. (1999). *Suspensions of Perception: Attention, Spectacle and Modern Culture*. Cambridge, MA: MIT Press.

De Beistegui, M. (2004). *Truth and Genesis: Philosophy as Differential Ontology*. Bloomington, NY: Indiana University Press.

Epstein, J. M. (2006). *Generative Social Science: Studies in Agent-Based Computational Modelling*. Princeton, NJ: Princeton University Press.

Funcke, B. (2005). 'Against Gravity: Bettina Funcke Talks with Peter Sloterdijk'. *Bookforum*, February/March (http://www,bookforum.com/archive/feb_05/funcke. html).

Galison, P. (2004). 'Removing knowledge', *Critical Inquiry*, 30: 229–43.

Gieryn, T. (2006). 'City as truth-spot: Laboratories and field sites in urban studies', *Social Studies of Science*, 36: 5–38.

Gitelman, L. (2006). *Always Already New: Media, History and the Data of Culture*. Cambridge, MA: MIT Press.

Glennie, P. and Thrift, N. J. (2008). *The Measured Heart: A History of Clock Times*. Oxford: Oxford University Press.

Haraway, D. (2006). 'Compounding', in C. A. Jones (ed.), *Sensorium: Embodied Experience, Technology, and Contemporary Art*. Boston, MA: MIT Press.

Igo, S. E. (2006). *The Averaged American: Surveys, Citizens, and the Making of a Mass Public*. Cambridge, MA: Harvard University Press.

Jacobs, J. M. (2006). 'A geography of big things', *Cultural Geographies*, 13(1): 1–27.

Jenkins, H. (2006). *Convergence Culture: Where Old and New Media Collide*. New York: New York University Press.

Kohler, R. E. (2002). *Landscapes and Labscapes: Exploring the Lab-Field Border in Biology*. Chicago, IL: University of Chicago Press.

Latour, B. (2007). 'A plea for earthly sciences', keynote lecture for the annual meeting of the British Sociological Association.

—— and Lépinay, V. (2007). 'L'économie, science des intérêts passionnés', preface to G. Tarde, *Psychologie Économique*. Paris: Les Empêcheurs.

Lazzarato, M. (2004). 'From capital-labour to capital-life', *Ephemera*, 4: 187–208.

Leadbeater, C. (2006). 'Are you thinking what I'm thinking?', *The Times*, 13 October, 2, 4–5.

McCracken, G. (2006). *Flock and Flow: Predicting and Managing Change in a Dynamic Marketplace*. Bloomington, IA: Indiana University Press.

Moggridge, M. (2006). *Designing Interactions*. Cambridge, MA: MIT Press.

Mokyr, J. (2002). *The Gifts of Athena: Historical Origins of the Knowledge Economy*. Princeton, NJ: Princeton University Press.

Mulvey, L. (2005). *Death 24X a Second*. London: Reaktion.

Porter, T. M. and Ross, D. (eds.) (2003). *The Cambridge History of Science, Volume 7: Modern Social Sciences*. Cambridge: Cambridge University Press.

Sebeok, T. A. and Danesi, M. (2000). *The Forms of Meaning: Modelling Systems Theory and Semiotic Analysis*. Berlin: Mouton de Gruyter.

Sheringham, M. (2006). *Everyday Life: Theories and Practices from Surrealism to the Present*. Oxford: Oxford University Press.

Sloterdijk, P. (1998). *Spharen I. Blasen*. Frankfurt: Suhrkamp Verlag.

—— (2005). 'Foreword to the theory of spheres', in M. Ohanian and J. C. Royaux (eds.) *Cosmograms*. New York: Lukas & Sternberg, pp. 223–40.

Spiller, N. (ed.) (2002). 'Special issue on reflexive architecture', *Architectural Design*, 72(3).

Standage, T. (2006). 'Your television is ringing', survey of Telecoms convergence, *The Economist*, 14 October.

Sterling, B. (2005). *Shaping Things*. Cambridge, MA: MIT Press.

Thrailkill, J. (2006). 'Emotive realism', *Journal of Narrative Theory*, 36: 365–88.

Thrift, N. J. (1996). *Spatial Formations: Theory, Culture and Society Series*. London: Sage.

—— (2004a). 'Remembering the technological unconscious by foregrounding knowledges of position', *Environment and Planning D: Society and Space*, 22: 175–90.

—— (2004b). 'Driving in the city', *Theory, Culture and Society*, 21: 41–59.

—— (2005a). 'Movement-space: The changing domain of thinking resulting from the development of new kinds of spatial awareness', *Economy and Society*, 33: 582–604.

—— (2005b). *Knowing Capitalism*. London: Sage.

—— (2006) 'Re-inventing invention: New tendencies in capitalist commodification', *Economy and Society*, 35: 279–306.

—— (2007). *Non-Representational Theory: Space/Politics/Affect*. London: Routledge.

Toscano, A. (2006). *The Theatre of Production: Philosophy and Individuation Between Kant and Deleuze*. London: Palgrave Macmillan.

Turk, S. (2006). 'Computer graphics: Tracing cybernetic flows', *Performance Research*, 11: 64–75.

Vertovec, S. (2005). *The Emergence of Super-Diversity in Britain*. Oxford: COMPAS, University of Oxford.

Wall, C. S. (2006). *The Prose of Things: Transformations of Description in the Eighteenth Century*. Chicago, IL: University of Chicago Press.

Webber, R. (2007). 'The metropolitan habitus: Its manifestations, locations and consumption profiles', *Environment and Planning A*, 39(1): 182–207.

Wheeler, W. (2006). *The Whole Creature: Complexity, Biosemiotics and the Evolution of Cultures*. London: Lawrence & Wishart.

Wood, M. (2005). *Literature and the Taste of Knowledge*. Cambridge: Cambridge University Press.

Zuboff, S. and Maxmin, J. (2002). *The Support Economy: Why Corporations are Failing Individuals and The Next Episode of Capitalism*. New York: Viking Penguin.

Notes

1. It counts as closer to the academic/business school end of the spectrum than some fads (being similar to more recent fads like open innovation) but it is a moot point whether it is therefore more effective.

2. 'Instant' is not meant to imply instantaneous. Rather, it suggests a conscious attempt to construct a community which does not allow the usual time constraints to apply. At the same time, it also points to the fact that technological advances like the Internet have provided a new set of means by which such communities can be built, means which have been seized upon by all kinds of interests to add more interest into the world.

3. Thus, propositional knowledge (knowledge of what, usually presented in systematic form in storage devices and requiring contemplative involvement) increasingly stands as a companion to prescriptive knowledge (knowledge of how, of technique, usually presented in embodied form), rather than as different moments set to one side (Mokyr 2002).

4. For example, the *Sage Advanced Quantitative Methods in the Social Sciences* series is up to Number 146 while the *Sage Introducing Qualitative Methods in the Social Sciences* series is at Number 21.

5. In making this argument I will not be arguing that research methods communities of practice are simply producing methods as an affirmation of prevailing values; methods are a means of exploring and interrogating the world with their own agency. They are not only a social construction, therefore, but an active presence in their own right.

6. After all, it was Repton who argued that 'a knowledge of arrangement or disposition is, of all others, the most useful' (cited in Wall 2006, p. 6).

7. Thus Sloterdijk retains Heidegger's radical emphasis on the recently discovered notion of the environment, as circumstances being adjusted to accommodate the entity in their midst.

8. In bringing forward this formulation, Sloterdijk is making a similar move to those approaches based on joint action that have become increasingly common.

9. As Turk (2006) points out, this cultural understanding of space is not far from those of many non-Western cultures which orient themselves along paths of directions in a dynamic response to features in the environment. The difference is that this new nomadic ability is made possible because of the tight interlocking of absolute geometrical coordinates.

10. This vision is not far from that offered by Sebeok and Danesi (2000) and others in which the world is a constant process of biosemiosis, but I want to argue that this vision which they regard as general needs to be historicized. It is a symptom.

11. Specifically, convergence refers to a process of technological convergence between the different media forms which provide kernels of thought but, more generally and usefully, it indexes a number of parallel but related processes of mediation, including the extension of markets stemming from moving content across different delivery systems, the synergy provided by the ability to own and control these different manifestations, and the franchising opportunities that arise from coordinated efforts to brand and market content under these new conditions (Jenkins 2006).

12. Talk of collective intelligence or 'we-thought' has itself become something of a fad, as evidenced by the way that Ségolène Royal used the latter term as a key part of her bid for the Socialist leadership in France.

13. The word 'psychological' is in scare quotes because Tarde does not use it to refer to a distinction between interior and exterior but to a more general condition.

14. Hence, the massive increase in social networking sites which allow individuals to contact other individuals.

15. My current favourite is subversive or guerrilla knitting (see, for example, microRevolt.com).

16. Although they can be called on by enterprises through various processes of open innovation (Thrift 2006).

17. In truth, this is a double-sided process in which consumers react to enterprises, which react to consumers, and so on in a constant iterative expansion of advantage and disadvantage. Take the case of media convergence as one example of this process (see also Standage 2006):

Media companies are learning how to accelerate the flow of media content across delivery channels to expand revenue opportunities, broaden markets and reinforce viewer commitments. Consumers are learning how to use these different media technologies to bring the flow of media more fully under their control and to interact with other consumers. The promises of this new media environment raise expectations of a freer flow of ideas and content. Inspired by these ideals, consumers are fighting for the right to participate more fully in their culture. Sometimes, corporate and grassroots convergence reinforce each other, creating closer, more rewarding relations between media producers and consumers. Sometimes, these two forces are at war. (Jenkins 2006, p. 18)

18. For example, place is clearly an important factor in how happiness and health are constituted.

19. As Gitelman (2006, p. 17) puts it: '[G]lobal media help to create a world in which people are not local only because of where they are or where they are from but also because of their relationships to media representations of localism and its fate.'

20. I am struck by how few commentators have likened these differences to the kinds of difference in scientific culture that are now routinely observed in social studies of science and which seem to me to be both extreme and likely to make it impossible to provide general groundings in research methods as if methods were just some kind of cookbook. But see Porter and Ross (2003) and Calhoun (2007).

21. An interesting study would be to look at the commerce between these different communities and how, in particular, methods move between them.

22. So, for example, people are starting to choose houses on the basis of the information able to be gleaned from these systems.

23. Indeed, I know of at least one research methods helpline for specialized social work communities, and I can see this principle being extended to the general public in time.

24. Similar events are happening in the historical domain where it is realized that reconstruction and re-enactment must be seen as more than the preserve of hobbyists and can yield valuable information not able to be gained in any other way.

25. Thus, markets can increasingly be represented at a considerable level of complexity, from the constant of traders' screens, spewing out data, to devices like Map of the Market.

26. Think, for example, of the 'weather' maps evolved to depict the state of telecommunications networks.

27. I think it can be argued that research methods communities of practice increasingly fit with the imperative of generating these worlds. They are an essential element in generating a world which is based on a mass individual logic, if that does not seem too much of a contradiction in terms. Thus, they increasingly bear the marks of the kind of worlding that is now prevalent; as I pointed out earlier, they are emergent and reactive and are working in more and more sensory registers. Of course, this progress is hesitant and it is by no means complete. Datasets are still infrequently collected – though there are signs that this is changing, as evidenced by the growing number of longitudinal datasets (especially in the socio-medical domain), the number of datasets that are intended to be comprehensive (as in the proposals in the UK for a

national children's database and the many datasets that are found internationally based on using electronic data), and the datasets that can be gleaned from the permanent to and fro of telecommunications and Internet systems (though these are still patchy and specific) as well as the proliferation of social network sites like MySpace and FaceBook. Similarly, true recursivity remains something of a pipe dream in many cases.

28. Understood as the sum total of information held individually by members of a group that can be accessed in response to a specific question.

PART II

Bridging Cognitive Distance

5

Cognitive Distance in and Between Communities of Practice and Firms: Where Do Exploitation and Exploration Take Place, and How Are They Connected?

Bart Nooteboom

5.1 Introduction

A central issue in theories of organizational learning concerns the relation between knowledge of individuals and knowledge on the level of an organization (Cohen 1991; Cook and Yanow 1993; Weick and Westley 1996). According to Weick (1991), organizational learning entails a process of acquiring common knowledge, beliefs, or norms, which includes the process of accepting and validating individually acquired knowledge as useful (Duncan and Weiss 1979). In this process there is an important intermediate level of 'communities', between an organization as a whole and individual people. There, knowledge links between individuals are achieved and common knowledge is acquired. The notion of 'communities of practice' (CoPs), initiated by Lave and Wenger (1991) and Brown and Duguid (1996), and identified as a mechanism through which knowledge is held, transferred, and created, has attracted much attention as well as considerable criticism and confusion (e.g. see Cohendet et al. 2001; Contu and Wilmott 2003; Bogenrieder and Nooteboom 2004*a*; Handley et al. 2006; Roberts 2006).

Here, I consider three issues. The first concerns the diversity of knowledge and interests, and hence dissonance, ambiguity, possible tensions and conflicts of interest, and differences of power, within a CoP, which are in danger of being neglected due to the connotation, intended or not, of a 'community' as being 'warm', consensual, and without conflict. A second issue, which forms the central subject of the present chapter, is whether, or to what extent, CoPs are fit not only for holding, sharing, and improving knowledge and competence, in exploitation, but also for creating new knowledge and competence, in exploration (March 1991). In exploitation there is plasticity of routines, but not the replacement of routines by new ones. The distinction between exploitation and exploration is comparable to 'first-order' in contrast with 'second-order' learning (Bateson 1973), and to 'single-loop', in contrast with 'double-loop' learning (Argyris and Schön 1978), and perhaps also to 'incremental' in contrast with 'radical' innovation. In the first, there is variation within a basic framework or set of principles, and in the latter there is a break of the framework. Or in yet other words, in the first there is improvisation and variation, while in the latter there is invention. The two issues of diversity and exploration are related. Exploratory learning requires diversity of knowledge, which may be combined into something new, in Schumpeterian 'novel combinations'. A third issue is that CoPs are defined in such wide and general terms that they could encompass a wide variety of groups of people working together.

According to Wenger (1998), members of CoPs establish relationships and norms of behaviour through *mutual engagement*, are bound together by an understanding and sense of *joint enterprise*, and produce a *shared repertoire* of languages, routines, artefacts, and stories. Wenger and Snyder (2000, pp. 139, 140) characterize a CoP as follows:

[a] group of people informally bound together by shared expertise and passion for a joint enterprise [which can] drive strategy, generate new lines of business, solve problems, promote the spread of best practices, develop professional skills, and help companies to recruit and retain talent.

This can be interpreted so widely as to allow for both exploitation and exploration. However, the 'shared expertise and repertoire' raise doubt concerning cognitive variety within a CoP, needed for innovation. The 'joint enterprise and binding together' suggest dense, strong, durable ties, while the social network literature suggests that for novelty ties should be sparse (non-redundant) and weak (Granovetter 1973; Burt 1992, 2000). With a set of criteria concerning the structure, content and strength of ties, and type and variety of knowledge or competence involved, Bogen-rieder and Nooteboom (2004*a*) provided a basis for a more precise classi-fication of a wide variety of learning groups according to how they score on those criteria. Interpreting CoPs in terms of that classification, in an empirical study of five learning groups, they found none that closely fitted that interpretation of CoPs.

In view of doubts concerning the innovative potential of CoPs, several authors (Haas 1992; Cowan et al. 2000; Steinmueller 2000; Cohendet, Creplet, and Dupouët 2001; Cohendet 2005) have proposed and discussed the contrasting notion of 'epistemic communities' (EC). EC are commonly defined as groups or networks of people who perform exploratory learn-ing. They engage in transdisciplinary and/or transfunctional activities, at the interstices between the various disciplines. In contrast with CoPs, they are not organized around a common discipline or practice but around a common topic or problem.

In a later paper, Wenger et al. (2002, p. 141, quoted in Roberts 2006, p. 626) acknowledged the 'downside' of CoPs, where 'the very qualities that make a community an ideal structure for learning – a shared perspec-tive on a domain, trust, a communal identity, longstanding relationships an established practice – are the same qualities that can hold it hostage to its history and its achievements'. Here, it is important to distinguish between learning in the sense of absorbing existing knowledge from others and learning in the sense of discovery or invention. For the first, a CoP provides an ideal environment, for an entrant in a CoP to learn its practices. For the second, there is great doubt.

The purpose of the present chapter is to further analyse the differences and connections between communities for exploitation and exploration. First, the chapter discusses the notions of exploitation and exploration, and an underlying 'activity theory' of cognition. Here, cognition is a wide notion, which includes both competence (knowledge, learning) and governance (moral norms, values, and feelings), and hence includes both rational evalu-ation and feelings and emotions. Second, it picks up the issue of variety within and between communities. It discusses and employs the notion of 'cognitive distance', as a construct for cognitive and moral variety, and its effect on collaboration and learning. In view of the broad notion of cogni-tion adopted here, cognitive distance includes the social and relational distance discussed in Chapter 8 (by Meric Gertler). Third, the chapter considers the cognitive and cultural identity of communities, as a basis for limiting (intellectual and moral) cognitive distance. Fourth, it analyses cognitive distance within CoPs, between CoPs within firms, and between firms, and the implications for the locus of exploitation and exploration. It ends with the proposition that CoPs serve primarily as units of exploitation, with limited cognitive distance and a certain focus on substantive issues and personalized governance, while between CoPs within a firm, cognitive distance is greater, with a wider focus of substantive issues yielding more exploration, but with still some limitation of cognitive distance, especially on moral issues, while between firms cognitive distance opens up further, also on moral issues, which further widens the potential for exploration.

5.2 Activity Theory of Cognition and Meaning

In their account of CoPs, Brown and Duguid (1996) and Lave and Wenger (1991) employed an 'activity theory' or 'situated-action theory' of knowledge (see e.g. Blackler 1995), inspired also by the work of Kolb (1984), in which action and learning feed each other, and where 'learning is a bridge between working and innovation'. Brown and Duguid employed the notion of 'canonical' and 'non-canonical' or 'procedural' (Cohen and Bacdayan 1996) knowledge. Canonical knowledge entails decontextualized, codified, and formalized rules for operation. Inevitably, such rules cannot cover the richness and the variability of practical contexts. It is by context-dependent deviations from canonical rules, with the ensuing need for improvisation and experimentation (Brown and Duguid employed Levy-Strauss' concept of *bricolage*) that learning arises, also in the sense of a shift of knowledge, in interaction between members of the community. This is based on 'storytelling', to capture and share context-bound experience, to guide experimentation. As a result, communities emerge from shared work practice rather than that they are designed *ex ante*.

The notion that cognition is *embedded*, and arises from interaction with the environment, goes back to Vygotsky (1962) and Piaget (1970, 1974), with their idea that 'intelligence is internalised action'.[1] In sociology, the idea that cognition arises from interaction of people with their (especially social) environment arises, in particular, in the 'symbolic interactionism' proposed by G. H. Mead (1934, 1982). In the organization literature, this has been introduced, in particular, by Weick (1979, 1995), who reconstructed organization as a 'sense-making system'.

The notion that cognition is embedded in practice and also rooted in the body arises also in recent work of cognitive scientists (Damasio 1995, 2003; Edelman 1987, 1992; Lakoff and Johnson 1999). In philosophy, it goes back to Merleau-Ponty (1964), who also argued that 'the light of reason is rooted in the darkness of the body'. Building on the philosophy of Spinoza, Damasio (2003) demonstrated a hierarchy of cognition, where rationality is driven by feelings, which in turn have a substrate of physiology, in a 'signaling from body to brain'. The process of association yields many un- or subconscious neural structures that constitute what we experience as intuition. Since those are automatic, they are often experienced as more 'authentic' and 'intrinsic' than rational evaluation. They do have the advantage of being faster than rational evaluation, and this fast response on the basis of mental routines has survival value, in the flight from danger and the spurt towards opportunity. Intuitions and reflexes are typically laden with emotion, which affects how deeply they are embedded and how easily, and on what occasions, they are triggered. Symbols typically trigger intuitions or reflexes with an appeal to their emotional content (Siemsen 2006).

Embeddedness of cognition goes together with embeddedness of meaning. The reference of terms is generally indeterminate without their embedding in a specific action context, *in combination with* the embodied web of largely tacit belief. John Searle used the notion of 'background', illustrated with the eating of a hamburger.[2] Unspecified, but obvious, is the condition that the hamburger enters the body not by the ear but by the mouth. I suggest that the background consists of the *cognitive* background, in a seamless web of cognition (Quine and Ullian 1970), of the observer, *and* the context, of words in a sentence, in a context of *action*. The latter triggers associations between connotations embodied in the former. In this way, embedding is needed to disambiguate expressions that by themselves are underdetermined in their reference.

A second effect of embeddedness of meaning, I propose, is that any event of interpretation, in a context of action, shifts meanings. Even memory is not simple retrieval, but reconstruction based on the context, and this reconstruction alters the memory. In sum, we grasp our actions in the world to both disambiguate and construct meaning. How do meanings of words change in their use? Neural structures provide the basis for categorization, that is assigning a perceived object to a semantic class, on the basis of patterns of connotations that distinguish one category from another. It seems, however, that the activity of categorization brings in novel connotations, or patterns of them, from specific contexts of action, and affects the distribution of connotations across categories. Then, an expression (sentence, term, sign) never has the exact same meaning across different contexts of action. Furthermore, I propose that any such act of interpretation shifts the basis for it. Associations between terms, on the basis of shared or linked connotations, shift the distribution of those connotations across terms.

In neurophysiological terms, this is embodied in selection and strengthening and weakening of connections between neuronal groups, as described by Professor Edelman. In the brain, association arises from neurons being activated ('firing') simultaneously, which, when repeated, yields novel physical connections between the neurons, as a result of which later activation of one of them triggers activation of the other. Could this be indicative of a more general logic of structuration where structures in their mutual influence can function efficiently while changing in the process?

There is much left to be investigated in the study of how the structuration of cognition, categorization, and meaning proceeds. How does the use of words change their meaning while maintaining stability of meaning for interpretation and meaningful discourse? Are there 'levels' of change, with 'minor change' that leads on, somehow, to 'large' or wider 'structural' change? How would that work? What happens in the brain in doing that? This yields a wide research programme, beyond the present chapter.

5.3 Exploitation, Exploration, and Cognitive Distance

An important implication of the activity theory of cognition, in the present context, is that while we can make a conceptual distinction between exploitation (practice) and exploration (invention), they build upon each other. Exploration arises from practice, and practice arises from exploration. The question for this chapter is whether that happens within or between communities. According to the notion of ECs, exploration arises within them. If CoPs are mostly exploitation-oriented, could exploration arise from interaction between them? How could that work? If organizations must somehow be involved, within the organization or in interaction with other organizations, in both exploitation, to survive in the short term, and exploration, to survive in the long term, how is that combination to be achieved?

Nooteboom (2000) proposed a 'heuristic of discovery', by which exploration and exploitation arise from each other in a series of stages or different levels of learning. In learning for exploitation, inventions from exploration converge on dominant technical and organizational designs. To move towards new exploration, such dominant practice needs to be subjected to novel challenges, in novel contexts of application, in a stage of 'generalization', needed to yield the motivation and the insight needed for change. When change is needed, to survive in novel conditions, it is typically first sought in 'proximate' change, to maintain exploitation as much as possible, by novel selections from existing repertoires of action, in the stage of 'differentiation'. When that does not suffice, more radical change is typically sought in the attempt to build in elements from newly encountered 'foreign' practices, in the new context of application, that appear to be successful where one's own practice appears to fail, in the stage of reciprocation or hybridization. This typically yields hybrids that are inefficient, or even inconsistent, but yield an opportunity to experiment and explore the potential of novel elements. When such potential emerges, it yields a motivation for more radical change of principles of design, principles or logic, and an indication of where that is to be sought, to realize emerging potential of novelty and to eliminate the inconsistencies or inefficiencies of the hybrid, in the stage of transformation or 'accommodation'. Bogenrieder and Nooteboom (2004*b*) applied the analysis to the 'emergence of learning communities'. Here, I go back one step to analyse the relationship between exploitation, exploration, and cognitive distance.

As a result of differences in physical and cultural environments that are embodied in cognition, the perception, interpretation, and evaluation by people are path-dependent and idiosyncratic to a greater or lesser extent. By path-dependent I refer, here, to the condition that cognition takes place on the basis of categories that have developed in interaction with a certain context of action, so that the latter predisposes cognition. Cognition depends, literally, on the path of cognitive development. Different people see the world differently to the extent that they have developed in different social and physical surroundings and have not interacted with each other. In other words, past experience determines 'absorptive capacity' (Cohen and Levinthal 1990). This yields what I call 'cognitive distance' (Nooteboom 1992, 1999).

Cognitive distance between people, resulting from variety of experience, presents both a problem and an opportunity. The opportunity is that variety of cognition is a source of innovation. This connects with the theme of this volume concerning the constructive role of dissonance and ambiguity, and the idea, discussed also in Chapter 9, by Patrick Cohendet and Laurent Simon, and going back to the seminal work of Brown and Duguid, that the friction of competing ideas can ignite innovation. The problem is that to the extent that cognition differs, it is more difficult to understand each other and to collaborate and utilize opportunities from cognitive variety. Note that cognition being a wide concept in this chapter, cognitive distance entails both difference in intellectual knowledge and difference in feeling and morality. As indicated before, here cognitive distance includes social and relational distance. Cognitive distance yields not only a difficulty of mutual understanding, or a limit to absorptive capacity (Cohen and Levinthal 1990), but also a wider difficulty of collaboration, including a mismatch of moral and motivational aspects of collaboration. In other words: distance includes issues of both competence and governance.

Optimal collaboration requires a trade-off between the upside and the downside of cognitive distance, seeking an 'optimal cognitive distance', large enough to offer variety for innovation, and small enough to enable collaboration. This is illustrated in Figure 5.1.

If ability to collaborate declines with cognitive distance, say linearly, to keep things as simple as possible, and novelty value increases with it, say linearly, and performance is proportional to the mathematical product of the two (potential x ability to utilize it), then performance is an inverted-U-shaped function of distance, yielding some optimal distance. Now for exploitation (Figure 5.1b), which is oriented towards efficiency, in a fine-tuning of complementary capabilities, where lack of error or mismatch is more important than novelty, the marginal utility of novelty is less (lower positive slope of the novelty line) than for exploration (Figure 5.1a), which is oriented at more radical novel combinations, and the marginal disutility of lack of understanding and ability to collaborate is greater (higher negative slope of the ability line). As a result, as illustrated in Figure 5.1, optimal cognitive distance is lower for exploitation than for exploration. In exploration cognitive distance has more relative advantage. This also

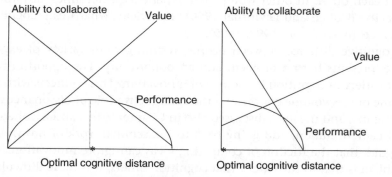

Figure 5.1: (*a*) Exploitation and (*b*) exploration.

illustrates the problem of combining exploitation and exploration in a single organizational unit: there is a tension between the needs for small and for large cognitive distance at the same time. We might now interpret Figure 5.1*b* as belonging to CoPs and Figure 5.1*a* as belonging to ECs.

One way to solve the problem of combining exploitation and exploration in one community is to specialize in either of the two, in a given community, and engage in collaboration with another community that specializes in the other. On the firm level, a classic example of this is that of small biotechnology firms that focus on the exploration of novel active substances or processes and then transfer the outcome to large pharmaceutical companies for its exploitation. However, there may be an alternative of combining different CoPs for the sake of exploration on the basis of cognitive distance between them. Or, in other words, could it be that several CoPs together may constitute a larger EC? But what is the meaning of cognitive distance if we shift from distance between individuals and distance between communities, or organizations?

5.4 Exploration by Interaction Between Communities

Nooteboom et al. (2007) applied the notion of optimal cognitive distance to collaboration between firms, in an attempt at an empirical test of the thesis of optimal cognitive distance. The hypothesis was that Figure 5.1 also applies on the level of organizations, in terms of cognitive distance between them. In that study, cognitive distance between firms was operationalized in terms of the dissimilarity between technology profiles of the firms involved, derived from patent data: profiles that arise on the basis of the incidence of a firm in (some 300) different patent classes. The hypothesis was that innovative performance (in terms of patent production) between firms was an inverse U-shaped function of such distance, and the hypothesis was corroborated on a data set of alliances between 116 firms in a period of twelve years.

That is not an unreasonable move, but how satisfactory is it to construct cognitive distance between groups in terms of the difference in the *collective* knowledge of those groups? An alternative would be to look at the difference in *individual* knowledge of those people from the different groups that actually interact in collaboration between those groups, that is the 'boundary spanners' between those groups? They may have limited distance between them and considerable distance to the other people in their respective groups. That distance is likely to be smaller than the distance in collective knowledge of the groups. To fulfil their role, boundary spanners must have an exceptionally large absorptive capacity, or ability to collaborate, in order to collaborate both with people within their own group and the boundary spanner of the connecting group. Boundary spanning is a delicate job. The boundary spanner's loyalty to his own group may be in doubt for the very reason that he is able to empathize with outsiders. He may be seen to engage in *illegitimate* peripheral participation. In the empirical study of Nooteboom and colleagues, such use of cognitive distance between boundary spanners rather than groups overall was not available in the data.

The following questions arise. How could boundary spanning between CoPs yield exploration? Are there any reasons why this should happen between communities within rather than between separate organizations? What is the identity of communities and organizations by which cognitive distance gets limited, not to exceed its maximum?

For an answer to the first question I turn to the 'logic of discovery' according to Nooteboom (2000) and summarized above. Collaboration across (greater or smaller) cognitive distance forces one to try and apply one's knowledge in a novel context, in this case the practice of the partner (generalization). There, one is faced with limitations in one's own view and competence, and the need to adapt. The first step would be to try and adapt by differentiating one's view according to existing repertoires of knowledge and competence (differentiation). If that is not sufficient, further interaction may yield the perception that one may try to adopt elements of what the partner is doing, which seem to function better than some elements of one's own practice, in experimentation with a hybrid (reciprocation). This, then, yields both the opportunity to explore the potential of novel elements and insight into where inefficiencies lie in the hybrid, as well as obstacles to the realization of the emerging potential of novelty, which provides both the incentive and some direction for a more radical change of principles of logic or design (accommodation). Note that what is different here from the original logic is that the process now is reciprocal. Partners can help each other in fitting in elements from their practice into hybridization of the partner's practice, trying to explain how it works, with clever use of metaphors, examples, mental experiments, or simulation. Next, they can try to jointly find novel design principles for a synthesis, in a new form.

From the process we can also derive other requirements for boundary spanning. One is that in the process of differentiation the boundary spanner has to liaise back to his own community to find new options from existing repertoires. This will be needed not only for reasons of competence but also for reasons for governance, in particular motivational reasons. The next stage of hybridization, with its attendant inefficiencies and possible inconsistencies, will hardly be popular with community members unless they have first had the opportunity to exhaust alternatives from their existing repertoires. In the more radical, fundamental change of basic design principles they will not be willing to go along unless they have experienced the benefits of the potential of novelty that is becoming manifest. Soon this process will go beyond the capacity and capability of any single boundary spanning, and the process is likely to be complemented with task forces and exchange of personnel between the partner communities, when its potential becomes manifest. At every step the peripherality of participation will have to be legitimated.

5.5 Organizational Focus

On the basis of the activity-based, social constructivist view of cognition, the literature on management and organization has developed the view that firms construct their own, more or less organization-specific meanings and interpretations, in the organization as a system of 'sense-making' (Weick 1995), 'collective mind' (Weick and Roberts 1993), system of 'shared meanings' (Smircich 1983), 'interpretation system' (Choo 1998), or a cognitive 'focusing device' (Nooteboom 2000).

In the present context, a cognitive focus, in the wide sense of including both substantive understanding (on the competence side) and morality (on the governance side), is needed, in communities and organizations, to limit cognitive distance from going beyond the optimum, given the orientation towards exploitation or exploration. Such focus is achieved on the basis of specialized semiotic systems, in language, symbols, metaphors, myths, and rituals. This is what we call organizational culture. Within communities focus is narrower, and culture tighter, than between communities within an organization. Organizational focus may be compared to the 'habitus' of an organization or community (Bourdieu 1986, 1990; Mutch 2003).

On the competence side, focus is needed to *enable* people to understand each other and connect complementary knowledge, without unduly restricting variety and creativity. How far variety (cognitive distance) is needed depends on orientation towards exploitation or exploration. On the governance side, focus is needed to *motivate* people to collaborate and share and connect knowledge, without unduly restricting autonomy, ambition, and competitive spirit. Governance is needed to control 'relational risk', within and between communities and organizations. Here, I distinguish three kinds of risk. One is risk of (particularly one-sided) dependence, which is close to the 'hold-up risk' of transaction cost theory. One cause of that risk may be the relation-specific investment one has to make in order to make the relationship work, for example to achieve mutual understanding and trust. One will make such investment only when confident that one will recoup it in the relationship. A second risk is that of competition due to knowledge spillover: in collaboration for learning, partners may run off with the knowledge one gives in order to compete, in profits, bonuses, or career prospects. A third risk is that of psychological safety (Edmonson 1999): one may be hesitant to show ignorance or lack of competence, for the loss of prestige and reputation that may yield. Such loss may also have negative effects on prospects for career and future partnerships.

Organizational focus also has a function of both selection and adaptation. In selection, it selects people, in recruitment but often on the basis of self-selection of personnel joining the organization because they feel affinity with it, and adaptation, in the socialization into the firm, and training, of incoming personnel. In between entry and socialization lies 'peripheral participation'. To perform these functions, focus must be embodied in some visible form. Such form is needed for several reasons. One is to function as a signalling device to outsiders. That is needed as a basis of the (self-)selection process of incoming staff, and for recognition and identification by other stakeholders, such as colleagues, customers, and suppliers. More for the internal function of coordination, we find the exemplary behaviour of organizational heroes, corresponding myths, war stories, and rituals.

This cognitive theory of the firm can be contrasted with earlier, contractual theories in economics (Alchian and Demsetz 1972; Williamson 1975, 1985; Hart 1995). The latter look at organizations as systems of contracts or material incentives, to control opportunism. However, increasingly it is has been recognized that for a variety of reasons *ex ante* incentive design is problematic. Due to uncertainty concerning contingencies of collaboration, and limited opportunities for monitoring, *ex ante* measures of governance are seldom complete, and need to be supplemented with *ex post* adaptation. Such uncertainties proliferate under present conditions of professional work and rapid innovation. Professional work is hard to monitor and evaluate, and requires considerable autonomy for its execution. Rapid innovation increases uncertainty of contingencies and makes formal governance, especially governance by contract, difficult to specify. If such specification is nevertheless undertaken, it threatens to form a straightjacket that constrains the scope for innovation (Nooteboom 1999). Furthermore, the attempt to use contracts to constrain opportunism tends to evoke mistrust that is retaliated by mistrust, while in view of uncertainty there is a need to operate on trust more than on contract (Nooteboom 2002). Organizational focus, provided by organizational culture, yields an epistemological and normative 'background' for *ex ante* selection of staff to suit organizational focus, and for *ex post* adaptation, as a basis for coordination, mutual understanding, mutual adaptation, decision-making, and conflict resolution.

5.6 Details and Differences of Focus

The question will arise: what, more precisely, is the difference between cognitive focus on the level of a community and on the level of an organization with several communities. I indicated before that within communities focus is narrower, and culture tighter, than between communities within an organization. What does that mean, more precisely?

Both inside and outside organizations, people have more goals, capabilities, roles, and relations than those that are governed by organizational focus (Dimaggio 1997). Ring and van de Ven (1994) made a distinction between organizational roles people play and their behaviour 'qua persona'. This was presaged by the distinction Simmel (1950 [1917]) made between a person's function in an organization, which takes up only part of his personality, and his full personality. So, one question is how far does organizational focus reach in affecting actions of people. Berger and Luckmann (1966) distinguished between primary socialization in family, as one grows up, and, building on that and moulding it further – secondary socialization in places of work.

The content and extent of cognitive alignment in organizations varies. In addition to the distinction between the competence and governance sides of focus, there are five dimensions for both. First, there is *width*, that is the range of different areas of competence and governance in a firm to which focus applies. This depends on the range of capabilities that a firm encompasses. Second, there is *reach*, that is the number of aspects within each area covered by the focus. Does it affect all or only some key aspects of a given capability? A third dimension is *tightness* versus *looseness*, that is narrowness of tolerance levels of standards or rules imposed by focus, versus allowance for slack and ambiguity, with improvised, unforeseen meanings, actions, etc. For exploitation focus needs to be tighter, and for exploration more loose.

Fourth, focus may have different *content*. In particular, on the governance side it may entail formal, that is depersonalized norms of legitimacy, which regulate what managers and workers can legitimately do and can expect from each other. Such norms render relations more impersonal and thereby reduce tensions associated with the exercise of personal power, and they enlist workers to participate in the control of their colleagues (Scott 1992, p. 306). The content of focus may also be more cultural, in the sense of offering guidance by more emotion-laden underlying values, expressed in symbolic entities, behaviours, events, or processes. The two types of content are related, since norms of legitimacy may be expressed culturally. One can have norms of legitimacy that are specified rigorously and formally, and one can have more informal, ambiguous, cultural features that go beyond norms of legitimacy. The first occurs more in exploitation and the second more in exploration.

Fifth, and this will turn out to be a central point, focus may relate to *surface regulations* concerning specific actions or to underlying more fundamental notions, in a *deep structure* of logic, principles, or cognitive categories that form the basis for surface regulation. A surface rule or regulation allows for a certain range of activities; a deep structure allows for a range of surface regulations. Simon (1976) already acknowledged that an organization controls not decisions but their premises. Nelson and Winter (1982) made a similar distinction, between routines and 'meta-routines' that guide the development of routines. Schein (1985) made a similar distinction in organizational culture. Below surface features such as specific rules, practices, symbols, myths, rituals, at the basis of organizational culture lie fundamental views and intuitions regarding the relation between the firm and its environment ('locus of control': is the firm master or victim of its environment), attitude to risk, the nature of knowledge (objective or constructed), the nature of man (loyal and trustworthy/self-interested or opportunistic), the position of man (individualistic or part of a community), and relations between people (rivalrous or collaborative), which inform content and process of strategy, organizational structure, and styles of decision-making and coordination. Schein also allowed for an intermediate level, connecting the fundamental cognitive categories with the surface level of specific structures and rules, in the form of general principles that express fundamental cognitive categories but are yet general and generic rather than specific to certain activities and contexts.

An attempt to schematically illustrate the difference between activities, surface regulation, and deep structure is given in Figure 5.2. On any level, a single point generates a range of action on the next higher level, and belongs to a wider range generated from the next lower level. A given deep-level 'philosophy' generates a range of possible operating procedures, on the middle level, each of which generates a range of specific actions. Here, for simplicity of exposition, the intermediate level of culture, indicated by Schein, is left out. On the middle level one can have a standard operating procedure, for operating a production unit, for prototyping, for interacting with customers, or an accounting or reporting procedure. An underlying cognitive category in deep-level structure enables a bundle of surface-level regulation. This could be a 'philosophy' of production, development, marketing, or control. The establishment of coordination on the surface level (routines, if one wants to use that term) leaves freedom for variety of underlying cognitive categories, but has to be set up ad hoc each time, and requires the solution of complications due to differences in underlying cognition. People having different 'philosophies' may well develop a shared operating procedure, but it will take time to bridge and integrate their perspectives sufficiently to achieve that task. The establishment of coordination on the deep level, in shared 'philosophies', yields more *ex ante* agreement for setting up surface regulation, and thus enhances flexibility and speed of action, but it reduces variety of cognition, due to shared 'philosophies', on the deep level. It entails more indoctrination. Thus, efficient exploitation is enhanced by deep-level coordination, and exploration is constrained by it.

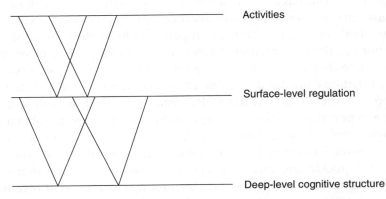

Activities

Surface-level regulation

Deep-level cognitive structure

Figure 5.2: Levels of coordination.

I will argue that organizations serve especially to coordinate on the deep level, with an advantage of easier and faster understanding and agreement, to enable exploitation, while collaboration between organizations operates more on the surface level, with the advantage of greater variety on the deep level, allowing for a wider scope of exploration. Organizational focus entails a certain myopia, which can be compensated with external relationships between firms, at greater cognitive distance. Here, the theory of the firm based on the notion of organizational cognitive focus entails a theory of inter-firm relationships.

The notion of cognitive distance entails a distinction between reducing and crossing cognitive distance. Reducing cognitive distance entails alignment on the deep level of cognition, so that people think more similarly. Crossing cognitive distance entails making surface agreements while maintaining differences on the deep level, with people continuing to think differently. When people who think differently continue interaction, starting from surface agreements, they may in time come to think more similarly, that is share underlying cognition, in a reduction of cognitive distance.

5.7 Why Communities Within Organizations?

If CoPs are needed primarily for efficient exploitation, and exploration can take place in ECs, or in interaction between CoPs, why have organizations that consist of more than one community? Why not have one organization or firm per community? In other words, what is the difference in cognitive focus between a community and an organization or firm? I propose that this has to do with the difference between the competence and governance sides of cognitive distance and organizational focus.

Very briefly and schematically, I propose that firms allow for considerable (but still limited) internal distance in competence between communities, while they limit distance in governance, on the basis of a certain style or 'habitus' on the moral side of collaboration, across a variety of contents of knowledge. Within CoPs, distance is small in both competence and governance. The advantage of this, compared to collaboration between different organizations, is that collaboration across different competencies, located in different CoPs, for the sake of exploration, can be set up quickly and relatively smoothly, compared to the problems of aligning interests and styles of collaboration across different organizations that differ more on the moral side. By contrast, within professional communities (PCs), extending across different organizations, there is limited distance on the competence side but considerable distance on the governance side. Between professionals there is easy understanding but not necessarily ease of collaboration. In other words, organizations combine variety in competence with some unity in governance, while in professions it is the other way around.

Next, I try to specify differences between organizations, CoPs, ECs, and PCs in more detail, in terms of the features of cognitive focus. This is summarized in Table 5.1.

According to Table 5.1, I propose that in organizations cognitive distance is limited in competence, allowing for some variety of potentially complementary competencies, and small in governance, with a cognitive focus that applies mostly to a limited range of moral categories (reach), but on a deep level of basic values, often with partly formal and partly informal (symbolic) features. In ECs, distance is limited in competence, aiming for variety but also complementarity, but they build on limited cognitive distance in governance, offered by organizational culture, and have limited, informal, and loose reach of aspects of behaviour, little depth of focus on top of that provided by the organization, and only some additional surface regulations. In CoPs, distance is small in both competence and governance, cognitive focus has a wide, pretty tight, typically informal reach, with considerable deep structure in addition to that provided by the organization. In PCs, across organizations, distance is small in competence, large in governance, and there is little reach of focus, but it is pretty tight and deep, in fundamental substantive principles or paradigms of the profession.

Together, these forms of organization are highly complementary, and together enable a system of exploitation and exploration that can be highly efficient. Organizations yield some variety of internal competence,

Table 5.1: Organizations, epistemic communities (ECs), communities of practice (CoPs), and professional communities (PCs)

	Organizations	ECs	CoPs	PCs
Cognitive distance				
In competence	Limited	Limited	Small	Small
In governance	Small	Small	Small	Large
Characteristics of cognitive focus				
Reach	Small	Limited	Wide	Small
Tightness	Large	Small	Large	Large
Content	Fairly formal	Informal	Informal	Formal or informal
Surface/deep level	Deep	Surface	Deep	Deep

though this is limited by the potential complementarity of competencies, with CoPs for efficient exploitation, ECs and interaction between different CoPs as sources of exploration, building on a relative ease of collaboration on the governance focus offered by the organization. Organizational focus by definition yields some organizational myopia, which limits exploration and innovation, but this can be compensated by inter-organizational collaboration, at larger cognitive distance. However, more time is needed there to set up surface regulation, or to develop some shared deep-level categories to facilitate collaboration. PCs across organizations serve to deepen professional expertise, in an exchange of experience across a variety of contexts of application.

Note that in the latter we see a reappearance of the 'logic of discovery' that was summarized before. When professionals get together to compare experience in different contexts of application, this yields a setting for 'generalization' that through 'differentiation' and 'reciprocation' may yield renewal and ultimately revolutionary change in the profession, although for the latter one may need novel combinations between different disciplines.

5.8 Conclusions and Further Research

The differences and relations between different kinds of communities, in particular CoPs and ECs, and the organization of which they may form a part, can be clarified on the basis of the activity-based theory of knowledge that is commonly used in the literature. That theory yields the notion of cognitive distance, and the trade-off between its advantage for novelty and its disadvantage in limited ability to collaborate. This yields the notion of optimal cognitive distance in a community, and the difference between CoPs and ECs. In organizations and communities, cognitive distance is limited by 'cognitive focus'.

Cognitive distance and organizational focus have a competence side, in substantive knowledge, and a governance side, in morality, that is norms and values of conduct. Exploitation takes place in CoPs. Exploration may take place in ECs or in interaction between CoPs, within and between organizations.

The way in which interaction between individuals and communities at a cognitive distance yields exploration can be understood from a 'logic' or heuristic of learning, with different stages, derived from earlier research. This has implications for the roles of boundary spanners that bridge the cognitive distance between communities. (For further details concerning levels of change in the interaction between communities, see Bogenrieder and Nooteboom 2004*b*).

While Table 5.1 applies to cognitive distance and relationships within communities, one can do a similar analysis concerning distance and relations between communities, as Cohendet (2005) did, and some of the logic developed here can be used to extend that analysis. However, that goes beyond the limits of the present chapter.

A central point of the present analysis is the following. There is a cognitive division of labour between communities and organizations. Within organizations there is some but limited distance in competence, and small distance in governance. In CoPs there is small distance in both competence and governance. In ECs there is small distance in governance and some distance in competence. In PCs there is small distance in competence and large distance in governance. Exploration in interaction between CoPs within an organization is facilitated by shared organizational focus in governance, but limited by the limited cognitive distance within an organization. The potential for exploration is larger between organizations, at larger cognitive distance, in both competence and governance, but requires more time and effort to set up and regulate collaboration. PCs enable professional development to tap into the diversity of application across organizations. Employing the potential of their cognitive complementarity, these different forms of organization can together yield efficient systems of exploitation and exploration.

Next to the effects of cognitive distance, there is analysis to be done of the effects of the structure, strength, and content of ties on novelty value and ability to collaborate. This will yield further insight into organizational structure, in the configuration of people in communities, and of communities in organizations, and their effects on exploitation and exploration. That goes beyond the present chapter, but for analysis and empirical tests for relationships between organizations, see Gilsing et al. (2008).

The distinction between CoP, EC, and PC is very schematic. In fact there is a greater variety of groups for learning or development, as demonstrated by Bogenrieder and Nooteboom (2004*a*). They used criteria of different kinds to categorize what, to avoid confusion, they called 'learning groups' rather than 'communities'. The structure, strength, and content of ties form part of those criteria. Structure has six dimensions and strength five. One dimension of strength is the frequency with which members meet and another is how long membership lasts. Content includes the subject of knowledge (technical, commercial, organizational), the type of knowledge in terms of tacit or more codified knowledge, and the level of learning, that is exploitation or exploration, involved. In addition, there are different types of relational risk (of dependence, competition, and psychological safety, cf. Edmonson 1999) and different instruments of governance to deal with them. By configuring these features in different ways one can generate a vast number of different potential kinds of learning groups.

Empirically, they found five groups. One was characterized as a project team, and had some similarity to the notion of a CoP. One aspect where it differed was that since the group was oriented at temporary projects, membership was shorter than one would expect for a CoP. None of the groups could be recognized as an EC, in the sense of being engaged in exploration of novel products or processes. Two groups seemed like PCs, but in different ways. One was aimed at the development of professional expertise, among members of the same profession, but all within the same organization, and the other was aimed at the development of behavioural and managerial skills among people from different professions, within the organization. This indicates that while in the discussion of communities we are inclined to think of technical expertise and skill, learning may be oriented also towards behavioural and organizational skills. The innovation literature used to have a similar bias towards technological innovation, but has learned to also look at organizational innovation. A fourth group was aimed at improvement of projects by exchange of experience from different projects. That group failed because the projects involved were too diverse, and required too much explanation of specific contents and conditions of projects before mutual understanding was established, with difficulties in codifying the tacit knowledge involved in the projects, and the stability of membership was too low to solve problems of psychological safety. This illustrates that in connecting different project teams or CoPs one must take the time to develop mutual absorptive capacity. This entails a specific investment in the sense of transaction cost theory, with the implication that the relationship must be expected to last sufficiently long to make that investment worthwhile. The group transformed itself into a group that was purely oriented at the exchange of location knowledge (Hutchins and Klausen 1996; Moreland 1999). Having established where interesting projects take place, people can contact them to develop a more intensive, durable, and psychologically safer relationship needed for mutual learning. Another group with a similar objective of project improvement was successful by replacing accounts of real projects by stylized, virtual cases that required less investment in attention upfront and solved the problem of psychological safety.

My conclusion is that the notion of ECs should be widened to include a wider variety of learning groups, and that the notion of PCs should be widened to allow for exchange of behavioural, organizational, or managerial professional competence next to more technical professional expertise. As a result, the analysis of the total system of exploitation and exploration will include a greater variety of learning groups, with a richer analysis of dimensions of cognitive distance and cognitive focus than provided in Table 5.1. However, the basic logic will still apply that the advantage of having such groups within an organization is that on the basis of organizational focus in governance they can be set up more easily than between different organizations. The disadvantage is that cognitive distance remains limited, yielding myopia, and outside relationships are needed to repair for that, at the price of more time and costs in setting them up.

References

Alchian, A. A. and Demsetz, H. (1972). 'Production, information costs, and economic organization', *American Economic Review*, 62(5): 777–95.

Argyris, C. and Schön, D. (1978). *Organizational Learning*. Reading, MA: Addison-Wesley.

Bateson, G. (1973). *Steps to an Ecology of Mind*. Boulder, CO: Paladin Books.

Berger, P. and Luckmann, T. (1966). *The Social Construction of Reality*. New York: Doubleday.

Blackler, F. (1995). 'Knowledge, knowledge work and organizations: An overview and interpretation', *Organization Studies*, 16(6): 1021–46.

Bogenrieder, I. and Nooteboom, B. (2004a). 'Learning groups: What types are there? A theoretical analysis and an empirical study in a consultancy firm', *Organization Studies*, 25(2): 287–314.

Bogenrieder, I. and Nooteboom, B. (2004b). 'The emergence of learning communities', in H. Tsoukas and N. Mylonopoulos (eds.), *Organizations as Knowledge Systems*. Basingstoke, UK: Palgrave, pp. 46–66.

Bourdieu, P. (1986). *Distinction: A Social Critique of the Judgement of Taste*. London: Routledge.

—— (1990). *The Logic of Practice*. Cambridge: Polity Press.

Brown, J. S. and Duguid, P. (1996). 'Organizational learning and communities-of-practice: Toward a unified view of working, learning, and innovation', in

M. D. Cohen and L. S. Sproull (eds.), *Organizational Learning*. Thousand Oaks, CA: Sage, pp. 58–82.

Burt, R. (1992). *Structural Holes: The Social Structure of Competition*. Cambridge, MA: Harvard University Press.

—— (2000) 'The network structure of social capital', in R. I. Sutton and B. M. Staw (eds.), *Research in Organizational Behavior*. Greenwich, CT: Jai Press, pp. 345–423.

Choo, C. W. (1998). *The Knowing Organization: How Organizations Use Information to Construct Meaning, Create Knowledge, and Make Decisions*. New York: Oxford University Press.

Cohen, M. D. (1991). 'Individual learning and organizational routine', *Organization Science*, 2(1): 135–9, reprinted in M. D. Cohen and L. S. Sproull (eds.) (1996). *Organizational Learning*. London: Sage, pp. 188–229.

—— and Bacdayan, P. (1996). 'Organizational routines are stored as procedural memory', in M. D. Cohen and L. S. Sproull (eds.), *Organizational Learning*. London: Sage, pp. 403–30; first printed in *Organization Science*, 5(4): 554–68, in 1994.

—— and Levinthal, D. A. (1990). 'Absorptive capacity: A new perspective on learning and innovation', *Administrative Science Quarterly*, 35: 128–52.

Cook, S. D. N. and Yanow, P. (1993). 'Culture and organizational learning', *Journal of Management Enquiry*, 2(4): 373–90; reprinted in M. D. Cohen and L. S. Sproull (eds.) (1996). *Organizational Learning*. London: Sage, pp. 430–59.

Cohendet, P. (2005). 'On knowing communities', paper presented at Conference Advancing Knowledge and the Knowledge Economy, Washington, DC, January.

Cohendet, P., Creplet, F., and Dupouët, O. (2001). *Communities of Practice and Epistemic Communities: A Renewed Approach of Organisational Learning within the Firm*. Strasbourg: BETA, Université Louis Pasteur.

Contu, A. and Wilmott, H. (2003). 'Re-embedding situatedness: The importance of power relations in learning theory', *Organization Science*, 7(2): 269–76.

Cowan, R., David, P. A., and Foray, D. (2000). 'The explicit economics of knowledge codification and tacitness', *Industrial and Corporate Change*, 9(2): 211–53.

Damasio, A. R. (1995). *Descartes' Error: Emotion, Reason and the Human Brain*. London: Picador.

Damasio, A. R. (2003). *Looking for Spinoza*. Orlando, FL: Harcourt.

DiMaggio, P. J. (1997). 'Culture and cognition', *Annual Review of Sociology*, 23: 263–87.

Duncan, R. and Weiss, A. (1979). 'Organizational learning: Implications for organizational design', *Research in Organizational Behavior*, 1: 75–132.

Edelman, G. M. (1987). *Neural Darwinism: The Theory of Neuronal Group Selection*. New York: Basic Books.

—— (1992). *Bright Air, Brilliant Fire: On the Matter of Mind*. London: Penguin.

Edmonson, A. (1999). 'Psychological safety and learning behaviour in work teams', *Administrative Science Quarterly*, 44: 350–83.

Flavell, J. H. (1967). *The Developmental Psychology of Jean Piaget*. Princeton, NJ: Van Nostrand.

Gilsing, V. A., Nooteboom, B., van Haverbeke, W., Duysters, G. M., and Oord, A. v.d. (2008). 'Network embeddedness and the exploration of novel technologies: technological distance, betweenness centrality and density', forthcoming in *Research Policy*.

Granovetter, M. (1973). 'The strength of weak ties', *American Journal of Sociology*, 78(6): 1360–81.

Haas, P. M. (1992). 'Introduction: Epistemic communities and international policy coordination', *International Organization*, 46(1): 1–35.

Handley, K., Sturdy, A., Fincham, R. and Clark, T. (2006). 'Within and beyond communities of practice: Making sense of learning through participation, identity and practice', *Journal of Management Studies*, 43(3): 642–52.

Hart, O. D. (1995). *Firms, Contracts, and Financial Structure*. Oxford: Clarendon Press.

Hutchins, E. and Klausen, T. (1996). 'Distributed cognition in an airline cockpit', in Y. Engestroem and D. Middleton (eds.), *Cognition and Communication at Work*. Cambridge: Cambridge University Press, pp. 15–34.

Kolb, D. (1984). *Experiential Learning: Experience as the Source of Learning and Development*. Englewood Cliffs, NJ: Prentice-Hall.

Lakoff, G. and Johnson, M. (1999). *Philosophy in the Flesh*. New York: Basic Books.

Lave, J. and Wenger, E. (1991). *Situated Learning: Legitimate Peripheral Participation*. Cambridge: Cambridge University Press.

March, J. (1991). 'Exploration and exploitation in organizational learning', *Organization Science*, 2(1): 71–87.

Mead, G. H. (1934). *Mind, Self and Society: From the Standpoint of a Social Behaviorist*. Chicago, IL: Chicago University Press.

——(1982). *The Individual and the Social Self*, unpublished work of G. H. Mead, edited by D. L. Miller. Chicago, IL: University of Chicago Press.

Merleau-Ponty, M. (1964). *Le visible et l'invisible*. Paris: Gallimard.

Moreland, R. L. (1999). 'Transactive memory: Learning who knows what in work groups and organizations', in L. L. Thompson, J. M. Levine, and D. M. Messick (eds.), *Shared Cognition in Organizations*. London: Erlbaum, pp. 3–31.

Mutch, A. (2003). 'Communities of practice and habitus: A critique', *Organization Studies*, 24(3): 383–401.

Nelson R. R. and Winter, S. (1982). *An Evolutionary Theory of Economic Change*. Cambridge: Cambridge University Press.

Nooteboom, B. (1992). 'Towards a dynamic theory of transactions', *Journal of Evolutionary Economics*, 2: 281–99.

——(1999). *Inter-Firm Alliances: Analysis and Design*. London: Routledge.

——(2000). *Learning and Innovation in Organizations and Economies*. Oxford: Oxford University Press.

——(2002). *Trust: Forms, Foundations, Functions, Failures and Figures*. Cheltenham, UK: Edward Elgar.

——Van Haverbeke, W. P. M., Duijsters, G. M., Gilsing, V. A., and Oord A. V. d. (2007). 'Optimal cognitive distance and absorptive capacity', *Research Policy*, 36(7): 1016–34.

Piaget, J. (1970). *Psychologie et epistémologie*. Paris: Denoël.

——(1974). *Introduction a l'épistémologie génétique*, I and II. Paris: Presses Universitaires de France.

Quine, W. V. and Ullian, J. S. (1970). *The Web of Belief*. New York: Random House.

Ring, P. and van de Ven, A. (1994). 'Developmental processes of cooperative interorganizational relationships', *Academy of Management Review*, 19(1): 90–118.

Roberts, J. (2006). 'Limits to communities of practice', *Journal of Management Studies*, 43(3): 623–39.

Schein, E. H. (1985). *Organizational Culture and Leadership*. San Francisco, CA: Jossey–Bass.

Scott, W. R. (1992 [1981]). *Organizations: Rational, Natural, and Open Systems*, 3rd edn. Englewood Cliffs, NJ: Prentice-Hall.

Siemsen, H. H. (2006). 'Applied research and technology transfer for globalisation development of emerging markets, providing a cognitive base for building innovation systems', PhD thesis, University of Iasi, Rumania.

Simmel, G. (1950[1917]). *The Sociology of Georg Simmel*, trans. by Kurt Wolff. Glencoe, IL: The Free Press.

Simon, H. A. (1976). *Administrative Behavior*, 3rd edn. New York: Free Press.

Smircich, L. (1983). 'Organization as shared meaning', in L. R. Pondy, P. J. Frost, G. Morgan, and T. C. Dandridge (eds.), *Organizational Symbolism*. Greenwich, CT: JAI Press, pp. 55–65.

Steinmueller, W. E. (2000). 'Will new information and communication technologies improve the "codification" of knowledge?', *Industrial and Corporate Change*, 9(2): 361–76.

Vygotsky, L. S. (1962). *Thought and Language*, ed. and trans. by E. Hanfmann and G. Varkar. Cambridge MA: MIT Press.

Weick, K. E. (1991). 'The nontraditional quality of organizational learning', *Organization Science*, 2(1): 163–74.

——and Roberts, K. H. (1993). 'Collective mind in organizations: Heedful interrelating on flight decks', *Administrative Science Quarterly*, 38L: 357–81.

——and Westley, F. (1996). 'Organizational learning: affirming an oxymoron', in S. Clegg, C. Hardy, and W. R. Nord (eds.), *Handbook of Organization Studies*. London: Sage, pp. 440–58.

Weick, K. F. (1979). *The Social Psychology of Organizing*. Reading, MA: Addison-Wesley.

——(1995). *Sensemaking in Organizations*. Thousand Oaks, CA: Sage.

Wenger, E. (1998). *Communities of Practice: Learning, Meaning and Identity*. Cambridge: Cambridge University Press.

——and Snyder, W. M. (2000). 'Communities of practice: The organizational frontier', *Harvard Business Review*, 78: 139–45.

——McDermott, R., and Snyder, W. M. (2002). *Cultivating Communities of Practice: A Guide to Managing Knowledge*. Boston, MA: Harvard Business School Press.

Williamson, O. E. (1975). *Markets and Hierarchies: Analysis and Anti-Trust Implications*. New York: The Free Press.

——(1985). *The Economic Institutions of Capitalism: Firms, Markets, Relational Contracting*. New York: The Free Press.

Notes

1. I am aware of the criticism of Piaget's views and methodology of research (cf. Flavell 1967). However, I still think that some of his basic intuitions and ideas are valid. Apart from methodological criticism of Piaget's work, a substantive point of criticism is that Piaget's view is under-socialized. Here, there was an interesting difference of interpretation between Piaget and Vygotsky. In language acquisition by children, a phenomenon on which Piaget and Vygotsky agreed was that at some point children engage in egocentric speech, oriented towards the self rather than social others, and that this subsequently declines. Piaget interpreted this as an outward movement *from* the self to the social other, a 'decentration' from the self. Vygotsky ascribed it to a continued movement *into* the self, in an ongoing process of formation and identification of the self and development of independent thought. The reason that egocentric speech declines is that overt speech is partly replaced by 'inner speech'. I think Vygotsky's interpretation is the correct one.

2. At a conference on cognition and economics in Great Barrington, United States, in 2003.

6

Project Work as a Locus of Learning: The Journey Through Practice

Harry Scarbrough and Jacky Swan

6.1 Introduction

This chapter speaks to the theme of 'bridging cognitive distance' by focusing on the role which projects play as a source of learning within organizations, and their links with other sources of learning. The need for such learning is often given as the major reason for deploying projects as a way of organizing work tasks (DeFillippi and Arthur 1998; Sole and Edmondson 2002). This approach to organizing work is seen as particularly useful in contexts typified by rapid changes in markets and technologies (Gerwin and Ferris 2004). Following this logic, organizations in both service and technology-based sectors are increasingly structuring work around projects and project teams (Huber 1999; Zenger 2002). The rich potential of projects as a source of learning needs to be set alongside a growing body of evidence that this potential is often neglected. Thus, while many organizations make conscious efforts to 'capture' the learning from projects (e.g. via post-project reviews), much of the available evidence suggests that these efforts experience only limited success (Hobday 2000; Keegan and Turner 2001). This inability to exploit the learning from projects has worrying implications for the growing popularity of the project form as a way of organizing work.

In this chapter, therefore, we are keen to explore the ways in which such learning becomes woven into the ongoing patterns of knowledge acquisition that occur within organizations. Equally, we seek to understand why many organizations continue to 'reinvent the wheel' by failing to capture and spread what has been learned from particular projects. This failure may have something to tell us about the possible limits on organizing for recombinance. Constraints on our ability to capture and exploit the learning from projects may be an indicator of possible trade-offs that exist between different organizational forms, on one hand, and the ability to accumulate and exploit knowledge on the other.

In exploring these features of project work, the chapter proceeds as follows. We begin with a brief review of existing perspectives on project-based learning. This contrasts practice-based and cognitive approaches to the topic. In the subsequent section (Section 6.3), we outline a practice-based approach to project work. The advantage of this approach is that it allows us to relate project-based learning to other sources of learning in organizations, particularly communities of practice (CoPs). Its implications are then further analysed by focusing on the characteristics of project work and how they relate to mainstream organizational practices. The theoretical framework produced by this analysis is explored through brief case-study descriptions of three projects which produced very different outcomes in terms of the generation, capture, and spread of learning. This allows us to derive some conclusions as to the factors influencing the role of projects as a source of learning within organizations, and the implications for attempts to exploit such learning as an organizational resource.

6.2 Perspectives on Project-Based Learning

Projects can be initially defined as the activities clustered around specified work tasks where there has been an allocation of resources and roles (e.g. a project manager) by a sponsoring organization to that task (DeFillippi 2001). Whereas the traditional view of projects saw them as rarely-to-be-repeated, time-bound, goal-driven activities, more recent research has recognized the importance of projects as sites for learning. In particular, it has underlined the need to distinguish conceptually between the learning *within* project teams (e.g. Huber 1999; Arthur et al. 2001; Sense 2003; Marks and Lockyer 2004), and learning *from* projects to the wider organization (Schindler and Eppler 2003; Williams 2003; Courtright 2004).

The dominant approach in many of these studies is based on a cognitive view of learning. This approach highlights changes in individual cognition – including perceptions, attitudes, and behaviour – as the characteristic form of learning within organizations. In this approach, project-based learning occurs through the operation of multiple mechanisms which impact on and reflect cognition. These include: the eliciting of existing knowledge though team-member expertise and their social networks (Ancona and Caldwell 1992); transforming such knowledge through a range of activities including the integration of disparate forms of expertise (Okhuysen and Eisenhardt 2002), reflection on and articulation of experience (Ayas and Zeniuk 2001; Zollo and Winter 2002), and the conversion of tacit into explicit knowledge (Nonaka and Takeuchi 1995); and, finally, the diffusion of the knowledge created, 'embrained' in the heads of project team members (Blackler 1995; Huber 1999) as they move on to new roles or projects within the organization, or to be made available as 'lessons learned' or 'after-project reviews' stored on company intranets or databases (Kotnour 1999).

Although studies adopting this cognitive approach are generally optimistic about the possibilities of project-based learning being shared with the wider organization, the existing empirical evidence is much more mixed. For example, the available evidence suggests that post-project review activities are not very successful in spreading knowledge to other groups (Keegan and Turner 2001; Von Zedtwitz 2002). This lack of success questions the assumption in cognitively oriented studies that exploiting project-based learning is largely a matter of having mechanisms in place to capture, store, and diffuse the knowledge. Rather, it suggests that a better understanding of the fate of project-based learning involves moving away from a focus on projects as isolated and self-contained activities (Engwall 2003). The alternative, as stressed in several recent studies (e.g. Sydow and Staber 2002), hinges on locating projects within their organizational context.

Emphasizing the organizational context for project work has a number of advantages. For one, it enables us to relate the learning which takes place within projects to other sources of learning in organizations. These include the individual learning of project participants, the group learning of the project team, the learning of wider CoPs, and ultimately the organizational learning through which new practices and routines become part of the mainstream operations of the firm. In addition, locating projects within their organizational context also highlights the variety of roles which projects may play depending on the strategy and structure of the organization.

This last point opens up a number of issues, but for the purposes of this chapter we will simply note that the character of project work varies across a continuum of organizational forms. At one extreme, we have settings where projects are organized infrequently to deal with specific needs and challenges – for example, change programmes. At the other extreme, we have what writers have labelled the 'project-based organization' – one which delivers its primary products and services through project working. Whilst there is a growing amount of work on this kind of organization, there is also considerable debate about whether 'pure' forms of such organization exist and, if they do, whether they are sustainable. Both Zenger (2002) and Foss (2003), for example, argue that hybrid organizations are inherently unstable and tend to drift towards more internally coherent bureaucratic or market-based forms. Organizations using cross-functional teams, for example, often continue to use hierarchically based incentive systems and, so, drift towards more bureaucratic forms of control (Barker 1993; Zenger 2002). Regardless of whether ideal or 'pure' types of project-based form exist, however, it is evident that many organizations that routinely deploy projects to complete tasks are not 'pure' project-based organizations. More typically, they will display some kind of internal 'hybrid' or matrix management structure which combines project work with work organized around functional or divisional specialization, thus mixing elements of both market and hierarchical governance (Zenger 2002). Within these matrix forms, some organizations (i.e. project-based) will privilege the project dimension whilst others will privilege the functional/divisional dimension (Knight 1977; Bresnen 1990; Lindkvist 2005).

6.3 A Practice-Based View of Project Work

There are many possible approaches to exploring the relationship between project-based learning and these other aspects of the organizational context. For the purposes of this chapter, however, we have adopted the lens of what has been termed the 'practice-based view' of knowledge (Gherardi 2001; Carlile 2002; Orlikowski 2002). Studies adopting this view take knowledge to be closely intertwined with the social practices which different groups and communities develop and participate in. Such studies can be contrasted epistemologically with the cognitive perspective on these issues in that it takes learning to be ' . . . an inseparable and integral part of all organizational practices' (Gherardi 1999, p. 113). They, thus, take knowledge out of the heads of individuals and place it within their practices and their accompanying social relations and identities.

Applying a practice-based view to project work is not unproblematic, as we outline below. However, the advantage of applying this lens is that it brings into sharp relief important features of the organizational context which the cognitive approach tends to leave in the background. Thus, previous work on learning within social practices has highlighted the role of shared practices in enabling the acquisition and spread of knowledge. Equally, it has also highlighted the way in which organization structure (e.g. functional specializations) creates divisions of practice. The latter are seen as creating boundaries to the acquisition and sharing of knowledge. As Brown and Duguid (2001, p. 203) note; 'it is at divisions of practice where knowledge sticks'. By focusing on the mainstream practices, and divisions in practice of the organization, therefore, we are able to develop a better understanding of the way in which project-based learning is assimilated into wider processes of knowledge acquisition in organizations.

Within the existing literature, most of the work on learning and social practices has focused on the development of CoPs. The latter involve 'a set of relations among persons, activity and world, over time and in relation with other tangential and overlapping communities of practice' (Lave and Wenger 1991, p. 41), and are seen as emerging over time through the recursive practices and social interactions of established social groups (Lave and Wenger 1991). Lave and Wenger (1991, p. 51), for instance, describe learning in terms of 'legitimate peripheral participation'. Learning is seen as involving a change in the individual, and is related to their socialization and identity formation within a particular community. As they put it, 'one way to think of learning is as the historical production, transformation, and change of persons' (p. 51). The contribution of such communities to organizational learning was also highlighted by Brown and Duguid (1991), who identified the role of story-telling in the sharing of non-canonical practice amongst a particular work community.

If we consider CoPs simply as distinct social entities, there seems to be little overlap between such communities and the learning which takes place in projects. In a stylized sense, projects are markedly different entities in that they are generally seen as involving highly time-bound social interaction, discrete forms of non-repeatable activity, formal objectives, and one-off tasks (Wenger and Snyder 2000). They, thus, typically lack the community-building effects (e.g. through strong ties, continued participation, common identities) found in localized, ongoing, and more routine work activities (Gherardi et al. 1998).

Table 6.1: Comparison of the characteristics of communities of practice and projects

Community of practice	Project work
No formally specified tasks	Predefined task
Open-ended work cycle	Time-bound
Emergent community participation	Conscripted participation
Primary identities forged within the community	Primary identities forged externally
Social motivation	Intrinsic and extrinsic motivation

Source: Based on Wenger (1998) and Sense (2003).

Again, 'legitimate peripheral participation' is not generally associated with projects, where the more usual image is one of disparate groups of individuals being assembled and dis-assembled in relation to specific tasks. These perceived differences between project work and CoPs as highlighted by the existing literature are briefly outlined in Table 6.1.

However, although this contrast points to differences in the way in which people learn within CoPs and projects respectively, it is too simplistic to say that project work and CoPs are wholly distinct activities. After all projects emerge out of and feed back into the embedded social practices of mainstream work organizations. It follows that it may be more useful to see the distinction between these sources of learning as fuzzy and relational rather than absolute, allowing that project activities draw on, are constrained by, and even influence the shared social practices sustained by CoPs. Thus, for the purposes of this chapter we see the concept of CoP as denoting not a discrete social grouping but rather historically specific expressions of the self-reinforcing relationships between learning, identity, group formation, and social practices. This definition not only admits of the wide variety of CoPs found empirically, but allows us to see CoPs as an emergent phenomenon, overlapping with, and not displacing, existing sociological categories such as work-group, occupation, and profession. Thus, in empirical terms, for example, we might identify CoP elements within a range of professional groups – these are described as 'networks of practice' by Brown and Duguid. By the same token, CoPs are equally amenable to the kinds of analysis applied to these other groupings, including the role of power relations in constituting and sustaining them (Contu and Willmott 2000).

Project work is also highly diverse in the forms it takes empirically. Again, specifying project work in terms of a given social group – that is, the project team – is problematic as project work may be undertaken by a variety of groups and individuals, inside and outside the focal organization, not all of whom are members of an identified team (the latter being in some sectors a highly fluid formation). Although many previous studies have emphasized the importance of team-based learning in projects, the characteristics of projects are not necessarily the same as the characteristics of teams. Psychological definitions of a 'team' emphasize characteristics of shared identity and continued psychological commitment to team membership where behaviour within the team is shaped by mutual interests and group-level norms. In contrast to these team-centred definitions, project work in some arenas may be temporary, fluid, interrupted, and distributed. Whilst projects typically entail formal role responsibilities, goals, and deliverables – they usually have a project manager and deadlines, for example – the boundaries of membership and role identities (i.e. who belongs to 'the team') are often not that clearly defined and/or not all that apparent to members of the project. For example, projects in construction typically involve site managers and construction engineers working alongside an extended range of other engineers, tendering experts, planners, and external subcontractors and architects. Different individuals (and organizations) enter and leave the project at different points in time, depending on particular issues that arise, and project members are often working on several projects at once. As such, the individuals involved may, or may not, see themselves as part of a (psychological) team and group goals and mutual interests may or may not develop. A suitably inclusive definition of project work, therefore, involves recognizing the shifting relationships between organizational tasks, group coordination, and resource allocation. Importantly, this definition suggests that projects may be differentiated from CoPs politically, inasmuch as their formal representation in the management structure and the resource dependencies which they command may make them significant political actors within the organization – some writers highlight the power of 'heavyweight' project managers, for example. In contrast, CoPs are less likely to mobilize as political actors but do operate as sites of resistance to such actors.

Adopting this relational definition suggests that project work may interact with CoPs in many different ways. Some of these interactions have been well described in the existing literature. Thus, in some sectors – for example, magazine publishing, advertising, and the movie industry – projects are assembled out of the competencies and networks sustained by wider sectoral and occupational communities (DeFillippi and Arthur 1998; Grabher 2002). In industries such as this the project form in effect creates the interface between the organization and these wider communities, providing a vehicle for the organization to exploit skills and competencies which it is not able to produce itself. The project enables the highly specialized practices of the wider industrial community to be applied, reproduced, and improved through their application to specific organizationally mandated tasks. It seems significant, however, that the role of the wider industrial communities in the sectors described above is centred on the creation and sharing of aesthetic forms of knowledge and sensibility – forms of knowledge which enable community learning outside the workplace through sociability and widely available artefacts. Indeed, this community learning may be much more important than organizational learning in certain sectors (Grabher 2002).

In other sectors, where critical forms of knowledge are more task- or firm-specific, the most important sources of learning are situated within organizational boundaries and CoPs are more rooted within particular organizational contexts. Here organizations typically encompass multiple CoPs, being a 'community of communities' as Brown and Duguid (1991) put it. Again, this suggests a number of possible interactions between such CoPs and projects. One possible interaction, for instance, is where project work is contained within and reproduces the practices of a particular CoP – for example, a subunit of the organization which delivers its offerings through project work. This kind of interaction is documented in a recent paper by Thompson who describes the development of a CoP within the 'E-Futures' subunit of a large multinational (Thompson 2005).

Where projects span subunit boundaries, however, and involve members of multiple CoPs, the possible interactions become more complex. Here, the CoP impact on projects may have as much to do with the divisions of practice which they reinforce as in the forms of learning which they sustain within the organization. Viewing the effect of CoPs in these terms suggests that they may have ambivalent effects on projects as sites for learning. On the one hand, these divisions of practice create significant opportunities for new *learning within* projects as members work to overcome practice boundaries in the accomplishment of tasks. For example, Carlile's (2002) study of cross-functional product-design teams observed the significant opportunities for learning and innovation entailed by team members overcoming the boundaries created by specialized practice. On the other hand, the same divisions in practice may constrain the *learning from* projects insofar as they make it difficult to assimilate such learning within the embedded social practices of the organization.

6.4 Project Features and Learning Processes

We have described above the ways in which project work may interact with other sources of learning within the firm and beyond. As discussed, the nature of these interactions and their learning outcomes depend generally on the way projects are positioned within the organizational context. To understand specific cases, however, we also need to address the way in which such positioning is worked out in terms of features of the project itself. Here, previous work highlights the importance of key features – task novelty, project autonomy, and project team membership – in shaping learning processes.

To review these briefly, task novelty is a classic explanation of the greater need for learning in projects. Situations involving new tasks and high levels of uncertainty have long been seen as a stimulus of learning (Burns and Stalker 1961; Mintzberg 1979). In turn, the related feature of project autonomy is seen as important for success by a number of writers. Studies in the biotechnology sector, for example, show how the innovative potential of projects is directly related to their relative detachment from mainstream organizational structures and processes (Powell et al. 1996; Oliver and Liebeskind 1998). Such findings suggest that the relative autonomy which projects enjoy, and hence their ability to generate learning, is important in allowing a set of practices to develop (e.g. highly pressurized and time-bound, see Lindkvist et al. 1998; Schultze 2000), which are distinctively different to mainstream organizational practices. Similarly, project team membership is also highlighted in the literature as an influence on learning (e.g. Senge 1993; Edmondson 1996; Argote and Ingram 2000). In particular, diversity of team-member backgrounds is seen as particularly conducive to learning when it produces tensions between the different cultures or worldviews. Such tensions, which can be related to the 'cognitive distance' described in previous chapters are said to 'ignite processes of deeper mutual (self) understanding and reflection' (Grabher 2002, p. 253).

What do these existing studies have to tell us about the relationship between project activities and learning within the wider organization? As noted above, task novelty is seen as requiring higher levels of learning and this is associated with greater project autonomy. It may be that such autonomy is important for learning precisely because it enables greater decoupling from existing organizational practices, thus allowing new practices to emerge which are distinctively different to the mainstream. One important ingredient in such decoupling may be the differences in time horizons which many writers see as a quintessential feature of project work, as compared to more routine organizational tasks (Bryman et al. 1987). Whereas organizational tasks are relatively open-ended and continuous, project work is both time-pressured and time-paced (Lindkvist, Soderlund, and Tell 1998). Even where projects are relatively long in duration (as, e.g. with automotive-design projects), they typically comprise multiple-phased subprojects or 'gateways', each with their own time-driven goals, milestones, and deadlines. This has significant implications for learning. The emphasis on milestones and deadlines triggers constant dialogue and compromise among project members between what is sufficient – or 'good enough' – and what is optimal to achieve performance. For example, 'corner cutting', ongoing problem solving, and improvisation is a 'normal' feature of project work. Deadlines, therefore, may induce project members, faced with non-negotiable goals, to abandon established organizational practices in favour of new, performative practices (Gersick 1989; Lindkvist et al. 1998).

Similarly, once we acknowledge that projects and teams are not coterminous, the value of a focus on practice rather than team dynamics or diversity becomes obvious. For example, where project membership is determined by established routines of project management, it seems more likely that existing practices will be applied to project work, and less likely that new practices will be developed. Diversity of membership in such settings may simply entail the application of a wide range of existing practices – as in complex, but routine projects, involving the programmatic deployment of different specialist skills. Conversely, where project membership is more stable or evolves according to the particular needs of the project itself, the diversity of membership may be an important ingredient in encouraging the development of new practices. It may operate in this way, partly because such diversity creates new challenges for knowledge integration (Okhuysen and Eisenhardt 2002) which cannot be addressed by existing practices, and partly due to the time-boundness of projects which 'prevents any single perspective from becoming corrupted by a hegemonic view... deadlines provide antidotes against lock-ins into particular cognitive or aesthetic patterns.' (Grabher 2002, p. 249)

To summarize the points above, the implications of task novelty, project autonomy, and project membership can be viewed to a large extent in terms of their effects on the relationship between project activities, existing CoPs, and divisions between practices. Thus, whether project activities involve the application of existing practices or the development of new practices has important implications for learning within projects, and this is likely to be linked to novelty, autonomy, and diversity of membership. In addition, even where projects see very little change in existing practices, they may have a learning effect through the development of new ways of integrating existing practices.

As noted earlier, the implications which these factors have for project-based learning as a locus of learning can usefully be considered in terms of both learning within, and learning from projects. In the former case, we have already noted that where the project is subsumed with in a particular CoP, learning within the project equates with learning by the CoP. However, even where projects span multiple CoPs, those communities may continue to influence the learning within the project by the importation of CoP artefacts and stories. Sense (2003), for example, suggests that project teams can become a 'dumping ground' for CoP artefacts. This particularly applies where project working is focused on low novelty tasks. In some project-based organizations, for example, specialist occupational practices may be applied across a variety of projects through the application of organizational routines for the coordination of project work. Where the organization possesses specialist project-management capabilities, the interactions between project members may be tightly regulated according to predetermined routines. There may be little or no need to create new forms of coordination when work is programmed and coordinated according to well-established norms and roles. Grant (1996, p. 379), for example, describes the 'closely coordinated working arrangements' of work teams where 'each team member applies his or her specialist knowledge but where the patterns of interaction appear automatic'.

On the other hand, where task novelty or project membership diversity create discontinuities, project settings may provide opportunities for the development of new practices through the process of interaction amongst project members. This may include a new repertoire of routines, words, tools, ways of doing things, stories, gestures, symbols, and actions which have become part of its practice (Wenger 1998). Brown and Duguid (2000, p. 127), for example, in describing one such group note how, 'in getting the job done, the people involved ignored divisions of rank and role to forge a single group around their shared task, with overlapping knowledge, relatively blurred boundaries, and a common working identity'. Clearly, this kind of project may provide an arena – more limited in learning scope and time than a CoP admittedly – in which individual learning is supplemented by the emergence of a group affiliation and social motivation (Sense 2003).

New project practices may also emerge where projects provide a boundary space which enables new forms of coordination and collaboration across existing practices. Such boundary spaces may involve the development of networking and brokering practices. Gherardi and Nicolini (2002, p. 419), for example, describe practices 'that traverse the boundaries of several communities...which...create a network of relations within a constellation of practices tied together by interconnected practices'.

Turning to the implications of project features for the organization's overall ability to learn from projects, a practice-based view of knowledge suggests that such learning may take a variety of forms, including the creation of artefacts and stories, with its spread across the organization being indicated both by the development of new practices and changes in the existing divisions of practice. By the same token, however, this view also suggests that the spread of learning from projects is likely to be mediated by existing practices and the communities which sustain them (Carlile 2002).

6.5 Cases of Project-Based Learning

The previous sections have identified a theoretical framework to apply to project-based learning based on major strands in the existing literature. In subsequent sections, we will explore this framework by drawing on empirical case-studies of projects and learning. These cases are drawn from a wider study, the initial findings of which have been presented previously (Scarbrough et al. 2004). The three cases[1] have been selected for their theoretical contribution more than empirical typicality, since they are deployed to highlight the effects of gross variation in contexts and outcomes (Pettigrew et al. 2001). Thus, the first case shows how sometimes there may be little learning within a project. The second case, in contrast, outlines a project where there were high levels of learning within the project, but little learning from the project. The third case completes the trio by providing an example where there was both learning within and learning from the project. Our aim in outlining these cases is simply to illustrate and explore the issues outlined above, and to derive some tentative findings for the wider appreciation of this topic.

6.5.1 Case A: The Thurrock project at BuildCo

This case focuses on a particular building project – the construction of a logistics warehouse – carried out by the Midlands regional division of

BuildCo, which is one of the largest building contractors in the UK. Logistics warehouses are considered routine in BuildCo. The Thurrock project started in February 2002 and was completed in July 2002. Importantly, the warehouse was to be built on a contaminated brown site, as opposed to a greenfield site where most such projects are done. This created significant contingencies, including the need to deal with the risk of contamination and with a large concrete slab, which remained after the demolition of previous buildings. As such, an important part of this project involved the development on site of a 'ground solution' that would address both problems.

The design and delivery of the Thurrock project depended, in practice, on two different teams – a tender team and a site team. The tender team was concerned with winning the work and agreeing the project specification and price (the tender) with the client. The site team was responsible for the construction of the building to agreed specifications. This way of organizing project practices (i.e. around sub-teams dealing with different project phases) was seen as typical of the way projects were approached in BuildCo, so the practices and forms of collaboration described below can be seen as reflecting institutionalized arrangements within the organization.

The tender team comprised staff who were all based at the regional headquarters. These staff were drawn from a variety of specialisms (including planning, architecture, commercial, and design) but each specialist also worked on several other projects at the same time. The tender team developed tenders on the basis of their understanding of the building process. Their work practices drew heavily on personal experience rather than any systematic review of previous projects. Tendering was viewed almost as a craft activity. The site team was similarly made up of a grouping of technical specialists, including a design and build coordinator, quantity surveyor, engineer, general supervisor, and a secretary. This group was led by the site agent, who was effectively the project manager and who, in contrast to the tender team, deployed a number of standardized project management tools and methods used in previous projects.

As was the norm in BuildCo, there was little overlap in activities and little interaction between the tender team and the site team in the development of the Thurrock programme. Moreover, the strict division in practices was not mitigated by any common membership or sense of shared identity – each team operated to its own sets of work parameters, objectives, and targets. The demarcation between tender and site project team thus sustained two different views of the practices surrounding construction. As the site agent noted (referring to the tender team): 'They hand over their strategy on how they see things, but the actual job, once that is handed over it has obviously got a different team looking at it. We are the guys that actually are going to build it . . . '

At a superficial level, the Thurrock project was actually successful on two counts. First, it was completed four weeks short of deadline – the tender team had planned for a twenty-six-week project but the building was actually delivered in twenty-two weeks. Second, the site team were successful in developing a ground solution that was more effective than the one originally proposed by the tender team. However, this 'success' was not based on learning across the two teams involved in the overall project. The reduction in timescale was effectively the result of a revision to the original tender by the site team, and this was made at the outset of site work. As the site agent put it: 'We were lucky to get a 26 week programme, so we knew we could shave off at least two or three weeks anyway.' Thus, the programme of work was revised according to the site team's knowledge from prior projects of proven methods and work practices in construction – knowledge which was not available to the tender team who devised the original programme. Similarly, the site team came to the view that the tender team's proposed solution to issues of ground contamination lacked an appreciation of the potential implications for the delivery of the project, and so they simply implemented a different solution.

The apparent success of the Thurrock project thus reflects a real failure to translate learning between tender team and site team. This lack of learning at a project level should not be confused, however, with the complete absence of learning. Certainly, individuals learned in that they adapted their own practices to the contingencies of the project. It was this individual learning which characterized project work, and which ensured that some of the experience of projects like Thurrock was recycled for future application.

The lack of project-based learning was thus linked to the 'craft' orientation, which individuals developed towards their work practices. A site engineer highlighted the importance of individual expertise as follows: 'If it is a minor problem I tend to fix it on the spot and that will be done and it will be locked away in my head. If it is anything a little bit major you would stay on the site team but probably go to the consultants and things like that and get information back from them. Anything else you tend to do it yourself.' This view could be related to the extent to which projects were seen as competitive environments in which individual performance was judged for career progression. This reinforced personal ownership of the learning acquired from projects, as reflected in the following comment by the site agent: 'The thing for me is obviously the more experience I gain obviously the better innovations that I can come up with. . . . It tends to be that the person who will benefit most out of it is me.'

The problems of lack of learning at project level were endemic within the company, as evidenced by the managerial initiatives which had been launched to exploit project-based learning more systematically. These included the creation of a new role of 'Regional Engineering Manager' where the explicit remit was to 'spread learning' across projects. They also included provision for formal 'post-project reviews' and 'quality alerts'. Such initiatives were largely ineffective, however, in stimulating project teams to identify, codify, and share the learning from their work. Post-project reviews occurred only rarely and quality alerts were a token gesture towards managerial requirements.

Relating the case to our previous discussion, the scope of learning within and between project teams in the Thurrock case was highly influenced by the project's position within a wider portfolio of projects undertaken by BuildCo. This seems to have been important in two ways. First, individuals came to the Thurrock project teams with experience of a number of previous, and similarly designed, projects behind them. Second, as part of a stream of 'repeat' projects, the overall Thurrock project was subject to a pervasive focus on efficiency through the application of standard methods. This reinforces findings from previous work which has emphasized the constraints on learning in the construction sector. Keegan and Turner (2001, p. 90), for example, note that in this sector 'the focus is clearly on capturing "deviations"'. Similarly, in the Thurrock case, where learning did occur, it was usually associated with errors or mistakes. As the planning manager on the tender team commented, 'We say bad news travels fast and good news never.'

6.5.2 Case B: Cataract treatment re-engineering project at Midlands Hospital

Midlands Hospital is one of a large number of trusts that together make up the National Health Service (NHS) of the UK. This case focuses on the re-engineering of the cataract diagnosis and treatment procedure at the hospital. This project was initiated by a dedicated 'transformation team' who had been charged with re-engineering hospital processes. Other projects initiated by this team included an initiative on lead-time reduction, a project on diabetes, and a project on hip-replacement surgery. The project to re-engineer cataract diagnosis and treatment commenced with the formation of a project team comprised of eye experts from both the hospital and the wider community to review possible ways in which to cut surgery lead times and improve patient satisfaction. Members of the cataract team included the head nurse in the eye unit, a hospital administrator, general practitioners (GPs), a set of optometrists from the local community, and a surgical consultant who was instrumental in championing the need for change and in leading the change process. Team meetings were held in the evening to facilitate attendance, and were led by a member of the transformation team who produced all minutes, flow charts, and other necessary documentation for the process, and distributed them to all team members after each meeting. In total, five project-team meetings and many more informal discussions were held over a six-month period.

The efforts of the project team were seen as justified by the need to address the inadequacies of the current process. Cataracts represent 96 per cent of the ophthalmology workload, but the surgery itself is only a twenty-minute procedure. However, the existing process for diagnosis and treatment involved a patient in a number of visits to various specialists. Typically, patients began at the optometrist (the high-street optician) because they believed that deteriorating eyesight required new glasses/contact lenses. However, the optometrist would quickly diagnose that the problem was actually cataracts, and would then refer the patient to his or her GP. After a visit to the local GP, who not being an eye specialist generally relies on the diagnosis of the optometrist, the patient would be forwarded to the hospital consultant for further examination. The patient then went on a waiting list and would eventually be called for a brief meeting with the consultant. This almost invariably confirmed the optometrist's diagnosis. Then, in a separate appointment, the patient would meet with the hospital nurse for a physical examination. Only when all these visits were completed would the patient get in the queue for obtaining a date for the cataract surgery. Post-surgery, another visit to the consultant would be scheduled to check on the patient, and then the patient would be referred back to the optometrist for a new pair of glasses. Therefore, it took patients at least six visits and often well over a year to have a routine, twenty-minute, outpatient, surgical procedure.

Work on the project brought together individuals from a diverse range of professional groups and backgrounds. One by-product of their working together was an increased understanding of the skills and capabilities of the members of other professional groups. This was particularly beneficial for the optometrists who traditionally had not been given the latitude to use their extensive training in eye-care treatment. The consultants and optometrists involved in the project gained new respect for each other, breaking down many preconceived prejudices. As one project member commented: 'We had never really got together before and that built great bridges.' However, team diversity was not without its costs. The project threatened existing work practices and professional demarcations, for example, and this led to resistance from certain groups (an issue which was also highlighted in Bart Nooteboom's analysis in Chapter 5). Professional barriers remained an issue for those consultants who had not been directly involved in the cataract project team. For example, certain consultants in Midlands Hospital still assumed that optometrists could not properly diagnose cataracts and were therefore unhappy about not making the diagnosis themselves. As one project member put it: 'There are a lot of other departments where people express reservations about the skills of optometrists who will be referring patients to them and they are not prepared to go down that route (i.e. the new cataract process) because of that.' The project team were able to overcome this resistance in large part due to the influence exerted by the team's ophthalmology consultant. By meeting formally and informally with his fellow consultants to discuss issues surrounding the change process, this individual was able to alleviate their concerns sufficiently to ensure acceptance of the project.

Once the project team had reviewed the existing process, they sought to develop a more streamlined approach which would deliver a significant reduction in the lead time for patients. A number of substantive changes to the existing process were made. Non-essential visits to the GP, the consultant, and the nurse were eliminated. Instead, optometrists were empowered to decide if a patient needed cataract surgery. In doing so, they were required to fill out a detailed form that provided the consultant with specific information about the nature and severity of the cataract, and to call the hospital and book a time for the patient's surgery. For their additional responsibility, the optometrists were given some extra training and received a small amount of compensation from the trust. The preliminary pre-operation physical was replaced with a self-diagnostic questionnaire that each patient was required to fill out and return to the hospital before surgery. Nurses would then telephone each patient before surgery to check the patient's details and answer any questions. Post-operation consultant appointments were also replaced with follow-up telephone calls.

The new cataract procedure resulted in dramatic efficiency gains. Lead times were radically reduced from over twelve months down to six to eight weeks. In addition, theatre-utilization rates improved due to the addition of an administrator whose sole responsibility lay in scheduling theatres. Finally, and most importantly, follow-up phone conversations with cataract patients indicated a dramatic improvement in patient satisfaction. The new re-engineering cataract process can, therefore, clearly be seen as transforming the Midlands Hospital's ability to deliver this service.

Despite the success in changing practices and the division of practice within the Midlands Hospital itself, attempts to *learn from* this project to the wider NHS organization were much less successful. Even in the face of significant efforts by project members and managers to champion the new procedure within the NHS more widely, staff in other hospitals remained sceptical of its relevance when it was presented to them as 'best practice'. This resistance was not greatly reduced even when the new team responsible for the new process were presented with an award by the prime minister for their efforts. Several factors can be adduced to account for this inability to spread the learning more widely. For one, the conditions at Midlands Hospital were especially conducive to the creation and implementation of the new process. The hospital's deployment of a transformation team was highly unusual within the NHS context, and this provided resources and expertise to facilitate the project. Also, the various professional groups involved in the design of the new procedure were willing and able to learn from each other and realign their roles and responsibilities accordingly. In contrast, these conditions were rarely found in other hospitals. Moreover, the learning which the cataract project generated was especially difficult to assimilate elsewhere; not only did it require a change in practices on the part of entrenched professionals, it also involved a change in the divisions in practice between groups which was even more difficult to orchestrate at other sites.

6.5.3 *Case C: The Lowlands projects at WaterCo*

WaterCo is one of the UK's leading water and sewage-treatment companies. It has a turnover of approximately £900 million. The company is organized on a functional basis, comprising the four main functions of asset procurement and investment, engineering, customer relations, and technology and development. The case focuses on a thirty-month, £60 million programme undertaken by WaterCo to redevelop and extend a sewage- and water-treatment works in a region of the UK. This site at Lowlands posed high-profile environmental problems and the works required a significant amount of asset renewal. The machinery was at the end of its working life and thus its reconstruction had significant planning and environmental aspects.

The programme was unique for WaterCo in many respects, being the largest capital scheme in the firm's development programme – such programmes were usually budgeted around £500,000 to £2 million in size. At the same time, the timescale was very demanding and the feasibility work, planning applications, assessment, and site investigations had all to be done at the same time rather than sequentially to meet an ambitious deadline. Finally, the programme was also unusual in its combination of civil engineering works with the complex mechanical and electronic tasks supporting an improved water-treatment process. Project activities were thus diverse, ranging from building a bridge over a river through to land remediation, additional infrastructures, and sophisticated software control systems.

A scheme of this size and technical complexity demanded the coordinated effort of a range of groups inside and outside WaterCo, including half a dozen of the UK's leading engineering and architectural consultancies. The primary external contractor, however, was ConstructCo, a major UK-based construction and building-design firm. Ultimately, despite the technical and organizational challenges confronting the programme, it was deemed a great success by WaterCo management. Not only were the treatment works successfully developed on time, but this was achieved to new specifications and a much tighter standard. Members of the programme believed that this success was closely related to important changes in the management of the programme over the course of three linked projects. As outlined below, these changes were significant in allowing the development of new patterns of project-based learning across these projects.

The management of the programme centred on the design of the organizational arrangements for the three sequentially linked projects (termed here Projects A, B, and C) which made it up. Project A was developed on the basis of standard project-management practices. This involved WaterCo management assembling a core team for the project which was made up of WaterCo and ConstructCo staff, each supported by their own regional head offices and their network of contractors and suppliers. WaterCo team members were all hand-picked and experienced specialists working full-time on the programme. The core team was carefully selected because WaterCo management felt that the timescale did not allow the project to be used as a learning environment for less-experienced staff. WaterCo's team on site was led by the site reconstruction manager, who possessed extensive experience of both sewage-treatment works within WaterCo and the site itself. Other WaterCo team members, however, were not based on site and worked on the project from their offices in the company headquarters. The tendering arrangements with subcontractors followed the conventional norm in WaterCo. Most of the design work was performed at the start of the project, and subcontractors tendered to produce predefined elements of the design. Design solutions were thus 'frozen' at the tender stage.

The learning which took place in project A was essentially technical in nature and driven by the need to redevelop the facilities to meet new environmental expectations. The core team sought to benefit from the experience of recently completed schemes and a significant amount of effort was devoted to benchmarking activities in technical areas, including chemical dosing systems, tank watertightness, and water-pump management. Such benchmarking initially focused on previous proprietary schemes and included visits to three water treatment works in the Midlands.

For Projects B and C, however, there was a significant change in Water-Co's approach which had major repercussions for the dynamics of project-based learning. This began with a spatial shift, as the site reconstruction manager decided to reorganize all members of the core project team (design, construction, and contract administration staff and a site supervision group) to locate them together on site with the external contractors. This, together with the shared responsibility over the final detailed design, gave the core team a certain degree of autonomy and independence from the main office.

In addition to the physical redistribution of team members, these subsequent projects were also subject to different contracting arrangements. Projects B and C were both procured with ConstructCo and related contractors on the basis of a single, one-off target price and an outline rather than a detailed design specification. Although each project was distinct in the sense of addressing a discrete set of tasks, the decision to link them contractually reflected a perceived complementarity between the tasks and skills involved – many of the tasks were the same or similar. This arrangement had important implications for the conduct of the project work. Although the projects continued to depend upon a form of inter-organizational collaboration, the linkage between them secured continuity of personnel across projects. At the same time, this arrangement incorporated a 'shared pain–shared gain' incentive arrangement between WaterCo and ConstructCo. The partners were to absorb whatever difference, either positive or negative, arose between the actual cost and the target price of the programme. Client and contractors were thus able to develop the detailed design together to optimize both the technical solution and the cost. This created new possibilities for collaborative design, shared ownership, and cross-fertilization between the partners.

The effects of these changes in management approach were to create a greater sense of shared goals and collaboration between WaterCo and its contractors. As ConstructCo's project manager put it:

Any problem that comes up, then there's that common goal of 'let's make the decision quickly to solve it and let's make it with the least cost in mind' . . . That means that people have the same objective rather than the opposite. In the old way of working we would try to maximize value and they would try to minimize it across the project, so you're working against each other.

Importantly, with this new arrangement, the project partners stood to benefit not only from any learning which they could take away from the project themselves (as we noted of the individual learning in the Thurrock case), but also from the learning applied to a future project. Any such learning across Projects B and C would improve overall project performance and hence create gains for all. This arrangement, together with the continuity of tasks and practices across projects, created a high level of motivation on the part of project members to ensure that anything learned in Project B was reapplied in Project C. Here, unlike the Thurrock case, project-based learning was viewed positively as a source of improvement and not as the 'bad news' associated with rectifying mistakes.

6.6 Analysis and Discussion

Our analysis of project-based learning within these cases begins with the simple observation that all our cases highlight the important role of existing CoPs, and existing divisions in practice, in mediating the generation and spread of such learning. In the Thurrock case, for example, learning was bounded by a separation between the ground-level learning of site contingencies which was the responsibility of site teams, and the tender teams' concern for the more abstract forms of knowledge accumulation applicable across local contexts. At one level, one might argue that this reflects the 'nested' nature of learning in organizations (Levinthal and March 1993). Thus, the one-off nature of many projects, solving specific or unique problems, was traded-off against the repeatability and specialization through which organizational learning was achieved. Moreover, this highlighted the influence of accumulated knowledge as reflected in the functional boundaries of the organization. The development of BuildCo had produced an accumulation of knowledge about project work within the firm, allowing the development of more standardized approaches to construction, the development of functionally specialized roles for individuals, and a broad division of labour between head office and site-based activities. This institutionalized separation between the two teams enabled the acquisition of abstract and professional knowledge regarding design and value engineering within the tendering process. Such knowledge could be applied across a variety of spatial environments and was developed at head office by a community of professional specialists rather than through exposure to the narrow contingencies of site work.

The separation of site activities from tendering and design also had the effect of promoting significantly different perspectives and practices amongst project participants. Tendering activities reflected the stories circulating about previous tenders as discussed between colleagues co-located at the regional head office. Building activities reflected experience on previous construction projects, although in this sphere communication between sites was limited. The strict demarcation between the activities of site teams and tender teams ensured that these bodies of specialized expertise were not confronted by experience which might be challenging or equivocal. This separation of practice, rather than any learning effect, seems to explain the difference between planned and actual outcomes in the Thurrock case. Given the differences in practice and the lack of interaction, the site team simply possessed greater knowledge about the site-level contingencies of building work than the tender team.

This tension between local variation and the standardizing pressures of organizational learning has been previously observed by a number of authors (e.g. Weick and Westley 1996). However, as Brown and Duguid (2001) note, the danger for organizations is that this trade-off actually reflects historic institutional demarcations (in the Thurrock case, between 'head' and 'hands') and is increasingly inappropriate when the local solutions produced by different communities are often critically important for innovation. In the Thurrock case, certainly, the emphasis on the standardization of methods meant that the rich experience of work on site was normatively evaluated as either conforming to or deviating from existing standards. Learning at the project level was associated with errors or mistakes.

In the NHS Trust case we see an example of a project which generates a significant amount of *learning within* the project. Through their interactions, project members are able to both bring about some change in their own practices – accepting new approaches to diagnosis and treatment – and, more importantly, in the division of practices between them. New protocols are established for the transfer of patients between the different professional groups involved and new inter-professional norms established for the way in which patients are treated.

Despite the significant benefits which this learning brought for the Midland Hospital itself, the failure to spread this learning more widely amongst other NHS hospitals highlights the difficulty of translating new practices across an organization. While new practices created within a project are likely to be localized, it is possible to envisage more widespread learning where such practices can be legitimized and translated through the institutions and norms of a functional or professional community (Greenwood et al. 2002). Changes in divisions in practice, however, may be more difficult to spread, in that they are more deeply embedded in the practices and norms of multiple groupings (Scarbrough 2003). Moreover, such changes would require organizational mechanisms for institutionalizing new divisions in practice which are either not available or are widely contested within the professionally dominated NHS.

Conversely, the Lowlands case highlights the extent to which new practices can be spread, at least from one project to another. Significantly, however, these changes in practice were only achieved when the project was able to achieve greater autonomy from its host organization. This enabled greater decoupling from mainstream organizational practices, and at the same time, the creation of conditions under which new, shared practices could be developed. That these changes in practice were then retained for a subsequent project seems to have been the result, first, of organizational and technical continuity between one project and the next – the same tasks could be addressed through the same practices and division of practice. And second, it seems to have reflected the project members' willingness to invest in these new practices in return for the gains which they could achieve together.

Taking our cases together effectively underlines the impact which existing communities and divisions in practice exert upon the organization's ability to exploit project-based learning. In each case, the opportunities and limitations for such learning were different. This seems to have reflected the importance, as noted previously, of the organizational contexts in which projects were positioned. These contexts involved an institutionalized ordering of different CoPs, and the relations of power and legitimacy between them (Contu and Willmott 2003), which facilitated certain kinds of learning but precluded others. Thus, in the Thurrock case, the BuildCo organization affirmed a traditional manual–mental division of labour between tender teams and site teams. The communities which evolved around these distinct practices thus promoted divergent forms of learning – centring for the tender teams on the discipline-based collation of technical data, and for the site teams on the individual learning of craft practices.

This can be contrasted with the Midlands Hospital case, where the conscious pursuit of innovative project goals achieved local success through diversity of team membership and high levels of learning within the project. However, the learning from this project was associated with artefacts and stories focused on an organizational innovation. These could not be readily assimilated within specialized practices which were reinforced and legitimized by formal professional bodies.

Significantly, the one case where we found both *learning within*, and *learning from* the project was the Lowlands case. Here, we identified a high level of project autonomy, but also the importance of the continuity from one project to another. Such continuity, when added to autonomy, meant that in some sense, the project became its own organizational subunit. One consequence of this was that the new practices created within the initial project did not have to be re-digested through an existing division of practice, but could be dynamically carried forward to the emerging activities of the follow-up project. The iteration of project work in this case also had political consequences, as the new contract arrangements effectively applied resource power to the project's innovative practices. This encouraged individuals to invest in these practices – in effect, creating an embryonic CoP – and, at the same time, forging a tighter partnership with contractors.

Consideration of the Lowlands case, however, also suggests a need to extend future research beyond locating the project in its organizational context to the positioning of the organization itself in wider institutional, technological, and market environments. This would complement the work described previously on project ecologies and regional effects, but focusing less on the movement of individuals across projects, and more on the organization's shifting powers and positions within wider labour-market and regulatory environments. Thus, developments in practice at Lowlands were made possible in part by a change in the relationship between BuildCo and its partner organization. This mandated the resources and business opportunity through which new practices could be sustained. In contrast, the Thurrock case shows an organization locked into the craft-based institutional logic of the UK construction sector, with important consequences (as with many other construction firms) for its ability to innovate. Finally, the Midlands Hospital case highlights the important influence of the wider professional, and explicitly political environment on the NHS' ability to bring about change from the level of practice – bottom-up change as it were – in its organizational processes (Child and Loveridge 1990).

6.7 Conclusions

In this chapter, we have attempted to develop a practice-based view of project-based learning. We noted that this view seemed to offer some advantages over alternative perspectives on such learning. Thus, cognitive-oriented views seemed to overstate the fluidity of project-based learning, neglecting the problems of embeddedness within organizational contexts. This may have helped to account for the limited effectiveness of cognitively based attempts to capture and transfer project-based learning. On the other hand, the existing literature on learning within teams has limited applicability to the dynamics of project work. Whatever autonomy projects enjoy, they are also interpenetrated by existing organizational routines (e.g. project-management routines) and practices. Learning within projects thus reflects not so much the localized development of the team as the way in which project members interpret and enact the interplay between project activities and existing organizational practices.

In the remainder of the chapter, we sought to explore a practice-based view of project work by focusing on its implications for, and indebtedness, to existing CoPs and divisions in practice. The comparison between our three cases suggests that these carriers of practice do indeed significantly influence the process and outcomes of project-based learning – certainly to a greater extent than is currently appreciated in much of the existing literature, which tends to isolate projects from the social practices which underpin their execution. We found that the scope and extent of *learning within* projects is influenced by the practices of established communities. Where projects were routine in nature, as in our construction example, the importation of existing practices was relatively straightforward, securing organizational efficiencies, but militating against the generation of learning within the project itself. In contrast, where the project was highly novel and project membership spanned a range of existing communities, a high level of learning was generated. However, the resulting organizational innovation encountered stiff resistance due to its challenge to existing practices within the wider organization.

The variation in these findings suggested that the influence of CoPs on project-based learning, and vice versa, needs to be related to their organizational contexts. Such contexts not only help to define the ordering and constitution of different CoPs – as, for example, between the craft-based and professionally based forms we found in BuildCo and Midlands Hospital respectively – but also the relative influence of existing divisions in practice on the learning potential of projects. As we noted previously, it is simplistic to see projects and CoPs as distinct entities. Rather, these different sources of learning within organizations overlap, reinforce, and sometimes conflict, depending on the relationship between project work and existing social practices. Thus, where projects map neatly onto established CoPs, one would anticipate an incremental pattern of learning, linked to existing practices and mediated by individual career paths and the development of the CoP. Conversely, where a project becomes a focal point for the development of new practices within an organization, or where it provides an interface to wider networks of practitioners outside the organization, the project may itself become an important, if likely short-lived, catalyst for the development of a new CoP. On the other hand, where project work cuts across existing CoPs, as in the Midlands Hospital case, there is potential for more radical breakthroughs in thinking and practice – 'learning within' as we have termed it. But this also increases the risk that the spread of any such breakthroughs will be blocked by the embeddedness of existing practices. Thus, by constraining change, existing CoPs may preserve one source of learning, but at the cost of 'reinventing the wheel' in successive projects.

References

Ancona, D. G. and Caldwell, D. F. (1992). 'Bridging the boundary: External activity and performance in organizational teams', *Administrative Science Quarterly*, 37(4): 634.

Argote, L. and Ingram, P. (2000). 'Knowledge transfer: A basis for competitive advantage in firms', *Organizational Behavior and Human Decision Processes*, 82(1): 150–69.

Arthur, M. B., DeFillippi, R., and Jones C. (2001). 'Project-based learning as the interplay of career and company non-financial capital', *Management Learning*, 32(1): 99–117.

Ayas, K. and Zeniuk, N. (2001). 'Project-based learning: Building communities of reflective practitioners', *Management Learning*, 32(1): 61–76.

Barker, J. R. (1993). 'Tightening the iron cage: Concertive control in self-managing teams', *Administrative Science Quarterly*, 38(3): 408–37.

Blackler, F. (1995). 'Knowledge, knowledge work and organizations: An overview and interpretation', *Organization Studies*, 16(6): 1021–46.

Bresnen, M. (1990). *Organising Construction: Project Organisation and Matrix Management*. London: Routledge.

Brown, J. S. and Duguid, P. (1991). 'Organizational learning and communities-of-practice: Towards a unified view of working, learning and innovation', *Organization Science*, 2: 40–57.

————(2000). *The Social Life of Information*. Cambridge, MA: Harvard Business School Press.

————(2001). 'Knowledge and organization: A social-practice perspective', *Organization Science*, 12(2): 198–213.

Bryman, A., Bresnen, M., Beardsworth, J., and Keil, E. (1987). 'The concept of the temporary system: The case of the construction project', in S. Bacharach (ed.), *Research in the Sociology of Organisations*, Vol. 5. London: JAI Press, pp. 253–84.

Burns, T. and Stalker, G. M. (1961). *The Management of Innovation*. London: Tavistock.

Carlile, P. R. (2002). 'A pragmatic view of knowledge and boundaries: Boundary objects in new product development', *Organization Science*, 13(4): 442–55.

Child, J. and Loveridge, R. (1990). *Information Technology and European Services: Towards a Microelectronic Future*. Oxford: Blackwell.

Contu, A. and Willmott, H. (2000). 'Comment on Wenger and Yanow: Knowing in practice. A delicate flower in the organizational learning field', *Organization*, 7(2): 269–76.

————(2003). 'Re-embedding situatedness: The importance of power relations in learning theory', *Organization Science: A Journal of the Institute of Management Sciences*, 14(3): 283–96.

Courtright, C. (2004). 'Which lessons are learned? Best practices and World Bank Rural Telecommunications policy', *Information Society*, 20(5): 345–56.

DeFillippi, R. J. (2001). 'Introduction: Project-based learning, reflective practices and learning outcomes', *Management Learning*, 32(1): 5–10.

——and Arthur, M. B. (1998). 'Paradox in project-based enterprise: The case of film making', *California Management Review*, 40(2): 125–39.

Edmondson, A. C. (1996). 'Group and organizational influences on team learning', Ph.D. thesis, Harvard University.

Engwall, M. (2003). 'No project is an island: Linking projects to history and context', *Research Policy*, 32: 789–808.

Foss, N. J. (2003). 'Selective intervention and internal hybrids: Interpreting and learning from the rise and decline of the Oticon Spaghetti Organization', *Organization Science*, 14(3): 331–49.

Gersick, C. J. G. (1989). 'Marking time: Predictable transitions in task groups', *The Academy of Management Journal*, 32(2): 274–309.

Gerwin, D. and Ferris, J. S. (2004). 'Organizing new product development projects in strategic alliances', *Organization Science: A Journal of the Institute of Management Sciences*, 15(1): 22–37.

Gherardi, S. (1999). 'Learning as problem-driven or learning in the face of mystery?', *Organization Studies*, 20(1): 101–23.

—— (2001). 'From organizational learning to practice-based knowing', *Human Relations*, 54(1): 131–9.

—— and Nicolini, D. (2002). 'Learning in a constellation of interconnected practices: Canon or dissonance?', *Journal of Management Studies*, 39(4): 419–36.

—— Nicolini, D., and Odella, F. (1998). 'Toward a social understanding of how people learn in organizations', *Management Learning*, 29(3): 273–93.

Grabher, G. (ed.) (2002). 'The project ecology of advertising: Tasks, talents and teams', *Production in Projects: Economic Geographies of Temporary Collaboration*: *Regional Studies Special Issue*, 36: 245–63.

Grant, R. (1996). 'Towards a knowledge based theory of the firm', *Strategic Management Journal* (Winter Special Issue), 17: 109–22.

Greenwood, R., Suddaby, R., and Hinings, C. R. (2002). 'Theorizing change: The role of professional associations in the transformation of institutionalized fields', *Academy of Management Journal*, 45(1): 58–80.

Hobday, M. (2000). 'The project-based organisation: An ideal form for managing complex products and systems?', *Research Policy*, 29(7–8): 871–93.

Huber, G. P. (1999). 'Facilitating project team learning and contributions to organizational knowledge', *Creativity and Innovation Management*, 8(2): 70–6.

Keegan, A. and Turner, J. R. (2001). 'Quantity versus quality in project-based learning practices', *Management Learning*, 32(1): 77–98.

Knight, K. (1977). 'Responsibility and authority in the matrix organization or is ambiguity a good thing', *R & D Management*, 7: 183–6.

Kotnour, T. (1999). 'A learning framework for project management', *Project Management Journal*, 30(2): 32–8.

Lave, J. and Wenger, E. (1991). *Situated Learning: Legitimate Peripheral Participation*. Cambridge: Cambridge University Press.

Levinthal, D. A. and March, J. G. (1993). 'The myopia of learning', *Strategic Management Journal*, 14: 95–112.

Lindkvist, L. (2005). 'Knowledge communities and knowledge collectivities: A typology of knowledge work in groups', *Journal of Management Studies*, 42(6): 1189–210.

—— Soderlund, J., and Tell, F. (1998). 'Managing product development projects: On the significance of fountains and deadlines', *Organization Studies*, 19(6): 931–51.

Marks, A. and Lockyer, C. (2004). 'Producing knowledge: The use of the project team as a vehicle for knowledge and skill acquisition for software employees', *Economic And Industrial Democracy*, 25(2): 219–45.

Mintzberg, H. (1979). *The Structuring of Organizations: A Synthesis of the Research.* Englewood Cliffs, NJ: Prentice-Hall.

Nonaka, I. and Takeuchi H. (1995). *The Knowledge Creating Company.* New York: Oxford University Press.

Okhuysen, G. A. and Eisenhardt, K. M. (2002). 'Integrating knowledge in groups: How formal interventions enable flexibility', *Organization Science,* 13(4): 370–86.

Oliver, A. L. and Liebeskind, J. P. (1998). 'Three levels of networking for sourcing intellectual capital in biotechnology', *International Studies of Management and Organization,* 27(4): 76–103.

Orlikowski, W. J. (2002). 'Knowing in practice: Enacting a collective capability in distributed organizing', *Organization Science: A Journal of the Institute of Management Sciences,* 13(3): 249–73.

Pettigrew, A. M., Woodman, R. W., and Cameron K. S. (2001). 'Studying organizational change and development: Challenges for future research', *Academy of Management Journal,* 44(4): 697.

Powell, W. W., Koput, K., and Smith-Doerr, L. (1996). 'Interorganizational collaboration and the locus of innovation: Networks of learning in biotechnology', *Administrative Science Quarterly,* 41(1): 116–45.

Scarbrough, H. (2003). 'The role of intermediary groups in shaping management fashion: The case of knowledge management', *International Studies of Management and Organization,* 32(4): 87–103.

——Swan, J., Laurent, S., Bresnen, M., Edelman, L., and Newell S. (2004). 'Project-based learning and the role of learning boundaries', *Organization Studies,* 25(9): 1579–600.

Schindler, M. and Eppler, M. J. (2003). 'Harvesting project knowledge: A review of project learning methods and success factors', *International Journal of Project Management,* 21: 219–28.

Schultze, U. (2000). 'A confessional account of an ethnography about knowledge work', *MIS Quarterly,* 24(1): 3–41.

Senge, P. (1993). *The Fifth Discipline: The Art and Practice of the Learning Organization.* New York: Century Business.

Sense, A. (2003). 'Learning generators: Project teams re-conceptualized', *Project Management Journal,* 34(3): 4–12.

Sole, D. and Edmondson, A. (2002). 'Situated knowledge and learning in dispersed teams', *British Journal of Management,* 13(3): S17–34.

Sydow, J. and Staber, U. (2002). 'The institutional embeddedness of project networks: The case of content production in German television', *Regional Studies,* 36(3): 215–27.

Thompson, M. (2005). 'Structural and epistemic parameters in communities of practice', *Organization Science,* 16(2): 151–64.

Von Zedtwitz, M. (2002). 'Organizational learning through post-project reviews in R & D', *R & D Management,* 32(3): 255–68.

Weick, K. E. and Westley, F. (1996). 'Organizational learning: Affirming an oxymoron', in S. R. Clegg, C. Hardy, and W. R. Nord (eds.), *Handbook of Organization Studies*. Thousand Oaks, CA: Sage, pp. 440–58.

Wenger, E. (1998). *Communities of Practice: Learning, Meaning, and Identity*. Cambridge, UK, and New York: Cambridge University Press.

Wenger, E. C. and Snyder, W. M. (2000). 'Communities of practice: The organizational frontier', *Harvard Business Review*, 78(1): 139–45.

Williams, T. (2003). 'Learning from projects', *Journal of the Operational Research Society*, 54(5): 443–51.

Zenger, T. R. (2002). 'Crafting internal hybrids: Complementarities, common change initiatives, and the team-based organization', *International Journal of the Economics of Business*, 9(1): 79–95.

Zollo, M. and Winter, S. G. (2002). 'Deliberate learning and the evolution of dynamic capabilities', *Organization Science*, 13(3): 339.

Note

1. The names of these organizations have been changed to protect the confidentiality of respondents.

7

Breakthrough Innovation and the Shaping of New Markets: The Role of Communities of Practice[1]

Aurélie Delemarle and Philippe Larédo

7.1 Introduction

This chapter focuses specifically on expert/high-creativity communities as defined by Amin and Roberts (Chapter 1). It analyses how the creation of new inter-organizational communities of practice (CoPs) helps to 'break out' of dominant technological paradigms. Our analysis is based on the emergence of asynchronous logic as a new option for chip design in microelectronics. Asynchronous logic provides an alternative circuit architecture to the prevalent one based on a clock-based logic. The latter is the dominant design on which all electronic circuits have relied since the beginning of the digital age. The accumulated infrastructure – including design and debug tools, engineers' training, and intellectual property blocks – builds and reinforces its predominance. The passage from synchronous to asynchronous logic corresponds to what evolutionary economics considers as a new technological paradigm, and what management describes as a breakthrough innovation.

The chapter examines the extension of the knowledge base from a small group of scientists in mathematics to a CoP bringing together scientists and engineers in electronics. The time span runs from the early 1980s through to the beginning of the new century. The chapter thus focuses on the building of such an expert/creative community, which has been neglected in the literature on CoPs compared to the question of the structure of such communities. We demonstrate that the CoP is a rich concept for accounting for the proliferation of scientific and technological options. However, it is of limited help in understanding the passage from the exploration to the exploitation phase, in so far as a CoP is unable to select a standard enabling the microelectronics industry to adopt a technology. In light of this, the role of inter-organizational expert CoPs can be positioned better in the deployment of breakthrough innovations: they contribute to building a space in which the option gains credibility. This point is crucial in the setting up of any new industry or market (Aldrich and Fiol 1994; Courtney et al. 1997).

How then can the emergence of an expert community based on science be facilitated? If it is acknowledged that such a CoP cannot be built in a top-down manner and if we recognize, like Roberts (2006, p. 634), that they 'do not develop and function in a vacuum', it is important to consider the selection mechanisms that favour the crystallization of the configuration of actors at various stages of the life of the option under consideration. In this respect – and we argue that it might be a general phenomenon for science-based breakthrough innovations – public policies have played a key role. What is, however, essential to analyse is the nature of incentives, depending upon the phases of the project. Here again, generic mechanisms (or, in other words, 'procedural policies') have been critical in fostering the emergence of the community and a wide exploration of potential directions, while specific mechanisms (requiring the policy to enter into the substance/content of the would-be innovation) have been instrumental in generating the standards necessary to open the road toward exploitation.

The chapter is organized in five main sections. Section 7.2 reviews our understanding of breakthrough innovation. Section 7.3 introduces the case study and analyses the role of the CoP in question, called Asynchronous Circuit Design (ACiD), in helping the new option – asynchronous logic – to gain credibility. Section 7.4 highlights the inability of ACiD to move from exploration to exploitation. This leads us to a more general discussion in Section 7.5, on the role of CoP in the development of breakthrough innovations, with particular emphasis on the passage from exploration to exploitation. Section 7.6 further elaborates on the incentives that support the creation of such inter-organizational expert communities and their productive deployment.

7.2 Breakthrough Innovation and the Exploration/ Exploitation Dilemma

Technological change results from a complex process that can be seen as gradual until it is punctuated by a major advance so significant that no increase in scale, efficiency, or design can allow other technologies to compete with the new one (Tushman and Anderson 1986). These are called breakthrough, disruptive, or radical advances, as they are often competence-destroying, both for the firm producing them and for users (they typically present a different package of performance attributes at the outset, not valued by existing customers). Evolutionary theories study technological dynamics and technological change as an evolution whose cycle is based on variation, selection, and retention. In the initial years (or even decades) of the cycle when the technology is still fluid, uncertainty is high, as actors do not know which option to select (Abernathy and Utterback 1978). This period has been characterized as a period of technological ferment and experimentation, with high rates of product variation (alternative forms compete), until a dominant design emerges as a synthesis of a number of proven concepts. This is associated with the emergence of product-class standards (Abernathy and Clark 1985). This period of variation is therefore crucial because choices made at this time orient further innovations. Numerous studies have demonstrated that the success of an innovation depends not only on its technical characteristics but also on necessity, history, social conditions (Akrich 1992; Bijker and Law 1992), individuals (Christensen 1997; Hamel 2000), and market demand (Nelson and Winter 1977).

Metcalfe and Boden (1992) complement evolutionary approaches with an insight on internal versus external selection environments: on the one hand, a firm has its own expectations concerning possible technological developments (internal selection mechanisms that influence the technological trajectories); on the other hand, there are the expectations of the rest of the environment (external selection mechanisms which have often been simplified as market or user factors but which also include regulation or general economic conditions). These two are not always aligned and may even contradict one another. The shaping of the environment and the alignment of actors (Callon 1992; Courtney et al. 1997) reduce the gap between internal and external environmental expectations so that the vision of the technology and of the market is shared and becomes a de facto standard. Even though many scholarly works describe the action of individual actors (e.g. Garud et al. 2002; Maguire et al. 2004), few deal with distributed creation, where no clear 'father' can be identified. Garud and Karnøe (2001) on path creation and Geels (2001) on evolutionary reconfiguration processes suggest that not one single central mechanism through which new technologies are explored lies in the deployment of an inter-organizational space which develops shared visions of the future world and shared repertoires.

In this chapter we expand on this approach in two directions: we first show that the initial deployment is linked to the emergence of an inter-organizational expert CoP but that the very nature of this community does not help in entering into a 'narrowing process'. This leads us, secondly, to question the selection environment. We highlight the role of public policies and the different mechanisms that support the innovation journey (Cheng and Van de Ven 1996).

7.3 Building Credibility of the Breakthrough Option: The Role of the ACiD Community of Practice

In the late 1940s the first electronic computers, as we know them today, were developed, thus ushering in the digital era. Almost seventy years later, the principles that regulate their functioning are still the same. Chips at the core of the computer (and of almost all digital machines) are based on a synchronous approach, meaning they use a single rhythm. This rhythm is imposed on all subsystems by a clock that governs the internal workings of the machine's microprocessor. However, in the infancy of the digital age (1946), both synchronous and asynchronous styles of designing chips existed. The synchronous design eventually prevailed because it was initially easier for engineers to design, test, and debug. Until now it has been able to meet the challenges and pace associated with Moore's famous law governing the microelectronic industry. Mathematical research on asynchronous logics nevertheless continued in a few places and a paper delivered at a major computer conference in 1989 revived interest in the subject (Sutherland 1989). Activity multiplied in computer departments, firms became interested, and a first generation of chips was produced from 1994 onwards. They did not however succeed in going beyond the demonstration phase (the few products marketed were unable to spread further than the small niches they started with). The proliferation of approaches, architectures, and design tools made it difficult to see 'product-class standards' emerge to support adoption. Only the intervention of the US Defense Advanced Research Projects Agency (DARPA) allowed the situation to evolve as it launched the 'Clockless Logic Analysis, Synthesis and Systems' (CLASS) project (2003–2006) with the aim of defining an industry-wide standard. In this section we study the conditions under which the first proliferation took place.

One significant aspect of breakthrough science and technology (see NEST project, Rip et al. 2005) relates to the cognitive and institutional isolation of promoters. By definition, new directions are not shared. They are often promoted simultaneously in different places by individuals or small groups that are marginal in their own field, in various senses: few people to discuss with, difficulty obtaining recognition, and embedded in the core research programme of the institutions or supporting bodies. This is why the emergence of an inter-organizational community is central. This is a long-standing issue in the analysis of the organization of science. 'Invisible colleges' are central to Mertonian analyses, but they are linked to established disciplines and cannot capture this type of situation for at least three reasons cited in the literature: first, there is no dominant established paradigm around which scientists gather; second, the interdisciplinary nature of the new paradigm being promoted, poses the difficulty of bridging the divide between pre-existing colleges; finally, resources mobilized are often heterogeneous, suggesting new 'architectures' (see Abernathy and Clark 1985) and lead to 'transepistemic arenas' (Knorr-Cetina 1982). While we share these observations, our argument is that they are based on the outcome and not on the dynamics of the processes of change. Dynamics require the development, over time, of a space which may not evolve within the boundaries of one organization but has all three main attributes which Wenger (1998) identifies as characteristic of a CoP: mutual engagement, sense of joint enterprise, and shared repertoire.

The asynchronous design case study[2] highlights the ways in which the ACiD CoP supported the emergence of this new science-based option. The 'ACiD working group' was initially created as a forum for scientists to exchange and communicate within the existing community and with the outside world; and develop a common language for the field so fluid that scientists, unable to speak the same scientific language and unable to build on each other's work, could 'get the work out to a lot of people' and develop 'some consensus on terminology' (van der Korst et al. 1992, p. 89). We show below how the Working Group on ACiD (ACiD-WG) was instrumental in shaping a relational space in which the breakthrough innovation could unfold, first by creating an expert community and then moving it towards becoming a professional one.

7.3.1 *A common understanding of the problem*

The first key dimension concerns a common understanding of the problem. In the case studied, asynchronous chip design, there was a 'shared perspective of the world', that is, of the limitations of the current dominant clocked paradigm. As early as the 1980s, a few researchers[3] thought that clocked chips had run their course and they expected asynchronous design to be able to solve technical issues that synchronous technology could not. As clocks went faster and systems became more complicated, physical limitations of the clock appeared. One was the inability of the signal to reach all components before the occurrence of the next clock tick (propagation of the signal problem), undermining the clock's synchronization role. Another was the clock itself taking space, which therefore reduced the possible number of components on the chip. A third limitation was that the coordination of millions of transistors each billionth of a second consumed a lot of energy, up to 30 per cent of the electrical power required by one chip[4] (Furber 1999). Finally, each tick of the clock triggered a switch of all gates, whether or not they are required to complete a function, which resulted in an increase in the temperature of the chip. A corollary is that logic transistors could spend up to 95 per cent of their time waiting for the next tick of the clock to tell them to act (Anthes 2002). This also involved security issues since the repetition of the sequence tick after tick was one of the main sources of information for hackers.

Developing a coherent argumentation against the dominant paradigm prompted members to build a common identity, answering – as Wenger suggests – simple questions such as 'who are we compared to the rest of the world?'. This positioned the community in its microelectronic environment. It is, however, not sufficient to become cognitively close to one another and to face or try to convince the rest of the world. We enter here into the realm of the second and third dimensions: the willingness to act together and the building of a shared repertoire.

7.3.2 *Building a willingness to act together resting on a specific context*

The funding[5] of ACiD-WG[6] was the first formal effort to structure actors in the field.

[This community] aims at improving the systematic exchange of information and the forging of links between teams which carry out RTD or take up activities around the theme of asynchronous circuit design. Its objectives are (1) to encourage excellence in S&T research pertaining to asynchronous circuits and systems,

(2) to facilitate the development of methods and tools that are usable by engineers for the design of asynchronous VLSI systems, and (3) to promote the adoption of asynchronous circuit design in industry. (ACiD-WG web site[7])

For such structuring to happen there is a need for a 'context' that favours initial encounters. In our case, there were at least three significant 'events' that set out the trajectory. First, there was one major scientific event with a unique paper (Sutherland 1989) that drew the link between abstract theoretical research and engineering possibilities, so that engineers who until then had focused on the clocked design could foresee the application potential of asynchronous logics. A second unexpected event was the breaking up of one of the theoretical 'hubs' of asynchronous logics, a research institute in the then Soviet-ruled Leningrad. As a result a number of its members were scattered throughout Europe in various universities. The third 'small event' was the recruitment by a major microelectronics company, Philips, of a post-doctoral student trained in the leading US research laboratory working on asynchronous logics, Caltech. This laboratory acted as a catalyser of the first ACiD offical meeting (Amsterdam 1992), attended by the core of the newly funded ACiD CoP.

7.3.3 *Building a shared repertoire*

The composition of ACiD-WG is significant: it comprised members from numerous universities but also from corporate R&D departments and from small high-tech firms (not yet called start-ups at the time). Over time its membership grew and continued to diversify (Table 7.1). For innovation specialists, this growing alignment of actors is proof of a productive 'journey'. From a CoP perspective, it shows that the activities developed have succeeded in creating a 'cognitive' and 'social' proximity.

To create a common repertoire from dispersed knowledge, ACiD-WG mobilized numerous mechanisms targeting both its members and non-members. Its activities started in 1992,[8] organized around the annual 'ASYNC' international symposium; workshops at which members of the Working Group and invited non-members presented their work, and special interest group meetings; exploratory visits to companies and tutorials at conferences; annual public overviews of the status of asynchronous design in industrial use; and summer schools and other teaching and training activities.

Apart from the usual features of CoPs mentioned by Wenger and others (common language, terminology, periodic generic gatherings, topic-oriented

Table 7.1: Asynchronous Circuit Design (ACiD) membership

Activities	1992–1995	1996–2000	2001–2005
Exchange and dissemination of information: ASYNC conferences and ACiD-WG workshop	2 conferences (average attendance: 90 participants) 5 workshops	3 conferences 4 workshops (average attendance: 40 participants)	2 conferences (average 105 participants) 4 workshops (average attendance: 53 participants)
Training (summer/ winter schools)	—	1 workshop (50 participants) + 10 courses	2 workshops (av. 75 participants)
Publications by members (ACiD database)	41	111 (+1 special issue)	161 (+2 books)
Members	11 (1 company + 10 public labs and universities)	10 (1 company + 9 public labs and universities) (+14 industrial affiliates)	21 (6 companies + 15 public labs and universities) (+9 industrial affiliates)

Source: Josephs (2004).

meetings, summer schools, and tutorials), there are two others that seem central to 'inter-organization' CoPs linked to breakthrough innovation. First, every year the working group prepared an annual overview of 'the status of asynchronous design in industrial use'. Firms, and especially the main players building the worldwide oligopoly of chip manufacturers, could thus have an idea of how relevant this approach might be for their competitors, requiring them to ask: 'Can I remain outside this potential development and risk missing having the adequate absorptive capacity if it turns out to be a relevant option?'. Second, the working group organized periodic presentations and discussions of results obtained by its members and, more widely, by their US colleagues. This aspect is consistent with a central feature of new disruptive technologies: during their initial phase, multiple options are explored and enter into competition to become the dominant design (or element of it). The technology can prosper only through this phase of 'ferment'. At this stage the issue is not to 'hide' one's developments; on the contrary, sharing is central for aggregating others around the proposed design and set of standards.

One critical aspect of radical innovation-oriented CoPs is thus to become an enabler of experiments and demonstrations. By organizing a 'space' where the prototype chips produced were discussed and compared, the working group was successful in arousing interest. This can be seen from Table 7.2, which lists the projects supported by the European

Table 7.2: European asynchronous chip projects

Projects	Period	Led by: companies	Partners: universities and public laboratories	Partners: companies	Number of partners only present in this project/participating in three or more projects
Amulet 1	1989–1992		4	9	6/2
Amulet 2	1992–1995	ARM*	5	2	4/1
Exact	1992–1995	Philips	5	5	7/1
Horn	1992–1996	SGS Thomson	10	5	10/1
DE2	1995–1997	ARM	1	4	1/2
Amulet 3	1997–1999	ARM	1	4	1/2

* ARM is a company located in Manchester, closely connected to the University ATP group, and present in five out of six projects. Both Philips and SGS Thomson (now ST Microelectronics) are present in two projects.
Source: Josephs (2004).

Table 7.3: Industrial interest in asynchronous design

Types of actors involved in asynchronous design	2002	2004
Start-up companies	6	7
Companies with asynchronous products	2	4
Companies with asynchronous research activities	5	7
Other industrial members & affiliates of the ACiD Working Group	?	5
Other companies declaring asynchronous interests	?	2

Source: Furber (2002, 2004).

Commission and their participation. Though there is a clear common core highlighted by the number of those who participate in three or more projects, they represent only a limited percentage compared to those that have been attracted and become involved in one project, thus developing their ability to assess the option. Another aspect to consider is the growing list of industry affiliates (Table 7.1) which testifies to the interest from industries (see also Table 7.3). We can thus conclude that ACiD-WG was instrumental in building the scientific credibility of this long-term option.

7.4 Framing the Conditions for a Future Market: Limits of the ACiD Community of Practice

How to move from exploration to exploitation? How to enter into this narrowing process once the option had raised interest and gained credibility? How to foster the emergence of a dominant design out of the variety that has been nurtured by the community? Our initial assumption was that the community would be in a position to compare approaches and to drive its members to choose between principles, define relevant architectures that ensure as much continuity as possible with present investments, and aggregate around design tools. These three dimensions are not mentioned by chance. They represent the key issues that need to be addressed in the microelectronics industry for an option to be embedded in the microelectronics road map, which plays a central role in organizing technology adoption by the industry.

7.4.1 *The inability of the community to set up a road map for the exploitation of the technology*

As De Laat and McKibbin (2003) argue, road maps are designed with the purpose of creating a path. They determine key drivers and parameters to be met so that technology can unfold. They typically are organized in working groups that consider the different aspects that need to be taken into consideration in a sequence, most of the time, along the following steps as summarized by De Laat and McKibbin:

- 'Step 1: definition of the markets (or a vision, objectives, guiding principles, requirements, etc.) at a 10-year time horizon. This should lead to a definition of future demand;
- Step 2: definition of the requirements of products that follow from this demand (supply side);
- Step 3: definition of key technologies or critical research necessary to develop these products and to create the associated infrastructures. This step normally leads to the Technology Road Map document.' (De Laat and McKibbin 2003, p. 3).

Many of these road maps (more than 50 examined in the above-mentioned review) have been initiated by public funding. Most are periodically updated and enriched. Very few have become 'autonomous' and independent from public funding, as in the case of the microelectronics road map managed by the International Technology Roadmap for Semiconductors (ITRS), which has now existed for twenty years and has turned into a major feature of the entire industry (in the last version, 839 international experts participated). Each road map extends over five successive generations, and each generation, following Moore's law, is renewed every eighteen to twenty-four months and represents a doubling of capacity (number of transistors in a similar size chip and number of operations per second).

The road map is a pre-competitive means to share one's own view with the community. In microelectronics this takes two main forms, relating to the main technological principles and the architectural designs that organize one generation. These act as quasi-standards which are further translated into the adaptation of the dominant design tool, Cadence, and are then implemented by each major producer (with its own in-house standards).

The road map thus articulates the two levels of exploration and exploitation. Following Walsh and Elders (2002), a road map allows its authors to present and defend their vision of the sector, including what the markets will be and how to construct them. If accepted by the various stakeholder communities, the proposed road map should speed up the R&D and commercialization process of disruptive technologies because the alignment of the various actors allows a better coordination of actions. Risks are reduced for all with the use of roadmapping: users feel more secure in using the emergent technology; suppliers can invest in production facilities and tools; manufacturers can adapt their production technologies to users' needs; and public policies can more easily support the actors and/or new technology.

This 'narrowing' has not happened in the case of asynchronous design and we think that crystallization is emerging from another completely different process, as we shall explain. This raises questions about the limitations of CoPs, or more exactly their role within the overall 'innovation journey' (Van de Ven et al. 1999).

7.4.2 ACiD's role in fostering a wide diversity of principles, architectures, and tools

7.4.2.1 PRINCIPLES AND ARCHITECTURES

As mentioned earlier, the ACiD community has fostered the exploration of many avenues. Quite a few firms have invested in developing demonstrators for very specific application contexts in order to prove the benefits of the new technology, such as low-consumption power, and high speed in data treatment or low signal emission. However, all but two have remained at the demonstrator level, and those two have been unable to move beyond their niche market (Table 7.4).

The reasons behind this lack of products relate to the diversity of the approaches taken in each of the projects: scientists, benefiting from the freedom of approaches that the project structure allowed, relied on different logics[9] organizing the communication of data within circuits. Each choice of logic has strong implications for the global architecture of the

Table 7.4: Industrial achievements related to asynchronous design

Company	Achievement	
Sharp	DDMP media processor	Product reached market in 1997
IBM	Rapid Single-Flux Quantum circuits	Never reached market
NTT	Fully asynchronous self-reconfigurable FPGA	Never reached market
Sun	Very high-speed asynchronous pipelines (GaSP)	Never reached market
Intel	x86 Instruction length decoder (1996)	Never reached market
Philips	80C51 microcontroller	Pager product reached market in 1997
MBDA	Clock-free circuitry embedded within an ASIC	Technology included in missiles
Myricom	Asynchronous techniques used for interfacing	Provides high-speed networking for connecting computers to form clusters

chip, that is, the organization of components on the chip. In an application-specific project, engineers specifically design the organization of components on the chip, by hand. They expect that the insertion of sequences (so-called Intellectual Property Blocks) that have already been validated (and that can therefore be reused as such to accomplish specific functions in different application contexts) will stimulate the interest of companies. However, in addition to different logics, engineers have also developed very different approaches to the overall architecture of chips,[10] which has entailed a second source of uncertainty for potentially interested companies.

7.4.2.2 DESIGN TOOLS

For demonstrations and even prototypes, design is done 'by hand', that is, tailored to the specific application context of the demonstration. Reaching the industrialization stage, that is, allowing asynchronous design to be used in a variety of contexts requires a move to less time-consuming and reproducible approaches. This explains why computer-assisted design tools have become central to the information technology (IT) industry. They allow players to benefit from standard intellectual property (IP) blocks that can be reused from one application to the next, and even traded. Owing to this, new chips are developed (designed and tested) in a shorter period of time (meaning shorter time to market) and in a less expensive way. Design tools are thus crucial to ensure the continuity with existing sunk capital. They also enable the articulation between actors, a growing issue with the enlargement of the mass-market producers that the semiconductor industry serves.

In the clocked paradigm, there is a de facto monopoly of one core design tool, Cadence, around which numerous complements and optimizations linked to specific situations have been developed not only by semiconductor firms, but also by a myriad of small design firms. When dealing with asynchronous design one requires a new generation of tools as the approach is radically different from the previous paradigm. Philips was the first to come up with a marketable tool but it took the company a decade to provide its team with an appropriate tool: Tangram. However, Philips has not been able to impose its solution and there are more than a dozen tools available today. Some are only PhD-based projects, whereas others have involved considerable investments by the diverse actors (Edwards and Toms 2004). Some are problem-specific, whereas others focus on a larger array of situations. The four most cited tools are: Tangram, developed by Handshake Solutions, a spin-off from Philips; Theseus logic tool, developed by a start-up initiated by Caltech students; Balsa, developed by Manchester University ATP group; and Tast, developed by the TIMA team at Institut Polytechnique de Grenoble. This variety of design tools is making the situation even more opaque for industry stakeholders.

Members of the community thus have had to compete over the three intermingled dimensions described (logic, architecture, and design tool), devising different strategies to 'align' stakeholders (as witnessed with design tools). The community, as such, has been unable to organize the narrowing down for the selection of a dominant design. This may well explain why DARPA launched the CLASS project in 2003. The objective of the project is clear: to incorporate asynchronous design into the road map. Core actors of the community were consulted and encouraged to join the effort (in Europe only Handshake Solutions was accepted). The aim was to build on existing competences, evaluate current products, and benchmark methods and tools to propose the most integrative solution. Demonstration chips were built for each of the main logics, which 'demonstrate clockless design in complex, highly constrained, DoD systems' (Objective 1; Brees 2006[11]). The promoters of the project presented a new design tool at the 2006 ACiD symposium in Grenoble: Mobius from Codetronix, based on the Null Convention Logic, but which also integrates the handshake logic to propose the largest spectrum of architectural possibilities within a single tool. This brings us to the second objective of the project, which is to 'develop clockless simulation, synthesis and libraries with commercial design tools'. Our recent interaction with key European members showed that, though the community worries about the access to the technology, it recognizes the value of such an initiative to eventually reach a standard and reap the fruits from more than twenty years of exploration.

7.5 Communities of Practice and Breakthrough Innovations

We have illustrated a case to show how the dynamics of breakthrough innovations are linked to the construction of a 'strong' CoP (as opposed to weak networks of practice proposed by Brown and Duguid 2001), whose activities are clearly summed up in the three dimensions put forward by Wenger (1998): mutual engagement, shared sense of a joint enterprise, and production of a shared repertoire of communal resources. CoPs dedicated to 'disruptive technologies' share three attributes recently highlighted in the literature. First, as mentioned by Roberts in her critical review of CoPs (2006, p. 630), radical innovation requires new communities: 'Radical change may be very difficult to bring about within existing communities and may be more easily introduced through the destruction of old communities and the emergence of new ones.' Second, such communities extend beyond the borders of one organization: 'CoP that exist independently of business organizations may take on an increasingly important role in the creation and transfer of knowledge' (Roberts 2006, p. 633). Thirdly, and most importantly, such communities are not geographically bound; as proposed by Amin and Cohendet (2003), they build spaces of relational proximity. They can be seen as 'one spatial form of knowing through communities' (Amin and Cohendet 2003, p. 16). For us, this notion of 'space' is central and makes it possible to move away from concepts such as the 'spaghetti' (Kolind 1996) or 'ambidextrous organization' (Tushman and O'Reilly 1996) that propose ways for companies to promote radical innovation. The space created through such CoPs provides the conditions enabling various members in different configurations (including an enlargement to non-members) to absorb the knowledge produced and to integrate it into their own product lines (see also Chapter 9 by Cohendet and Simon in this book). This justifies the development of 'demonstration projects' aimed at developing prototypes of asynchronous chips. However, the space has limited organizational power to encourage actors to enter into a narrowing process and to be in a position to produce the necessary 'framework conditions' for the proposed option to be included in the microelectronic road map: it has no selecting capacity over competing principles, architectures, and design tools.

This leads us to suggest that the construction of a CoP is a key ingredient in building the credibility of an approach but not in crystallizing it so that a market can be shaped and product-class standards emerge. But it also pushes us to further explore the role of the selection environment and, more specifically for breakthrough innovations, the role of the public environment in the unfolding of such innovations.

7.6 The Role of the Public Environment in Shaping Inter-organizational Bodies: From Generic to Specific Interventions

Roberts (2006, p. 634) concludes that CoP 'do not develop and function in a vacuum'. She mentions the context and broad socio-cultural factors, and wonders whether these might be nation-specific. This suggests the need to reconsider the conditions under which the ACiD community and space have developed, and the events that are crystallizing (or at least we assume so) the unfolding of the option. In this last section, we would like to put forward two complementary hypotheses.

The first one, for breakthrough innovation, concerns public intervention as a critical dimension of the selection environment. Every stage of the process is associated with public funding. The initiation of the ACiD community started from a project; we know that CoPs 'can emerge from a project'. The initial group was extended twice, so that over one decade the community could evolve and stabilize (we should, perhaps, reflect on the paradox of a 'slow community' aiming at radically changing the business environment). During this period the numerous experiments mentioned were all funded under the EU ESPRIT programme. Similarly, the crystallization process that started in 2004 is the result of a US DARPA initiative. We thus have here an active public selection environment that has been an enabler of community emergence, development, and crystallization.

It is however important to consider the concrete mechanisms at work, which may well link to 'nation-specific' contexts, or more exactly to evolving nation-specific contexts, provided that in this discussion one accepts the equation of the EU to one 'nation'. Here the case emphasizes the role of 'generic' public mechanisms at the exploration level, and 'specific' ones for the crystallization phase.

7.6.1 *Generic mechanisms to foster exploration*

First we consider the two complementary generic mechanisms which act as incentives for the emergence of the community and enable the testing of a variety of directions. For any new approach or option to have a chance to exist (and expectations linked to it to be expressed), 'space-building' or 'community-building' is essential. In fluid phases, new directions are not shared but are often promoted simultaneously in different places by individuals or small groups that are marginal in their own place (few people to discuss with, and difficulty being recognized). Alignment of actors is therefore central. How can actors be helped to align? The EU ESPRIT programme had a simple device: any set of actors could apply for 'working group' funding. Criteria for allocation required that the applicants demonstrate widespread interest from the academic community and industry. The budget allocated supported meetings, distribution of knowledge and tools, training courses, and similar activities (where funding is on a marginal basis).

There nevertheless need to be complementary actions concerning the evolving issues that cause the community to come together. To initiate interest from colleagues and economic actors, initial learning by promoters is required. This exploration period is often characterized by a multiplication of options with no shared directions. It is thus very difficult to develop an argumentation that can convince any selection group based on peer reviewing. How then did asynchronous design evolve even though asynchronous logic was not on the agenda of the established national and European public programmes? The fact that the second half of the 1990s witnessed nearly a dozen ESPRIT projects with activities on asynchronous chip design, can only be explained by the implementation approach chosen by this EC programme. While it mainly supported 'prototypes' that were near to the market (i.e. corresponding to the road map established), it also required each project to invest part of the expenses associated with the funds granted, into longer-term research and options. Clockless design flourished, based on this procedural choice by researchers themselves, whereby the selection remained bottom-up at the project level.

In combination, these two very different 'bottom-up' mechanisms provided strong incentives both for enabling the space to emerge, and for filling it with activities; an essential aspect for maintaining the community on the move and increasing its visibility in the microelectronics world as a whole.

7.6.2 *Specific mechanism to allow crystallization and exploitation to occur*

These 'generic' mechanisms did not however prove adequate for encouraging the community to enter into a selection process through the standardization of the three dimensions required for the inscription of asynchronous chip design on the microelectronic road map. The striking aspect of the cross-Atlantic shift observed, is not the fact that the USA took over or that it has been supported by a defence agency (note that the Internet emerged as an innovation from this same defence agency), but that the massively mission-oriented federal funding of R&D provided an adequate selection environment. DARPA does not work with open calls for proposals, but uses working groups for assessing the potential interest of emerging breakthrough technologies and then, through focused processes, shapes an alliance in charge of promoting it. Sometimes this alliance may bring major surprises as compared to recognized capabilities. In the present case the choice of Boeing and Theseus was a major shock.

Does this reflect lasting 'nation-specific' differences, as suggested by Roberts? We do not think so. One only has to consider the key role of European programmes ten years earlier, in organizing top-down the space which 'chose' the GSM standard. Or witness the way the successful European megawatt windmill programme was organized, promoting the development of four prototypes and organizing the gathering of over forty utilities to define the safety and quality standards as well as the economic conditions under which wind energy could flourish. It seems more relevant, rather, to study the developments that have rendered the EU incapable of continuing this type of approach. Our example shows that crystallization requires the selection process to become 'specific' and enter into the content of the future world proposed by the breakthrough innovation. There can be numerous forms of crystallization (Larédo 2006), but the example considered here highlights one central mechanism that is both top-down (with public intervention requiring actors to choose one set of standards and design tools) and bottom-up (what is created is only a space for selection, leaving open the concrete solution finally selected).

7.7 Conclusion

Using the case of asynchronous design, we have tried to demonstrate the importance of expert inter-organizational CoPs in the exploration phase of breakthrough innovations. Their main characteristics are to develop 'spaces of relational proximity', both between geographically distant actors, and between actors, from different organizations. The latter aspect is central to building the credibility of the potential breakthrough innovation. However, and importantly, probably because of their very loose connection with organizations (an issue still to be explored further), such communities may be very weak at entering into the narrowing process that shapes product-class standards, paving the way for effective developments and innovations. Finally, based on our case study, the role of the public-selection environment cannot be ignored, both in the emergence of breakthrough innovation-oriented CoPs, and in the crystallizing phase. The case study allows us to posit that the former depends on 'generic' forms (or procedural forms) of public intervention, while the latter requires that public intervention enters into the substance of the proposed innovation. This makes for 'specific' or 'ad hoc' interventions, with strong implications for the ongoing debates about the content of 'innovation' and 'industrial policies'.

References

Abernathy, W. J. and Clark, K. B. (1985). 'Mapping the winds of creative destruction', *Research Policy*, 14: 3–22.

—— and Utterback, J. M. (1978). 'Patterns of industrial innovation', *Technology Review*, 6(7): 40–8.

Akrich, M. (1992). 'The de-scription of technical objects', in W. Bijker and J. Law (eds.), *Shaping Technology/Building Society: Studies in Sociotechnical Change*. Cambridge, MA: MIT Press, pp. 205–24.

Aldrich, H. E. and Fiol, C. M. (1994). 'Fools rush in? The institutional context of industry creation', *Academy of Management Review*, 19(4): 645–70.

Amin, A. and Cohendet, P. (2003). 'Geography of knowledge formation in firms', DRUID Summer Conference on Creating, Sharing and Transferring Knowledge: The Role of Geography, Institutions and Organisations, Copenhagen, 12–14 June.

Anthes, G. (2002). *Computer Clocks Wind Down – Clockless, or Asynchronous, Circuits March to Different Drummer*, www.computerworld.com

Bijker, W. E. and Law, J. (eds.) (1992). *Shaping Technology/Building Society: Studies in Sociotechnical Change*. Cambridge, MA: MIT Press.

Brees, R. (2006). '*CLASS*', Presentation to the ASYNC'06 Symposium, Grenoble, France.

Brown, J. S. and Duguid, P. (2001). 'Knowledge and organisation: A social-practice perspective', *Organization Science*, 12(2): 198–213.

Callon, M. (1992). 'The dynamics of techno-economic networks', in R. Coombs, P. Saviotti, and V. Walsh (eds.), *Technical Change and Company Strategies*. London: Academic Press, pp. 73–102.

Cheng, Y. T. and Van de Ven, A. H. (1996). 'Learning the innovation journey: Order out of chaos', *Organization Science*, 7(6): 593–614.

Christensen, C. L. M. (1997). *The Innovator's Dilemma: When New Technologies Cause Great Firms to Fail*. Boston, MA: Harvard Business School Press.

Courtney, H., Kirkland, J., and Viguerie, P. (1997). 'Strategy under uncertainty', *Harvard Business Review*, 75(6): 67–79.

De Laat, B. and McKibbin, S. (2003). *Positionnement du RNRT par rapport aux grandes ⟪Road\maps⟫ Européennes du secteur des Télécommunications*. Paris: Technopolis, p. 42.

Edwards, D. A. and Toms W. B. (2004). *Design, Automation and Test for Asynchronous Circuits and System*, IST Programme, 3rd edn. London: IST.

Furber, S. (1999). *The Return of Asynchronous Logic*, http://www.cs.manchester.a-c.uk/ apt/async/background/return_async.html (last accessed 12 June 2007).

——(2002). *Industrial Take-Up of Asynchronous Design*, www.scism.sbu.ac.uk/ccsv/ ACiD-WG/Workshop2FP5/Programme/Furber1Slides.pdf (last accessed 16 November 2007).

——(2004). 'Industrial take-up of asynchronous design', in D. A. Edwards and W. B. Toms (eds.), *The Status of Asynchronous Design in Industry*. London: ACiD WG.

Garud, R. and Karnøe, P. (2001). 'Path creation as a process of mindful deviation', in R. Garud and P. Karnøe (eds.), *Path Dependence and Creation*. Mahwah, NJ: Erlbaum, pp. 1–38.

——Jain, S., and Kumaraswamy, A. (2002). 'Institutional entrepreneurship in the sponsorship of common technological standards: The case of Sun Microsystems and Java', *Academy of Management Journal*, 45(1): 192–214.

Geels, F. (2001). 'Technological transitions as evolutionary reconfiguration processes', Conference on The Future of Innovation Studies, Eindhoven, ECIS 20–3 September.

Hamel, G. (2000). *Leading the Revolution*. Boston, MA: HBS Press.

Jolivet, E., Larédo, P. and Shove, E. (2002). *Managing Breakthrough Innovations: The SOCROBUST Methodology*, Final report, EC TSER Programme. Paris: Centre de Sociologie de l'Innovation.

Josephs, M. (2004). 12 *Years of Support from the European Commission for Asynchronous Circuits & Systems*, www.ics.forth.gr/async2004/ presentations/12_year_support_eu.ppt (last accessed 12 June 2007).

Knorr-Cetina, K. (1982) 'Scientific communities or transepistemic arenas of research?', *Social Studies of Science*, 12: 101–30.

Kolind, L. (1996). 'The revolution at Oticon: Creating a spaghetti organisation', *Research Technology Management*, 39(5): 54.

Larédo, P. (2006). 'Transformation des régimes de recherche: implications pour les interventions publiques', *Lettre de la Régulation*, 56, December.

Maguire, S., Hardy, C. and Lawrence, T. B. (2004). 'Institutional entrepreneurship in an emerging field: HIV/AIDS treatment advocacy in Canada', *Academy of Management Journal*, 47(5): 1–23.

Metcalfe, J. S. and Boden, M. (1992). 'Evolutionary epistemology and the nature of technology strategy', in R. Coombs, P. Saviotti, and V. Walsh (eds.), *Technological Change and Company Strategies: Economic and Sociological Perspectives*. London: Academic Press, pp. 49–71.

Nelson, R. R. and Winter, S. G. (1977). 'In search of useful theory of innovation', *Research Policy*, 6(1): 36–76.

Rip, A., Larédo, P., Williams, R., Propp, T., Delemarle, A., and Spinardi, G. (2005). *ATBEST*, Final Activity Report to NEST, Contract No. 508929. London: NEST, 247p.

Roberts, J. (2006). 'Limits to communities of practice', *Journal of Management Studies*, 43(3): 623–39.

Sutherland, I. (1989). 'Micropipelines', *Communications of the ACM*, 32(6): 720–34.

Tushman, M. L. and Anderson, P. (1986). 'Technological discontinuities and organizational environments', *Administrative Science Quarterly*, 31: 439–65.

Tushman, M. L. and O'Reilly III, C. (1996). 'Ambidextrous organizations: Managing evolutionary and revolutionary change', *California Management Review*, 38(4): 8–30.

van der Korst, M., Peeters, A., and Schols, H. (1992). 'Design and implementation of asynchronous circuits, Proceedings of the Workshop, Amsterdam, Royal Netherlands Academy of Arts and Science, 10–14 November 1991.

Van de Ven, A. H., Polley, D., Garud, R. and Venkatraman, S. (1999). *The Innovation Journey*. New York: Oxford University Press.

Walsh, S. and Elders, J. (2002). *International Roadmap in MEMS, Microsystems, Micromachining and Top-Down Nanotechnology*. Naples, FL: MANCEF, pp. 614–630.

Wenger, E. (1998). *Communities of Practice: Learning, Meaning and Identity*. Cambridge: Cambridge University Press.

Notes

1. We acknowledge the work undertaken in the ATBEST project (NEST-SSA 508929). Assessment Tools for Breakthrough and Emerging Technologies (ATBEST) as an EC FP6 project funded by the New and Emerging Science and Technology (NEST) programme as well as the Minatec project funded by the Commissariat à l'Energie Atomique (CEA). We also wish to thank the participants of the workshop that originated this book for their comments.

2. We used an approach to data collection based on the actors own mapping of the world, starting from a single project (Esp@sIS) in 2004–2005. We stopped the interviews when no new names came up. This allowed us to historically track the evolution of asynchronous design, follow the controversies, dead ends, closures, and crystallizations; and to map the world of asynchronous design.

- Actors from Esp@sIS: CEA-Leti (public laboratory, France, 5 interviews); INPG-TIMA (university laboratory, France, one interview); ST Microelectronics (private research laboratory, France, three interviews)

- Further actors in the field: ATP Group (University of Manchester, UK, three interviews); Philips (private research laboratory, the Netherlands, one interview); Handshake Solutions (spin-off from Philips, the Netherlands, one interview); London South Bank University (UK, one interactive exchange).

All crucial actors initially involved in the field were interviewed or interactively contacted by email with the exception of two, who were approached but who showed no willingness to answer our questions: Martin's group at the California Institute of Technology, and DARPA, the US agency supporting defence research. Therefore, we used the interviewees' knowledge as well as web searches to recreate the puzzle for the most recent period under investigation.

We asked interviewees to describe their way of seeing the world they were involved in, recreating both a past image but also picturing future developments. In a way, we used a light version of the Socrobust methodology (Jolivet et al. 2002). Selection mechanisms were revealed during this process because the actors themselves highlighted the role of such or such a programme in the successful unfolding of asynchronous design.

We then based our analysis on industry and scientific reports (EU-IST reports, ACiD members' presentations and articles, DARPA web site, ATP web site), industrial news (IEEE news and reports) alerts and conferences presentations (ASYNC Symposium, ACiD WG conferences), and checked with the actors involved the veracity of our interpretations. This strategy allowed us to follow the unfolding of asynchronous design until the latest developments in 2006.

3. Only a few islands of 'asynchronicity' still existed in the 1980s, the most important being Manchester, Eindhoven, and St Peterburg in Europe, and the University of Utah and the California Institute of Technology in the USA.

4. This characteristic is particularly important for battery-powered equipment which accounts for an increasingly large share of the overall computer market.

5. ACiD was funded as ACiD-Working Group (WG) by the ESPRIT-specific programme, in the third European framework programme. ESPRIT devoted a specific share of its budget to funding 'Basic Research Groups', to allow emerging communities to explore promising research avenues.

6. ACiD and ACiD-WG labels refer to the same entity, although, ACiD-WG is used to point to the specific procedure which allows the community to structure itself. The term ACiD as such refers to its CoP characteristics developed in the long run.

7. http://www.bcim.lsbu.ac.uk/ccsv/ACiD-WG/ (last accessed 11 June 2007).

8. These activities were still up and running in 2006.

9. As there is no global clock to organize the flow of data between blocks, distributed control mechanisms need to organize the communication flow of various

components within a chip. Chips become distributed systems instead of being organized on the basis of a single centralized clock system. However, there are different ways to organize the flow of data, that is, there are different logics that could be applied. As Furber (1999) writes 'there are many different flavours of asynchronous logic, and they are as different from each other as they are from synchronous logic'. Below we present two very different competing principles that have been used in projects.

- 'Dual-rail' circuits: two wires allow the transistors to send bits but also signals to indicate when work has been done (also called handshake, a solution supported by Philips and its spin-off, Handshake Solutions). This solution is promoted for applications requiring low consumption levels and low signal detection.
- 'Null convention logic': allows the transistor to answer the question 'is the work completed' with 'yes', 'no', or 'no answer yet' responses (this is supported by Theseus Logic in the USA). This solution is described as 'robust' (i.e. IP blocks are well determined) but is not well suited to applications focusing on speed of data treatment or on a small size of the chip.

10. Two main architectures have been proposed in the different chip designs to associate synchronous and asynchronous elements.

- Globally Asynchronous Locally Synchronous (GALS) is an approach 'in which little synchronous islands operating at different clock speeds communicate through some kind of asynchronous buffer or fabric' (Anthes, 2002). For Furber (1999) GALS should solve large System-on-a-Chip (SoC) clock distribution problems (SoCs could in the future count hundreds or even thousands of IP blocks and complex interconnected topologies).
- Locally Asynchronous Globally Synchronous (LAGS) is in which asynchronous logic is used only within given IP blocks to solve problems that the conventional clocked system has difficulty overcoming.

They exemplify very different approaches to the articulation with existing knowledge bases and firm intellectual capital. Facing these, some experts are trying to find more progressive approaches and new architectures were proposed at the last 2006 ACiD conference in Grenoble.

11. http://tima.imag.fr/conferences/ASYNC/Technical_Program/Tuesday/Industrial_Session/Brees_Roger.pdf (last accessed 29 June 2007).

Part III

Achieving Relational Proximity

8

Buzz Without Being There?
Communities of Practice in Context[1]

Meric S. Gertler

8.1 Geography and Community

At the very foundation of the contemporary literature in economic geography is the idea that proximity matters. According to the widely accepted view, the geographical clustering of economic actors facilitates the exchange of knowledge between them, through both traded and untraded means. The interaction that supports this – planned and unplanned, formal and informal – is said to be enabled by spatial concentration. The same conditions enrich close, collaborative, and vertical interaction with local customers and suppliers, in which learning-through-interacting generates mutual benefits for technology users and producers alike (Lundvall 1988; Gertler 1995). The geographical clustering of firms in the same industries also accentuates competition – and the innovative dynamism arising from it – by enhancing firms' ability to learn from one another through observation and monitoring (Porter 2000; Malmberg and Maskell 2002). In short, 'being there' underpins the joint production, circulation, and sharing of knowledge.

More recently, this mainstream view has been challenged on a number of fronts. Its apparent infatuation with locally sourced knowledge has been characterized as both unrealistic and undesirable, since truly innovative economic activity relies on the combination of locally and non-locally sourced knowledge. Furthermore, scholars have demonstrated that the most dynamic city-regions not only excel in generating and circulating specialized knowledge locally, but also maintain strong linkages to other sites of concentrated knowledge production elsewhere (Bathelt et al. 2004).

The literature on economic communities – including both communities of practice and the related idea of epistemic communities – has offered a fresh perspective on this issue (Brown and Duguid 1996; Wenger 1998), by attempting to show how knowledge is actively produced inside teams of expertise – teams whose members are as likely to be spatially dispersed ('distanciated') as they are to be spatially proximate to one another. These communities of practice are largely autonomous, self-organizing groups of people working inside one or more organizations. They are constituted by actors who share a number of commonalities: shared expertise, joint work experience, and focus on a common goal. These collections of individuals – and the relationships that bind them together – are alleged to be the key mechanism for the production of both strategic and routine knowledge within firms. These teams are also the primary force behind the circulation of knowledge within and between firms, *both locally and at a distance*. The latter is supported by the achievement of relational proximity – a social-quality underpinning interaction between economic partners, which may or may not coincide with geographical proximity.

While this argument makes sense conceptually, its limits – both theoretical and empirical – have not yet been fully explored. A key unanswered question is: under what conditions should we expect relational proximity to be achieved effectively at a distance? In this chapter, I suggest that the evidence accumulated thus far to support the argument that communities of practice can support distanciated learning remains underdeveloped. Empirically, the literature still rests upon on a small sample of sectors and geographical/institutional settings. Moreover, the arguments have remained somewhat undertheorized, since they lack any systematic attempt to identify critical determinants of relational proximity. Following a brief review of recent debates in the literature, this chapter outlines recent findings from a number of case studies in which distributed teams participating in joint problem-solving projects have attempted to engage in long-distance learning and knowledge translation, with varying degrees of success. Deterrents to effective distanciated learning are both logistical and institutional in nature. The frictional effects of distance are shown to depend to an important extent on the types of knowledge base supporting innovation in each case. I argue that it is through this kind of analysis that we might begin to develop more compelling answers to questions like: under what circumstances will relational proximity be stronger or weaker?

What are the conditions that facilitate long-distance circulation of knowledge, or its joint production by distanciated actors?

8.2 The Advantages of Being There – or Not

Much of the recent literature in economic geography and related fields suggests that a key source of competitive advantage for firms located in geographically proximate clusters is their ability to produce and use unique, specialized knowledge in the form of product and process innovations. Moreover, this ability rests on the opportunity to interact with other local economic actors – customers, suppliers, competitors, research institutions, government agencies, and other elements of the regional innovation system (Lundvall 1988; Porter 2000; Maskell 2001*b*; Asheim and Gertler 2005). Proximity to critical sources of knowledge, whether they are found in public or private research institutions or embedded in the core competencies of lead or anchor firms, facilitates the process of acquiring new technical knowledge, especially when the relevant knowledge is located at the research frontier or involves a largely tacit dimension. Knowledge of this nature is transmitted most effectively through interpersonal contacts and the mobility of skilled workers between firms in the same region.

The success of these local knowledge production and circulation processes rests on 'the high level of embeddedness of local firms in a very thick network of knowledge sharing, which is supported by close social interactions and by institutions building trust and encouraging informal relations among actors' (Breschi and Malerba 2001, p. 819). Common conventions and norms, readily available knowledge about the reliability and trustworthiness of individual economic actors, and the ability to utilize the full array of verbal and non-verbal modes of communication further support the local flow of knowledge – both tacit and codified – within local industry clusters (Storper and Leamer 2001). Storper and Venables (2004) characterize this localized flow of specialized, highly tacit knowledge as the 'buzz' that distinguishes economically dynamic centres of innovation. In their view, local presence and the frequent opportunities for face-to-face interaction not only enable but virtually ensure that economic actors will enjoy the unique, knowledge-based benefits of 'being there'. In their view, it is almost impossible to avoid acquiring information about other firms in the cluster and their activities through the myriad opportunities for interaction that exist locally.

But must local concentrations of firms in the same and related sectors rely exclusively on local sources of knowledge? Is it not reasonable to expect that such clusters of firms will also depend on non-local sources of knowledge for their competitive and innovative dynamism? While the above rendition dominates the literature on innovation and learning within economic geography and related disciplines, recent contributions have begun to question the view that local interaction and knowledge circulation are the only source of innovative dynamism for firms. Instead, they posit that non-local (inter-regional and international) networks, relationships, and knowledge flows are critically important sources of vitality, supplementing and complementing the local 'buzz' that is said to be the defining characteristic of the local economic cluster (Bathelt et al. 2004; Owen-Smith and Powell 2004; Gertler and Levitte 2005).

On further reflection, it stands to reason that few, if any, local economies are likely to be completely self-sufficient in terms of the knowledge base from which they draw. Indeed, it may be both unrealistic and undesirable for economic regions to aspire to this kind of self-sufficiency. Bathelt et al. (2004) maintain that the most innovative local economies are home to firms and research institutions that succeed in building and managing a variety of channels and networks for accessing specialized knowledge from around the globe. Following Owen-Smith and Powell (2004), Bathelt et al. address these non-local knowledge flows through the concept of global pipelines, which refer to channels of communication used in the interaction between firms in different knowledge-producing centres located at a distance from one another. They argue that global pipelines create real economic advantages for local firms by providing access to a more variegated set of knowledge pools from which to draw. Seen from the perspective of evolutionary economics, pipelines increase the variety of locally available knowledge by linking firms to knowledge arising from multiple selection environments. Access to a more diverse knowledge base in turn stimulates local innovation: in other words, non-local learning brings its own economic advantages (Sturgeon 2003; Powell and Grodal 2005).

Appealing as these arguments may be, they consist largely of a set of logical assertions awaiting broader elaboration and substantiation. Among other critical gaps, we do not yet have a well-developed understanding of *how* knowledge is supposed to flow across long distances via global pipelines, or under what circumstances this is more – or less – likely to be the case. In other words, both the precise mechanisms and the conditions that facilitate the flow of knowledge over long distances are not very fully specified.

The recent literature on communities of practice provides another important perspective on this debate, arguing that such communities have become vehicles for supporting learning at a distance (distanciated learning). Communities of practice are defined as groups of workers informally bound together by shared experience, expertise, and commitment to a joint enterprise (Lave and Wenger 1991; Brown and Duguid 1996, 2000; Wenger 1998). These communities normally self-organize for the purpose of solving practical problems facing the larger organization(s) in which they are embedded, and in the process they produce innovations (both product and process) that generate new economic value. The joint production and sharing of knowledge – tacit and codified, strategic and routine – occurs through collaborative problem-solving, employing a number of discursive devices for circulating knowledge. This process is said to be facilitated by the commonalities shared by members of the community.

In this view, the joint production and diffusion/transmission of tacit and codifiable knowledge within and between organizations is made considerably easier when it is mediated by these communities. Furthermore, knowledge may also flow across regional and national boundaries if relational proximity is strong enough. In other words, learning (and the sharing of tacit knowledge) need not be spatially constrained if relational proximity is present. Thus, large, multinational firms with 'distributed' knowledge bases and multiple sites of innovation may actively encourage the formation of communities of practice, supported by advanced means of electronically mediated communication, to overcome the friction of geographical separation. Thus, according to this approach, it is relational proximity, rather than geographical proximity per se, that supports the joint production and sharing of tacit knowledge between economic actors (Allen 2000).

Amin and Cohendet (2004) pursue this idea still further, in espousing the concept of relational proximity as the force that underlies successful learning dynamics between two or more actors. In their view, relational proximity can link together 'sites that might appear distant and unconnected on a linear plane', while also creating 'the possibility of no relational links between co-located sites' (p. 93). In other words, one should not assume that spatial proximity implies relational proximity, or that the latter requires the former. So long as other social affinities are sufficiently strong, these can compensate for the absence of spatial proximity and enable long-distance learning. Moreover, this kind of distanciated learning offers further advantages to the organization by allowing it to tap into spatially distributed competences more effectively. Amin and Cohendet describe relational proximity as relying on a host of things: cultural and experiential commonality; corporate organization and practices to enhance engagement, enrolment, and translation; advanced communication technologies supporting virtual interaction; and travel to support occasional face-to-face meetings when necessary.

The alternative view described above, incorporating both the global pipelines construct and the communities of practice approach, offers a compelling corrective to a number of problematic assumptions that have become widespread in recent years. In particular, it throws into question the assumption that innovative regions are self-reliant when it comes to the production of knowledge, or that spatial proximity necessarily guarantees successful joint learning and knowledge sharing, while spatial separation necessarily undermines this process.

Important as this contribution is, there may nevertheless be a risk of overstating the case (Morgan 2004). It would be clearly unhelpful to suggest that spatially distributed communities of practice are *always* effective substitutes for 'being there'. In other words, we need to achieve a more nuanced synthesis of the two broad approaches outlined above, in which the limits to the effectiveness of communities of practice as a mechanism for distanciated learning are better understood. In this sense, the question driving our analysis should be: under what circumstances is distanciated learning likely to be facilitated and more effective – or, alternatively, more difficult to achieve? What are the conditions that facilitate the long-distance circulation of knowledge, or its joint production by distanciated actors? If relational proximity depends on the presence of social affinities, what specific kinds of affinities facilitate learning (local or non-local)?

8.3 Social Affinities and Learning

We know from recent knowledge-based theories of innovation and learning dynamics that the potential for learning between two economic actors is greatest when two conditions apply: (*a*) they each know 'different things' – that is, their respective stocks of knowledge are sufficiently different that there is something to be gained from the sharing of knowledge between them, and (*b*) the two actors are similar enough in other respects to be able to understand one another and engage in a productive dialogue. Nooteboom's (2001) path-breaking work employs the concept of optimal cognitive distance to capture this idea (see also Maskell 2001*a* for a geographical application). Optimality in this sense is achieved when two parties know different things, but have sufficient affinity – and/or absorptive capacity (Cohen and Levinthal 1990; Drejer and Vinding 2007) – to communicate effectively with one another, thereby enabling knowledge sharing (mutual learning) and the joint production of new knowledge.

This insight leads quite naturally to another set of questions: what roles do communities of practice play in bridging the cognitive distance between their members? How much cognitive distance is too much for a community of practice to overcome? Finally, what are the fundamental sources or determinants of cognitive distance or proximity?

There is strong consensus that the transfer of specialized knowledge, particularly that which contains a strong tacit component, depends on shared cognitive frameworks between the parties involved. As Lam (2005: 125) puts it, 'its transfer requires social interaction and the development of shared understanding and common interpretative schemes'. This development is said to occur over time, through repeated, practice-based interaction (shared work experiences) amongst the members of a particular community. According to Lam, '[P]ractice provides a social activity in which shared perspectives and cognitive repertoires develop to facilitate knowledge sharing and transfer.' Using a metaphor from the world of information and communication technologies, Powell and Grodal (2005, p. 60) put it this way: 'Parties that develop a broader bandwidth for communication are, in turn, more capable of transferring complex knowledge.'

The preconditions and components of this shared cognitive and interpretative framework – this 'broader bandwidth' – are multilayered. Given that the basic building block in this process is the individual worker/ manager/researcher, it stands to reason that particular attributes of the individuals involved will have an important impact on their ability to understand one another as they engage in collective learning and innovation processes. At the most basic level, sharing the same spoken and/or written language is an obvious precondition for effective social learning based on mutual comprehension. This trait in itself may also be a proxy for other more basic commonalities such as similarity in national, ethnic, or cultural origin, although the widespread use of particular languages in multiple national and regional settings – for example, English, Spanish,

French, and German – suggests that one cannot map language onto cultural origin in any kind of simple, one-to-one manner.

Other individual traits that may underlie social affinity include a common educational background, common work experience, and common occupational identity. It is widely acknowledged that one's particular educational history shapes one's affinities with others in both general and more specific ways. At a general level, there is much truth to the widely shared observation that 'all engineers think alike', that 'MBAs see the world in a particular way', or that 'economists reduce the world to a set of price signals and incentives'. A large part of the educational process is the imparting of a vocabulary of terms and concepts, a portfolio of analytical frameworks and models, and a dominant mindset or world view that shapes the interpretive outlook of all those who graduate with a particular kind of degree. At a more specific level, one can differentiate between distinctive groups within these discipline-based populations, most obviously on the basis of the university or college at which one studied. Hence, a Chicago MBA might be significantly differentiated from a Harvard, Stanford, or Wharton MBA, on the basis of real or perceived differences in the nature of each programme. The upshot is that when two economic actors have a similar educational background, they are more likely to be productive interlocutors with one another. If they have studied at the same university, their affinity is likely to be even stronger. Finally, if they happen to have been classmates, the commonalities between them are likely to be stronger still.

Similarities in work experience represent another important dimension of potential social affinity. Setting aside for the time being the issue of specific employers (addressed below), there are other major attributes of work experience that shape one's outlook, mindset, and capabilities: for example, a history of working in the public (or private, or non-profit) sector, international versus domestic work experience, a background working within large, multinational (or small, entrepreneurial, start-up) organizations, and so on. Sharing similar kinds of work histories with other economic actors is likely to contribute to greater ease of mutual understanding and 'broader bandwidth' of communication.

Occupational identity is also well recognized as an important source of social affinity. To a large extent, the notion of 'occupation' can be understood as a combination of educational background plus work experience, so many of the above observations apply here as well. The phenomenon of occupation-based communities is exemplified by formal and informal organizations such as professional associations, expert groups, professional

user groups, and epistemic communities, which act as effective governance mechanisms to facilitate the circulation of specialized knowledge
(Powell and Grodal 2005). Hence, a shared occupational identity between
two actors is likely to constitute an important form of social affinity
supporting knowledge sharing and effective collaboration.

The extensive literature on innovation and learning in organizations
underscores that organizations themselves tend to develop characteristic
shared rules, practices, routines, models, and cognitive frameworks
(Nelson and Winter 1982). Together, these organizational practices, norms,
and routines have the potential to create a distinctive competitive advantage for the firm by enabling more effective social-learning dynamics
within the organization (Nonaka and Takeuchi 1995; Nonaka et al. 2000;
Lam 2005). These attributes – which may be recognized as part and parcel
of the more familiar concept of 'corporate culture' – come to be shared by
those who work in a given organization for any significant period of time,
regardless of their individual educational, experiential, or occupational
background. If such corporate cultures are strong enough to pervade the
overseas branches of the global firm, two people working for the same firm
in different countries may still enjoy a significant degree of social affinity
with one another, to the extent that they are able to work collaboratively
in the joint production and exchange of knowledge.

Another dimension shaping affinity between economic actors is the
industrial sector in which one currently works, or has worked in the
past. The literature on sectoral systems of innovation suggests that
the nature of the innovation process – the elements of the innovation
system, the relationships between them, the dominant knowledge bases,
the nature of industrial organization, and the influence of competitive
and regulatory dynamics – tend to vary systematically by industry (Pavitt
1984; Malerba 2005).

Here again, this dimension may operate independently of educational,
experiential, occupational, or organizational identities if there are particular forms of technological and market knowledge, competitive challenges,
and regulatory regimes that dominate within a given industry. Hence,
a shared background within the same industry can also provide the foundation for enhanced bandwidth and mutual understanding between
economic actors.

The degree to which two economic actors can establish effective
mutual understanding is also likely to depend on more than just linguistic, educational, experiential, occupational, organizational, or industrial
commonalities. The institutional context within which they are situated

has a major influence over the 'rules of the game', 'how things are done', motivations and expectations, and how learning is organized (Cooke and Morgan 1998; Whitley 1999; O'Sullivan 2000; Hall and Soskice 2001; Edquist 2005). What we might think of as institutional affinity consists of the shared norms, conventions, values, expectations, and routines that arise from commonly experienced frameworks of institutions existing within a national and regional setting (Gertler 2003, 2004). Consequently, when two actors share a common institutional identity, based on country/region of origin or extended periods of living and working within the same institutional system, this provides a crucially important source of social affinity that facilitates greater understanding between them.

The preceding discussion of individual, organizational, industrial, and institutional sources of social affinity provides a framework outlining the primary dimensions of 'relational proximity'. In the absence of these forms of social affinity, geographical proximity alone is likely to be an insufficient basis for supporting effective communication and mutual understanding between economic actors. That said, when relational proximity is strong, all else being equal, physical co-presence – 'being there' in a literal sense – still provides advantages for mutual understanding and knowledge sharing that are well established (Maskell and Malmberg 1999; Morgan 2004; Storper and Venables 2004). The geographical literature suggests that the advantages of being there are likely to be especially strong when the knowledge being produced and exchanged is highly specialized and resists codification – either because of its strongly tacit character or because it is highly novel and economically valuable. This leads us to consider more fully the nature of knowledge and its impact on the ease of communication between economic actors at a distance.

8.4 Knowledge Type and Distanciated Learning

For the past ten to fifteen years, innovation scholars have shown a keen interest in the different types of knowledge that figure into the innovation process, and the consequences of this for the geography of innovative activity. Following the work of Nelson and Winter (1982) and, more recently, Nonaka and Takeuchi (1995), the distinction between tacit and codified forms of knowledge has received much attention within the recent literature in economic geography and evolutionary economics (Cowan et al. 2000; Johnson et al. 2002; Gertler 2003). The prevailing view is that, because tacit knowledge is – by definition – more difficult to share in written, symbolic form, and because it is strongly context-specific, it tends to be more effectively transmitted through direct, face-to-face interaction. Consequently, those economic actors and firms for whom innovation depends heavily on tacit knowledge transmission and application will tend to cluster spatially with other entities involved with them in the innovation process (including customers, suppliers, and other partners). Conversely, when codified forms of knowledge are relatively more important, economic actors will be less compelled to agglomerate spatially, since the knowledge with which they are working is relatively easy to be understood intact at a distance.

Compelling as this distinction may appear, it has been criticized from a number of angles. First, as Nonaka and Takeuchi (1995), Nonaka et al. (2000), and Johnson et al. (2002) point out, the process of producing and using new knowledge involves a dynamic interplay between, and transformation of, tacit and codified forms of knowledge in virtually all sectors of the economy. The process of understanding knowledge that is shared in codified form requires the prior assimilation of tacitly held codes of communication and/or cognitive structures. In other words, these two forms of knowledge are complements, not substitutes, to one another.

Second, as noted earlier, there is a well-established consensus that knowledge bases tend to vary systematically by industry – and so too does the nature of the innovation process. It therefore stands to reason that the geography of knowledge flows and the possibilities for distanciated learning are also likely to vary systematically by sector. Recent analyses of this question, building on the work of Laestadius (1998), have found the distinction between analytical, synthetic, and symbolic knowledge bases to be helpful in this regard (Johnson et al. 2002; Coenen et al. 2004; Asheim and Gertler 2005; Asheim et al. 2007; Moodysson et al. 2008).

As summarized in Table 8.1, *analytical* knowledge predominates in those industries where new scientific knowledge is highly important, and where knowledge creation is normally based on formal deductive models, scientific laws, and the highly structured knowledge production and verification processes inherent in the scientific method. Primary examples of such industries are drug development and biotechnology. Here, the core activity generating new products and processes is systematically organized, formal research and development, both inside the individual firm and in collaboration with universities and other research organizations. Knowledge inputs and outputs in this type of knowledge base are more predominantly codified (or readily codifiable) in the form of scientific papers and patent descriptions. Acceptance of this kind of new knowledge is based on

213

Table 8.1: Knowledge bases: A typology

Analytical	Synthetic	Symbolic
Know why: developing new knowledge about natural systems by applying scientific laws	Know how: applying or combining existing knowledge in new ways	Know who: creating meaning, aesthetic qualities, affect; symbols, images
Scientific knowledge, models, deductive	Problem-solving, custom production, inductive	Creative process
Collaboration within and between formal research units	Interactive learning with customers, suppliers	Learning-by-doing, in studio, project teams
Strong codified knowledge content; highly abstract, universal	Partially codified knowledge; strong tacit component; more context-specific	Strong semiotic content; importance of interpretation implies very strong context specificity
Meaning relatively constant between places	Meaning varies substantially between places	Meaning highly variable between places
Drug development	Advanced machinery	Advertising

principles of peer review, replicability, and controlled trials. The new knowledge produced in such industries is more likely to lead to products or processes that constitute radical rather than incremental innovations.

Because of the highly formalized and abstract form of communication used to document the production of new analytical knowledge, and in light of the fact that the systems of codification with which such knowledge is expressed are universally shared and understood, at least by all those with the appropriate educational background (Kuhn 1970), the meaning inherent in analytical knowledge varies little by place. That is, it will be understood in much the same way, no matter where the producer and consumer of such knowledge happen to be located.

In contrast, a *synthetic* knowledge base dominates industrial settings where innovation takes place mainly through the application or novel combinations of existing knowledge. Innovation in such industries tends to be driven by the need to solve specific problems arising in the interaction with clients and suppliers. Classic industry examples come from sectors within advanced industrial engineering (such as the development of specialized machinery). In such sectors, research is less important than development. When it occurs, it tends to take the form of applied research, but the most prevalent form of innovative activity is incremental product or process development by firms with the objective of solving technological or production problems presented by customers. Knowledge tends to be created inductively rather than deductively, through a process of design, experimentation, trial-and-error, and testing. While the knowledge embodied in technical solutions is at least partially codified (e.g. in the form of operating manuals and blueprints), tacit knowledge tends to be very important, since shop floor or office experience, on-the-job training, and learning-by-doing, -using and -interacting are crucial to knowledge generation. Much of this knowledge resides in concrete know-how, craft, and practical skill.

Synthetic knowledge also tends to be much more context-specific, because it is created in response to specific demands by customers, and is tailored for use in settings that are strongly shaped by the surrounding cultural, institutional, and regulatory environment. A case in point might be advanced industrial machinery, which works most effectively when it is paired with a set of operators and managers possessing the appropriate skills, training, and norms with respect to practices such as maintenance and investment returns. Because of the context-specific nature of synthetic knowledge, it will be understood or interpreted in different ways in different places – particularly when those places are differentiated along cultural or institutional lines. In other words, its meaning could potentially vary substantially by location.

Finally, *symbolic* knowledge is distinguished by its strongly aesthetic, affective, and semiotic nature. According to Asheim et al. (2007), it is strongly present within a set of rapidly growing cultural industries such as film, television, publishing, music, fashion, and design, in which innovation 'is dedicated to the "creation" of new ideas and images and less to their physical production process' (p. 664). Hence, symbolic knowledge may be embedded within tangible goods such as furniture or electronic devices (in the form of a distinctive design), but its impact on the consumer – and its economic value – arises from its intangible (aesthetic, or 'sign value') character. It also comprises the primary form of knowledge in service industries such as advertising. As it is produced increasingly through short-term team projects, 'know-who' (knowledge of actual or potential team partners, or access to reputational knowledge about potential partners) is of considerable importance to the ultimate success of the creative project.

Symbolic knowledge is highly context-specific, since the interpretation of symbols, images, designs, stories, and cultural artefacts 'is strongly tied to a deep understanding of the habits and norms and "everyday culture" of specific social groupings' (Asheim et al. 2007, p. 664). Indeed, the symbolic knowledge embedded within industries such as advertising has been shown to be very highly shaped by its social and cultural context – witness the infamous accounts of how an advertisement that is highly effective in one cultural setting often meets with a very different reception when it is implemented in another market. For these reasons, we can conclude that the meaning associated with symbolic knowledge varies widely between places.

Of course, just as all innovation processes make use of both tacit and codified forms of knowledge, so too do many industries draw significantly upon analytical, synthetic, and symbolic forms of knowledge, though perhaps to varying degrees. A case in point is the medical devices and technologies sector, in which product development draws upon knowledge from a wide range of fields including bioscience, information and communication technology (ICT), software, advanced materials, nanotechnology, and mechanical engineering. It should also be pointed out that different forms of knowledge may become more prominent within the same industry over time, as it moves through different stages of the product life cycle. For example, Moodysson et al. (2008) demonstrate how the dominant type of knowledge changed over the life of specific innovation projects within the Swedish drug development and functional food industries, with analytical and synthetic forms of knowledge dominating at different phases of each innovation's evolution over time – a point to which I shall return subsequently.

8.5 Case Studies in Distanciated Learning

We now have a set of implicit hypotheses concerning the conditions under which communities of practice might best be able to achieve relational proximity in the absence of geographical proximity. The discussion in the previous two sections (Sections 8.3 and 8.4) of this chapter implies that distanciated learning – within communities of practice or otherwise – will be more difficult under certain circumstances than under others. In particular, it suggests that successful distanciated learning will be more difficult to achieve when the parties involved speak different languages; come from different educational, experiential, occupational, or industrial backgrounds; work for organizations with different prevailing practices, routines, and cultures; and come from different national business systems, innovation systems, or varieties of capitalism. Moreover, these challenges are likely to be further compounded when they are working primarily with synthetic or symbolic forms of knowledge.

How do these hypotheses stand up when subjected to empirical scrutiny? Table 8.2 summarizes the relevant characteristics from three recent

Table 8.2: Distanciated learning: Three cases compared

Key characteristics	Advanced manufacturing technology	Industrial software development	Drug development
Location of partners	Germany, Canada, USA	Germany, Canada	Sweden, USA
Linguistic affinity	Moderate	Moderate	Moderate
Occupational affinity	High	High	High
Organizational affinity	High to low	Low	Low
Industrial affinity	Moderate to high	High	High
Institutional affinity	Low	Low	Low
Dominant knowledge type	Synthetic	Analytical/synthetic	Analytical
Success in knowledge transfer	Low	Moderate	High

case studies in which distributed teams participating in joint problem-solving projects have attempted to engage in long-distance learning and knowledge translation. A review of the findings from these cases provides some preliminary support for this line of analysis.

The first case, extensively documented in Gertler (2004), involves a set of collaborative projects focused on the development and implementation of advanced manufacturing technologies for use in sectors such as automotive products, electronics, fabricated metal products, and plastic and rubber products. The partners in these collaborative communities of practice were a set of machinery producers in several different regions of Germany, and their industrial customers in Ontario, Canada and the Midwest, Northeast, and Southeast regions of the United States. Because of the highly specialized nature of these production technologies, they were custom-designed to suit the needs of individual customer firms, through a process that required considerable interaction and cooperation between technology producers and users over an extended period of time (measured in months and, in some cases, years). In some of the cases considered, the 'partners' involved were actually different branches of the same corporate entity, with one branch responsible for producing the capital goods used in the production of other downstream commodities. More commonly, however, the collaborating partners were employed by unrelated firms.

Because the German engineers responsible for machinery design and production were reasonably conversant in English, we can say that at least moderate linguistic affinity was achieved between them and their North American customers. As the participants from both sides tended to be trained in mechanical engineering, their occupational affinity was generally high. Organizational affinity was strong in those cases that involved different branches of the same firm, while in other cases, this form of affinity was weaker. Given the well-established institutional differences between Germany and the North American economies – manifested most vividly in their divergent systems of labour-market regulation, workplace organization, corporate governance, and finance – we can describe the degree of institutional affinity between innovation partners as low. Finally, it is clear that, with the focus on mechanical engineering, the dominant type of knowledge being jointly produced within these projects was synthetic in nature. The resulting degree to which this knowledge was successfully transferred across long distances was unequivocally low, with frequent operational problems, breakdowns, and conflicts between the technology users and producers.

In the second case, the goal of transatlantic collaboration was to develop jointly new software to enable technical-service staff to debug problems with electromechanical engineering products. The innovation partners comprising the community of practice in this case were software writers based in media research laboratories in Toronto, Canada and Stuttgart, Germany working collaboratively to produce a viable software solution for an industrial partner in Germany (Wolfe et al. 2001).

As with the first case, linguistic affinity was moderate and occupational affinity was high (since all the partners were trained in computer science and software development). Since they worked for different organizations within the same general sector, organizational affinity was low while industrial affinity was high. For the same reasons outlined above, the institutional affinity between the partners was low. A significant point of difference between this case and the previous one stems from the predominant forms of knowledge being produced and shared. The software component of the project was predominantly analytical in nature, based on the shared use of formally structured and universally recognized programming languages. However, since the goal was to produce software that would guide repair staff through the steps needed to solve operational problems or determine maintenance needs of the machinery in question, there was a strong synthetic component to the knowledge being jointly produced. In this case, the degree of success of knowledge-sharing between the German and Canadian members of the communities of practice was moderate. After engaging in extended exchange of personnel between the two laboratories, the team was eventually able to produce a software product that met the client's needs, though the timeline for completion of this project was considerably longer than originally planned.

Case number three involved a joint Swedish (Scania) and American (New Jersey) project to development a new antibody-based drug for HIV therapy (Moodysson et al. 2008). The community of practice that came together to work on this innovation was comprised of a leading university, a research institute, and a biotech company in Sweden, as well as a bio-medical firm in New Jersey that possessed distinctive capabilities which complemented those of its Swedish partners. Once again, linguistic affinity was moderately high, as all the Swedish scientists involved spoke English reasonably well. A common background in the biological sciences generated a high degree of occupational affinity. While the variety of employers involved meant that organizational affinity was low, a shared focus on biological research and drug development created a high degree of industrial affinity between the participants. Nevertheless, the institutional differences between Sweden and the USA are considerable, with the former resembling a northern European system reminiscent of the German model of capitalism.

As the collaboration was strongly based in biological science, the knowledge that was jointly produced within this international community of practice was primarily analytical in nature. In line with the prediction arising from our earlier analysis, the distributed participants in this collaborative project experienced little difficulty in jointly producing and sharing knowledge associated with this successful innovation, with the drug development process moving in orderly fashion to phase II clinical trials being conducted at a hospital in London (yet another partner). As the authors (Moodysson et al. 2008) of this case study conclude, 'it is important to specify the actual content of this global collaboration as being heavily based on analytical knowledge creation'. They further note that '[I]t is easier to transform important knowledge in easy-to-transmit codes and numbers that can be understood by other researchers that speak the same scientific language in other parts of the world. Geographical proximity is not much of an issue here'.

Looking across these three cases of distanciated learning for further insights, in all cases the occupational affinity amongst the participants was high. On the other hand, the institutional divide between the collaborating partners was substantial and imposed a significant potential barrier to effective knowledge-sharing. In those cases where the knowledge underpinning the innovation process contained a strong synthetic component, the geographical and institutional divides proved more difficult to overcome. In other words, low levels of institutional affinity appear to trump other shared social attributes. Alternatively, when analytical knowledge was the dominant form – as in the third case – other forms of social affinity prevailed, forming the basis for a successful distributed-learning process to unfold.

It is important to acknowledge that the process of achieving and maintaining relational proximity often rests on deliberate actions and investments of time and resources. Common strategies include the staging of creative brainstorming sessions – typically at an early stage in the project – in which all or most of the members of the community of practice are brought together in the same place for a short period of intense interaction (Wolfe et al. 2001; Gertler 2004; Coenen et al. 2006). This may be complemented by periodic team meetings and/or the longer-term exchange of personnel between different innovation sites, as a way of renewing or boosting relational proximity at later stages in the project. Meanwhile, in between actual face-to-face meetings, team members communicate on a day-to-day basis through ICT-mediated means such as email, teleconferencing, Voice-over Internet Protocol, or videoconferencing (Brown and Duguid 2000; Asheim et al. 2007).

This implies a kind of life cycle to spatially distributed communities of practice, in which they are typically launched through an early phase of intensive, face-to-face interaction, followed by the establishment of a well-defined division of labour between team members (or subgroups of team members). The sense of community is then sustained over time by periodic air travel and frequent electronic interaction. The division of labour established between team members and/or subgroups means that the work of the community of practice is geographically distributed, but with localized centres of innovative activity corresponding to the location of each team member/subgroup. In later stages in the life of the community of practice, much of the distanciated interaction between members is focused on coordination, rather than joint problem-solving (Coenen et al. 2006; Moodysson et al. 2008).

Setting this discussion within the broader context of knowledge practices implemented by multinational firms, recent research highlights a number of analogous strategies for promoting relational proximity between managers and professionals who work within globally distributed corporate networks (Ichijo et al. 1998; von Krogh et al. 2000; Faulconbridge 2006; Jones 2007). Included here are mobile 'knowledge enablers' who travel almost continuously between the global firm's far-flung branches, circulating knowledge of core practices and cultures. At the same time, regular global, national, and regional company meetings and conferences play a similar role by complementing small-group, day-to-day interaction with larger events. It has recently been suggested that trade fairs constitute a mechanism for both circulating established knowledge as well as enabling the formation of interactive relationships between potential members of learning communities, through the temporary but repeated opportunities for interaction that they support (Maskell et al. 2006).

Another key finding from the recent literature is that extended, close, face-to-face interaction at some point in the past – what might be called 'proto-proximate' relations – often forms the necessary foundations for successful distanciated knowledge-based relationships in the future (Coenen et al. 2006). This idea resonates with our earlier discussion of experiential affinity, and is also reinforced by recent findings (Agrawal et al. 2006), based on the geographical analysis of patent citations between inventors, which show that a past workplace association (working in the same organization at the same time) has a strong positive influence over subsequent citation patterns, even after one (or both) of the citing partners has moved to another location. As the authors of this study put it, 'once relationships are established, individuals can remain socially close even when they become geographically separated' (Agrawal et al. 2006, p. 589). This underscores the need to set one's analysis of the current effectiveness of learning communities within a longitudinal or evolutionary perspective.

8.6 Conclusions: Buzz Without Being There?

I began this chapter by noting that the conventional wisdom within economic geography – that 'proximity matters' – has been challenged recently by an alternative perspective emphasizing the possibilities for non-local learning and innovation dynamics. In this alternative vision, communities of practice have emerged as one of the primary mechanisms for enabling and facilitating distanciated learning. I then posed a question about the limits to this alternative argument. While there are undoubtedly particular circumstances in which spatially distributed communities of practice serve as an effective substitute for 'being there', will this always be the case? Under what conditions can we expect such distanciated learning processes to be successful – that is, to generate and circulate 'buzz without being there'?

The remainder of this chapter explored the limits to this idea, showing how the relational proximity on which successful distanciated learning rests is itself constituted by a set of specific social affinities at the individual, organizational, industrial, and institutional scales. Moreover, I argued that the possibilities for joint knowledge production and innovation at a distance are highly dependent on the type of knowledge that predominates in this process. This led us to a set of propositions about the circumstances under which effective distanciated learning would be easier or more difficult to achieve. A review and comparison of three case studies of distributed innovation within distanciated communities of practice lent at least preliminary credence to the conceptual framework outlined in this chapter. In particular, the analysis highlighted the impacts of institutional distance and knowledge type on innovation outcomes. As a result, we now have the basic elements of a framework for understanding the specific circumstances in which we could expect distributed communities of practice to be effective generators of 'buzz without being there'.

The resulting geographies of innovation and joint knowledge production turn out to be considerably more complex and contingent than first imagined. While spatial proximity continues to offer important advantages in fostering mutual understanding between interacting economic actors, spatially distributed innovation processes can function and flourish in the presence of strong-enough social affinities. Such geographical configurations also yield particular economic advantages by, for example, enabling firms to tap into a wider array of specialized expertise and experience than can be accessed in any single location. Moreover, it seems likely that the dominant mode of knowledge-based interaction will vary over the life of an innovation project, so that the members of a community of practice will find face-to-face encounters to be essential in certain phases of the project, but less important in others.

Finally, while the analysis offered in this chapter helps open up the black box of relational proximity, nevertheless it also confirms the ongoing significance of spatially proximate, face-to-face interaction. Although the latter should no longer be seen as the necessary and sufficient condition for achieving effective knowledge production and sharing between innovation partners, it is far from obsolete. Indeed, the rapidly growing literature on the evolving geography of the biotechnology industry underscores this point most vividly. After all, despite the strong predominance of analytical knowledge and the well-established practice of international collaboration between innovation actors, this industry continues to exhibit very high degrees of geographical concentration in a surprisingly small number of major centres (Asheim and Gertler 2005). In this world of globally connected local innovation nodes, 'being there' still provides its own rewards.

References

Agrawal, A., Cockburn, I., and McHale, J. (2006). 'Gone but not forgotten: Knowledge flows, labor mobility, and enduring social relationships', *Journal of Economic Geography*, 6: 571–91.

Allen, J. (2000), 'Power/economic knowledge: Symbolic and spatial formations', in J. R. Bryson, P. W. Daniels, N. Henry, and J. Pollard (eds.), *Knowledge, Space, Economy*. London: Routledge, pp. 15–33.

Amin, A. and Cohendet, P. (2004). *Architectures of Knowledge*. Oxford: Oxford University Press.

Asheim, B. T. and Gertler, M. S. (2005). 'The geography of innovation: Regional innovation systems', in J. Fagerberg, D. C. Mowery, and R. R. Nelson (eds.), *The Oxford Handbook of Innovation*. Oxford: Oxford University Press, pp. 291–317.

——Coenen, L., and Vang, J. (2007). 'Face-to-face, buzz, and knowledge bases: Sociospatial implications for learning, innovation, and innovation policy', *Environment and Planning C: Government and Policy*, 25: 655–70.

Bathelt, H., Malmberg, A., and Maskell, P. (2004). 'Clusters and knowledge: Local buzz, global pipelines and the process of knowledge creation', *Progress in Human Geography*, 28: 31–56.

Breschi, S. and Malerba, F. (2001). 'The geography of innovation and economic clustering: Some introductory notes', *Industrial and Corporate Change*, 10: 817–33.

Brown, J. S. and Duguid, P. (1996). 'Organisational learning and communities-of-practice: Towards a unified theory of working, learning and innovation', in M. Cohen and L. Sproul (eds.), *Organisational Learning*. New York: Sage, pp. 58–82.

————(2000). *The Social Life of Information*. Boston, MA: Harvard Business School Press.

Coenen, L., Moodysson, J., and Asheim, B. T. (2004). 'Nodes, networks and proximities: On the knowledge dynamics of the Medicon Valley biotech cluster', *European Planning Studies*, 12: 1003–18.

————Ryan, C., Asheim, B. T., and Phillips, P. (2006). 'Comparing a pharmaceutical and an agro-food bioregion: On the importance of knowledge bases for socio-spatial patterns of innovation', *Industry and Innovation*, 13: 393–414.

Cohen, W. M. and Levinthal, D. A. (1990). 'Absorptive capacity: A new perspective on learning and innovation', *Administrative Science Quarterly*, 35: 123–38.

Cooke, P. and Morgan, K. (1998). *The Associational Economy*. Oxford: Oxford University Press.

Cowan, R., David, P. A., and Foray, D. (2000). 'The explicit economics of knowledge codification and tacitness', *Industrial and Corporate Change*, 9: 211–53.

Drejer, I. and Vinding, A. L. (2007). 'Searching near and far: Determinants of innovative firms' propensity to collaborate across geographical distance', *Industry and Innovation*, 14: 259–75.

Edquist, C. (2005). 'Systems of innovation: Perspectives and challenges', in J. Fagerberg, D. C. Mowery, and R. R. Nelson (eds.), *The Oxford Handbook of Innovation*. Oxford: Oxford University Press, pp. 181–208.

Faulconbridge, J. R. (2006). 'Stretching tacit knowledge beyond a local fix? Global spaces of learning in advertising professional service firms', *Journal of Economic Geography*, 6: 517–40.

Gertler, M. S. (1995). ' "Being there": proximity, organization, and culture in the development and adoption of advanced manufacturing technologies', *Economic Geography*, 71: 1–26.

——(2003). 'The undefinable tacitness of being (there): Tacit knowledge and the economic geography of context', *Journal of Economic Geography*, 3: 75–99.

——(2004). *Manufacturing Culture: The Institutional Geography of Industrial Practice*. Oxford: Oxford University Press.

——and Levitte, Y. M. (2005). 'Local nodes in global networks: The geography of knowledge flows in biotechnology innovation', *Industry and Innovation*, 12: 487–507.

Hall, P. A. and Soskice, D. (eds.) (2001). *Varieties of Capitalism*. Oxford: Oxford University Press.

Ichijo, K., von Krogh, G., and Nonaka, I. (1998). 'Knowledge enablers', in G. von Krogh, J. Roos, and D. Kleine (eds.), *Knowing in Firms*. London: Sage, pp. 173–203.

Johnson, B., Lorenz, E., and Lundvall, B-Å. (2002). 'Why all this fuss about codified and tacit knowledge?', *Industrial and Corporate Change*, 11: 245–62.

Jones, A. (2007). 'More than "managing across borders?" The complex role of face-to-face interaction in globalizing law firms', *Journal of Economic Geography*, 7: 223–46.

Kuhn, T. S. (1970). *The Structure of Scientific Revolutions*. Chicago, IL: University of Chicago Press.

Laestadius, S. (1998). 'Technology level, knowledge formation and industrial competence in paper manufacturing', in G. Eliasson, C. Green, and C. R. McCann (eds.), *Microfoundations of Economic Growth: A Schumpeterian Perspective*. Ann Arbor, MI: University of Michigan Press, pp. 212–26.

Lam, A. (2005). 'Organizational innovation', in J. Fagerberg, D. C. Mowery, and R. R. Nelson (eds.), *The Oxford Handbook of Innovation*. Oxford: Oxford University Press, pp. 115–47.

Lave, J. and Wenger, E. (1991). *Situated Learning: Legitimate Peripheral Participation*. Cambridge: Cambridge University Press.

Lundvall, B-Å. (1988). 'Innovation as an interactive process: From user-producer interaction to the national system of innovation', in G. Dosi, C. Freeman, G. Silverberg, and L. Soete (eds.), *Technical Change and Economic Theory*. London: Pinter, pp. 349–69.

Malerba, F. (2005). 'Sectoral systems: How and why innovation differs across sectors', in J. Fagerberg, D. Mowery, and R. Nelson (eds.), *The Oxford Handbook of Innovation*. Oxford: Oxford University Press, pp. 380–406.

Malmberg, A. and Maskell, P. (2002). 'The elusive concept of localization economies: Towards a knowledge-based theory of spatial clustering', *Environment & Planning A*, 34: 429–49.

Maskell, P. (2001*a*). 'Knowledge creation and diffusion in geographic clusters', *International Journal of Innovation Management*, 5: 213–37.

—— (2001*b*). 'Towards a knowledge-based theory of the geographic cluster', *Industrial and Corporate Change*, 10: 921–43.

—— and Malmberg, A. (1999). 'Localised learning and industrial competitiveness', *Cambridge Journal of Economics*, 23: 167–86.

—— Bathelt, H., and Malmberg, A. (2006). 'Building global knowledge pipelines: The role of temporary clusters', *European Planning Studies*, 14: 997–1013.

Moodysson, J., Coenen, L., and Asheim, B. T. (2008). 'Explaining spatial patterns of innovation: Analytical and synthetic modes of knowledge creation in the Medicon Valley life science cluster', *Environment and Planning A*, 40 (forthcoming).

Morgan, K. (2004). 'The exaggerated death of geography: Learning, proximity and territorial innovation systems', *Journal of Economic Geography*, 4: 3–21.

Nelson, R. R. and Winter, S. G. (1982). *An Evolutionary Theory of Economic Change*. Cambridge, MA: Harvard University Press.

Nonaka, I. and Takeuchi, H. (1995). *The Knowledge Creating Company*. Oxford: Oxford University Press.

—— Toyama, R., and Nagata, A. (2000). 'A firm as a knowledge-creating entity: A new perspective on the theory of the firm', *Industrial and Corporate Change*, 9: 1–20.

Nooteboom, B. (2001). *Learning and Innovation in Organizations and Economies*. Oxford: Oxford University Press.

O'Sullivan, M. A. (2000). *Contests for Corporate Control: Corporate Governance and Economic Performance in the United States and Germany*. Oxford: Oxford University Press.

Owen-Smith, J. and Powell, W. W. (2004). 'Knowledge networks as channels and conduits: The effects of spillovers in the Boston biotechnology community', *Organization Science*, 15: 5–21.

Pavitt, K. (1984). 'Sectoral patterns of technical change: Towards a taxonomy and a theory', *Research Policy*, 13: 343–73.

Porter, M. E. (2000). 'Locations, clusters, and company strategy', in G. L. Clark, M. P. Feldman, and M. S. Gertler (eds.), *The Oxford Handbook of Economic Geography*. Oxford: Oxford University Press, 253–74.

Powell, W. W. and Grodal, S. (2005). 'Networks of innovators', in J. Fagerberg, D. C. Mowery, and R. R. Nelson (eds.), *The Oxford Handbook of Innovation*. Oxford: Oxford University Press, pp. 56–85.

Storper, M. and Leamer, E. E. (2001). 'The economic geography of the Internet age', *Journal of International Business Studies*, 32: 641–65.

—— and Venables, A. J. (2004). 'Buzz: Face-to-face contact and the urban economy', *Journal of Economic Geography*, 4: 351–70.

Sturgeon, T. J. (2003). 'What really goes on in Silicon Valley? Spatial clustering and dispersal in modular production networks', *Journal of Economic Geography*, 3: 199–225.

von Krogh, G., Ichijo, K., and Nonaka, I. (2000). *Enabling Knowledge Creation*. Oxford: Oxford University Press.

Wenger, E. (1998). *Communities of Practice: Learning, Meaning and Identity*. Cambridge: Cambridge University Press.

Whitley, R. (1999). *Divergent Capitalisms: The Social Structuring and Change of Business Systems*. Oxford: Oxford University Press.

Wolfe, D. A., Moore, G., Mills, L., and Gertler, M. S. (2001). 'The role of institutions in shaping innovation – CoMedia: A case study', report to International Science and Technology Agreements, Ontario Ministry of Energy, Science and Technology, Toronto, June.

Note

1. The author gratefully acknowledges the valuable comments received on an earlier version of this chapter when it was first presented at the DIME conference at the University of Durham, 27–8 October 2006. He would especially like to thank the editors of this volume for their guidance, support, and intellectual stimulation during the writing of this chapter. The research from which it draws much of its inspiration has been generously funded by the Social Sciences and Humanities Research Council of Canada, as well as the Goldring Chair in Canadian Studies at the University of Toronto. This chapter has also benefited greatly from the author's past opportunities for face-to-face interaction with David Wolfe, Harald Bathelt, and other members of our PROGRIS research group at the Munk Centre for International Studies, University of Toronto, Björn Asheim and his colleagues at CIRCLE, University of Lund, Phil Cooke and Kevin Morgan at Cardiff University, Anders Malmberg and colleagues at CIND, Uppsala University, and Peter Maskell at the Copenhagen Business School.

9

Knowledge-Intensive Firms, Communities, and Creative Cities[1]

Patrick Cohendet and Laurent Simon

9.1 Introduction

A major trend in research on the economics of innovation is the recognition of the metropolis/city as a locus of knowledge creation and integration (Krugman 1991; Lucas 1993). This trend has included introduction of the idea of the 'creative city' to mainstream thinking (Florida 2002), an idea that has generated considerable interest among urban policy-makers and cultural activists, and an equivalent level of criticism from the academic community (Scott 2005).

This chapter departs from a generic and uncritical understanding of the so-called creative city, to propose an empirically grounded theoretical reflection on the 'creativity' of the city and its dependencies with creative or knowledge-intensive firms (hereinafter, 'KI firms'). Using Montreal as an example of a creative city that offers a unique range of important KI firms – such as Ubisoft in the videogame industry (Cohendet and Simon 2007), Le Cirque du Soleil in entertainment activities, or Cossette and Sid Lee in advertising – our aim is to contribute to a more robust theorization of the role of KI firms in creative cities. Our approach is based on a critical analysis of studies of the creativeness of the city (Stolarick et al. 2005; Stolarick and Florida 2006), and on empirical fieldwork in some Montreal-based KI firms inspired by traditional approaches of organizational ethnography.

A remarkable characteristic of KI firms such as Le Cirque du Soleil or Ubisoft is that they do not have large research and development (R&D) departments or worldwide subsidiaries to tap into for external creative ideas, nor do they access creative knowledge through their participation in global networks of diverse partners. Furthermore, these KI firms do not develop the kind of internal organization with a virtuous knowledge spiral (SECI model) as advanced by Nonaka and Takeuchi (1995). None of these classical ways to enhance creativity is present in these KI firms. Our view is that the creativity of these firms relies in the existence and interactions of a myriad of *communities*[2] which are the active units of the many creative projects of the KI firms, but which find their inspiration and creativity in the *fertile soil* of the creative city itself.

Our main argument is that KI firms in creative cities tend to adopt a very specific mode of organization: they concentrate internally on the govern-ance of multi-project activities, which contribute, thanks to the creative role of communities of knowing, to the generation, exploitation, and development of '*creative slack*' as a source of growth for the firm. At the same time, they tend to place their indirect capabilities, and in particular their absorptive capabilities, in the soil of a creative city. Thus, it is as though these KI firms, while concentrating internally on the formation and exploitation of creative slack as their key internal core competence, delegate the building of creative capabilities of the communities to the local milieu of the city, in particular, the development of *absorptive capabilities*.

In short, we argue that creative cities tend to favour a specific 'ecology of knowledge' where some major KI firms tend to emerge and grow through a specific form of co-evolution with the city: the city nurtures the KI firm with flows of specialized knowledge and creativity, and in turn, the main KI firms nourish the creative soil of the city through a flagship or anchor role (Agrawal and Cockburn 2003). This chapter, thus, aims to highlight the co-evolution between KI firms and the creative city, and to demonstrate that different types of communities mediate this co-evolution.

9.2 The Knowledge-Intensive Firm: The Delicate Balance Between Formal and Informal Architectures of Knowledge

Following Boland and Tenkasi (1995, p. 351), we can view KI firms as organizations composed of multiple communities with highly specialized technologies, expertise, and knowledge domains:

Organizations are characterized by a process of distributed cognition in which multiple communities of specialized knowledge workers, each dealing with a part of an overall organizational problem, interact to create the patterns of sense making and behaviour displayed by the organization as a whole. Organizations are necessarily characterized by distributed cognition because their critically important processes and the diversity of environments and technologies to be dealt with are 'too complex for one person to understand in its entirety'... Communities develop unique social and cognitive repertoires which guide their interpretation of the world. (Brehmer 1991, p. 4; Nersessian 1992)

We consider that the main reason explaining the growing role of communities within KI firms is that when facing a rapidly changing environment, these firms are confronted with a major constraint: coping with the fixed (sunk) costs associated with building specialized knowledge. The ability, in a given firm, to integrate an ever-diverse number of specialized bodies of knowledge is not infinite: firstly, because ever-growing absorptive capabilities (which are far from being a free good) are required for understanding external knowledge; secondly, because the ability to design cognitive platforms of integration is required to shape the external knowledge into a form suitable for further exploitation by the firm; and thirdly, because in this system the firm is compelled to specialize even further in its domain of specialized knowledge. This requires the building of an infrastructure of knowledge (models, grammar, codes, etc.) that generates ever-increasing sunk costs.

These conditions explain why as the knowledge-based economy expands, communities play an increasing role, since they can assume a significant part of the 'sunk costs' associated with the process of generation or accumulation of specialized parcels of knowledge (e.g. see Cowan and Foray 1997). These costs correspond for instance, to the progressive construction of languages and models of action and interpretation that are required for the implementation of new knowledge, and that cannot be covered through the classical signals of hierarchies (or markets). This setting is likely to compensate for some organizational limitations (learning failures) that firms face when confronted with the need to continuously innovate and produce new knowledge.

Our vision is that the creation of new knowledge within a KI firm is the result of a delicate balance between the new ideas that emerge from formal units (such as a research laboratory, or an artistic department in charge of the conception of new projects) and the new knowledge produced within the different communities. We will in particular emphasize that through the dynamic interaction between communities, new configurations of knowledge may emerge by creating new meanings or new linguistic routines. The creation of new knowledge in an organization is often the result of an open-system transformation of that organization's communities of knowing, as they question and revise routines and create new processes and relationships between themselves. Producing knowledge to create innovative products and processes in such firms requires the ability to voice strong opinions within a community, as well as the ability to take the perspective of another into account.

However, if communities can absorb the sunk costs associated with the building of specialized domains of knowledge, there is still the need to integrate the diverse bodies of specialized knowledge in an efficient manner, in an organized and formal structure. This is precisely where the critical role of the hierarchy of the firm comes into play: to organize efficient formal platforms of knowledge (the hard architecture) within the firm in order to facilitate the interaction between knowing communities.

Thus KI firms tend to combine a 'hard architecture of knowledge' in the form of administrative functional units and hierarchical structures with a 'soft architecture of knowledge' that delegates to communities the role of creating, nurturing, and enhancing the bodies of specialized knowledge that are needed for their creative business. In an intense-knowledge context, the organization of firms tends towards a specific structure that articulates on the one side a hierarchical formal part in charge of the strategy, the definition of competences, the contractual activities, and the formal organization of a multi-project activity, and on the other side an informal part composed of diverse knowing communities in charge of the production, accumulation, and circulation of competitive knowledge.

From this perspective, an important question relates to the types of competence the firm should keep internally, and those it should place in the external environment, as suggested by Loasby (1991) who distinguishes between the firm's internal and external organization by differentiating between 'knowledge how' (knowing how to do things for yourself) and 'knowledge that' (knowing how to get things done for you). The firm can thus maintain its direct capabilities internally and place its indirect capabilities in its external environment (Loasby 1998, p. 9). Some firms may try to keep most of their competences and communities within the internal boundaries and delegate to the external environment basic supplier needs, while others may extensively rely on external competences and communities dispersed across a global network.

As illustrated by Figure 9.1, our view is that KI firms in creative cities tend to adopt a very specific mode of organization: they concentrate internally on the governance of multi-project activities which contribute to the generation, exploitation, and development of 'creative slack' as a source of growth for the firm, while placing their indirect capabilities, and in particular their absorptive capabilities captured by the knowing communities, in the soil of a creative city.

9.3 Knowledge-Intensive Firms: Projects and the Role of Communities

When considering KI firms such as Ubisoft, Le Cirque du Soleil, or Cossette Communication, the following common organizational characteristics can be found. Firstly, they do not have large R&D departments. Secondly, when looking at their organizational structure, one finds traces of functional traditional departments such as accounting personnel, financial staff, human resource employees, and diverse administrative units. However, trying to understand the creative potential of these KI firms from an analysis of these functional departments would be misleading. The functional departments primarily act as administrative support to the organization of projects which are the main element of the 'hard architecture of knowledge' (the formal architecture of knowledge which is shaped and controlled by the hierarchy) in these companies. The KI firms usually conduct several projects simultaneously (shows, series of videogames, advertising projects), and therefore correspond to the type of 'project-based firms' identified in the literature (De Fillippi and Arthur 1998; Gann and Salter 2000; see also Scarbrough and Swan in this book). Even if most of these projects are driven by a creative tension (mutual prescriptions) between technological developers and creators of content, they are multidisciplinary in essence and involve the integration of diverse sets of knowledge, skills, and expertise from very different fields.

What is remarkable is that the sources of creativity in these KI firms are hardly visible on an organizational flow chart. From our observations, the creativity of these KI firms relies on the existence and interactions of diverse informal *communities*. More precisely, the main element of the 'soft (or informal) architecture of knowledge' and the source of creativity relies on the functioning of communities, on what we refer to as *communities of 'specialists'* (script writers, game designers, graphic artists, sound designers, software programmers, etc.). They are *communities of specialists* because each of them is composed of members with the same background, working on the same type of assignments, who share on a daily basisz

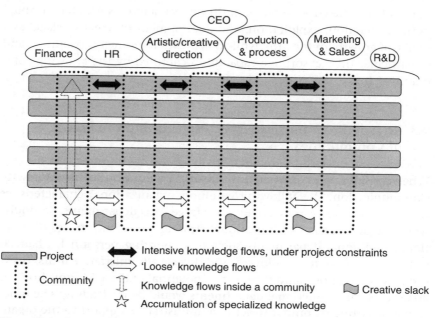

Figure 9.1: Creative knowledge-intensive project-based firm: A model.

information, knowledge, and insights about their work in and outside the formal framework of projects. However, the very reason why we refer to *communities* instead of well-defined *professions* or *jobs* as in traditional industries is because these groups of people, essentially composed of young professionals, are bound by emerging and weakly formalized bodies of knowledge.

Most of the diverse knowing communities are focused both on the production and accumulation of knowledge in the domain of their specialized practice. At one level, communities of specialists broadly fit the definition of *communities of practice* as their members use the same technical 'jargon', share practical knowledge, and exchange the tricks of their trade based on trial-and-error experiences to increase their competence in a given field of knowledge (thus focusing on *exploitation* activities). At another level, they clearly also have an epistemic dimension, which means that they are focused on the production of new knowledge (*exploration* activities). As Cowan et al. (2000) have shown, epistemic communities constantly refer to a *procedural authority*. For instance, these communities may gather around the appreciation of one 'genre' of games or one 'style' of graphic design. In these formats, communities would fit the definition of *epistemic communities*.

As a result, most of the communities of specialists in the KI firms engage in both the exploration and exploitation of knowledge. The balance varies from one community to the other; for instance, the community of game designers probably puts the most weight on exploration. However, the coexistence of many diverse communities having both exploration and exploitation dimensions is one of the distinctive characteristics of cultural industries and explains why these types of organization finally succeed in matching creativity and efficiency.

In order to better understand the formation of creativity we must explore the various channels through which communities establish permanent informal interactions with the outside world in order to confront ideas, tap creative practices from other domains of knowledge, and engage with communities of consumers to check the relevance of their creative endeavours. This reveals a complex maze of creativity, with intense connections across global space mainly through virtual exchanges of knowledge (see Gertler, Chapter 8 in this book) as well as those with deep roots in the local milieu, which plays the role of a large and complex forum, home of myriads of knowing communities which promote creativity in very diverse activities and modes.

However, what is distinctive about KI firms, compared to traditional industries, is that members of a given *community of specialists* – even when they are assigned to a specific project – remain connected to their community on a daily basis. They continue to exchange and interact with the other members of the community and enrich the knowledge of their community by bringing the experience gained during the project they are assigned to. Such a situation offers three distinctive advantages: providing a structure for interactions between communities, helping to couple or decouple creative and routine work, and reinforcing the common culture of the company. In this dynamic process, individuals clearly cope with a dual identity, as members of a given project and as members of a given community. We address these advantages in turn below.

Firstly, dual identity favours direct interactions between communities. Members of a community who have participated in a project progressively build cognitive links with colleagues of other communities, and tend to bring the knowledge gained to their community through their daily interactions. Step by step, the cultural and cognitive distance (Nooteboom 1999) between the different communities of specialists is reduced and leads to a reasonable level of mutual understanding, increasing the potential for innovation and creativity. Too great a distance between communities within a firm will not lead to innovative solutions, while if the cognitive distance between communities is too small, the innovative potential of the firm will fade away.

As an example, in a videogame project, game designer A, quite naively, asked a programmer to develop an animated piece of rope as an element of decor in a medieval setting for the next day. The programmer bluntly refused, and entered into open conflict with the now-disconcerted game designer. As the argument unfolded, the conflict escalated to the programmer's manager and the lead game-designer. A technical discussion followed, during which the manager explained that programming a rope is not a simple task, that it involved sophisticated calculus of flexibility and elasticity, and that this object was not absolutely required unless it played an important role in the gameplay. The game designer backed off, and acknowledged that he had learnt something and finally apologized to the programmer. Cognitive distance was reduced and would allow for smoother collaboration in the future. A few months later, the lead game-designer formally requested that programmers developing subprograms of animated ropes should be included in future designs and used as an element to stimulate the creation of new gameplays.

While dual identity favours a reduction of cognitive distance between distant communities, it may in turn have a beneficial effect within a given community by introducing a continuous flow of new ideas from members scattered in dozens of projects running in parallel. Thus, the cognitive distance within members of a given community can be maintained at a level which prevents both too much uniformity and lack of creativity.

Our view is that in the long run, this mutual understanding between communities may drastically modify the way of managing projects in KI firms, in particular in building modularity. In theory, modules (communities) are not supposed to interact directly. Their interactions are mediated by the cognitive platform designed by the hierarchy. However, in the case where mutual understanding between communities becomes very high, we can envisage governance by the community alone, with hierarchy needed only to 'authorize' or 'enact' the organizational forms produced by the interacting autonomous communities. In particular, the cognitive platform itself can become an emerging by-product of the constant interactions between communities. The organization could come to operate largely in a self-organized manner. In such a mode of 'management by enactment', the unceasing efflorescence of communities would allow the organization to innovate constantly (Ciborra 1996).

Secondly, dual identity helps to solve the *distance paradox*. As underlined by De Fillippi et al. (2004) organizations attempting to solve the dilemma between creativity and efficiency may physically separate creative units from more units of routine work. 'Such de-coupling presumably favours lateral thinking "outside the box" that is free from the practices and conventions of the routine work of the organizations' (Bilton and Leary 2002, p. 52). However, the implementation of such a solution introduces a major risk of dissonance when creative inputs and creative work practices have to be introduced into the rest of the organization. The *de facto* 'dual identity' of project employees in KI firms helps to eliminate this risk and bypasses the need for decoupling/re-coupling the organizations, by providing a specific mode that guarantees a permanent connection between the routine work required in the management of projects and the creative work within communities.

One of the advantages of this permanent connection is that it provides opportunities for feedback between the micro-creativity that emerges from the daily activities of the project, and the macro-creativity that is the expected output of the creative communities. The creativity of a project should not be confined to the macro-creativity set up at the beginning of the project by the project managers. A creative project should be able to incorporate new ideas and innovative suggestions and all the micro-creative inputs that emerge from the day-to-day activities during a project. This micro-creativity compensates for one of the main drawbacks of the hierarchical conduct of any project: if the hierarchy exercises strict control over the timing of a project, it can exclude significant feedbacks, and thus also stifle creativity by restricting the micro-inputs of creativity. Dual identity mitigates this risk, by allowing permanent interactions between micro- and macro-creativity. In practice, this permanent interaction can lead to two main outcomes. Firstly, it may allow a micro-creative idea that has emerged during a project to circulate between communities through regular exchanges, be improved and validated through these exchanges, and be adopted by the project. Secondly, micro-creative ideas that emerge during a project may be absorbed into the active memory of some communities of specialists, as a form of creative slack that could be used in other projects.

9.4 Knowledge-Intensive Firms: The 'Creative Slack'

The notion of *creative slack* deliberately echoes the notion of *organizational slack* as originally proposed by Penrose (1995 [1959]), who suggested that organizations always have some stock of unused, or underused, resources (knowledge, relationships, reputation, managerial talent, physical assets, etc.) that inevitably accumulate in the course of developing, producing, and marketing any given product or service. In her view, these unexploited or underexploited productive resources are primary factors determining both the extent and direction of the firm's growth; the dominant motivation of firms, limited only by its administrative capacity.

Our view is that in KI firms organizational slack is essentially a creative force, one that acts as an important reservoir of opportunities to generate innovative knowledge, and therefore also the growth of the organization. In line with Penrose's vision, our thesis is that the firm that has accumulated creative slack is better prepared than any other organization to derive benefit from the creative potential of the slack. Creative slack is shaped by the culture of the firm and is essentially understandable through the language of the organization. Because of such idiosyncrasies, it may be much cheaper to valorize slack *within* a firm than through other firms and organizations (including through any isolated community), even though some may argue that the creative slack acts as a *cushion of redundancy* that is costly to maintain.

We consider that the specific conditions necessary for the formation of creative slack in KI firms – relying on the functioning of autonomous communities that produce and conserve knowledge in their domain of specialization – is a guarantee of the efficiency of maintaining creative slack at low cost. The significant point is that the slack is diffused across the diverse communities of specialists in the firm that have memorized (thanks to the knowledge accumulated by their members) aspects of learning gained during projects. Although it is well known that organizations have extreme difficulties in memorizing what has been learnt during a project, the interest of communities with regards to this issue is that they rather easily memorize the routines practiced by their members. As Cohendet and Llerena (2003, p. 273) suggested, 'a routine that has naturally emerged within a community of economic agents sharing strong common social norms will probably have a much stronger power of replication than a routine which results from the functioning of a temporary team project constituted from heterogeneous agents who never met before'.

Thus creative slack has an ambivalent characteristic: it provides a specific advantage for the firm which is the only entity able to take benefit from it, yet at the same time it is held, nurtured, and maintained at low cost by diverse communities, sometimes even without an explicit awareness of the managers. This raises the key question of the source of the creativity of communities of specialists. Our view is that in certain locations where large numbers of KI firms are clustered, the creativity of communities in KI firms is rooted in the soil of the creative city itself. It is as if the KI firms, while concentrating internally on the formation and exploitation of creative slack as their key core competence, have delegated the building of creative capabilities of the communities to the local milieu of the city, in particular, the development of *absorptive capabilities*.

If creative communities in firms are seen as elementary units of specialized knowledge, they might be seen as providing a new asset for the firm, that is, an addition to the firms' absorptive capabilities. Knowing communities are never bound within the limits of organizations. They permanently interact in their specialized domain of knowledge with the outside world, collecting new ideas and benchmarking the best conditions of practice. They nurture the organization by continuously bringing new pieces of specialized knowledge which have just been tested and validated in the outside world. The different communities in the organization could thus been seen as a set of diverse sources of absorptive capabilities that potentially allow firms to benefit from a diversity of knowledge. As Cohen and Levinthal (1990, p. 131) argue:

[D]iversity of knowledge plays an important role: in a setting in which there is uncertainty about the knowledge domains from which potentially useful innovation may emerge, a diverse background provides a more robust basis for learning because it increases the prospect that incoming information will relate to what is already known. In addition to strengthening assimilative power, knowledge diversity also facilitates the innovative process by enabling the individual to make novel associations and linkages.

The contribution of the urban milieu in the formation, enhancement, and development of absorptive capabilities activated by the communities is discussed in Section 9.5. Before doing so, we would stress that not all absorptive capabilities are 'externalized' to the creative city. The KI firm certainly develops and retains some absorptive capabilities, in particular in its professional domain. We would also acknowledge that each project of the KI firm acts as a source of knowledge creation and literally feeds the members of every community involved in the project, indirectly increasing the creative potential of all communities and of the firm itself. However, based on our observations of KI firms in Montreal, we believe that the essential driver of creativity is anchored in the soil of the creative city which provides places and events for the fertile intertwining between creative communities.

9.5 The Creative City: A Fertile Ground for Developing Absorptive Capabilities

As we have seen, KI firms rely on the functioning of 'communities of specialists'. In each community, members communicate regularly with each other about their practice through informal cognitive spaces with more or less open boundaries, where people meet and trade knowledge in a not-so-organized fashion. These work spaces are not fully monitored through the formal corporate process. They are not necessarily aligned with corporate goals and strategy. They are also somewhat disconnected from the daily pressure of producing an efficient output designed for a specific market. These informal socio-cognitive spaces allow people to meet, wander, confront ideas, build daring assumptions, and validate new creative forms.

Tracing the sources of creativity starts with the knowledge platforms on which the members of each respective community of specialists interact. Exploring each of these platforms will then lead us to discover their connections to other informal creative places of knowledge exchange in which these communities of specialists find the sources of their inspiration. Members of the communities of specialists of KI firms constantly communicate with similar specialists in the outside world, through global virtual platforms, sometimes even with members of competing firms who share the same interest for a given practice. They also directly interact through informal routes with communities of users. Moreover, they have deep local roots in the 'creative city'. To better understand the role played by the city as a source of creativity for a myriad local communities, we start by describing the particular case of Montreal.

9.5.1 *Montreal as a creative city*

The socio-political and economic development of Quebec society in the 1950s and 1960s, a period known as the 'Quiet Revolution' (*La Révolution Tranquille*), allowed Montreal to play an active role as the culturally, socially, and economically innovative city in Canada. Two defining international events helped to showcase Montreal as a different, innovative, and creative city – Expo '67 and the 1976 Olympic Games. The city and its people developed a culture of large projects requiring a shared vision and popular involvement. The urge to innovate and create became part of the culture of the city and creativity became one defining element of the local and international image of Montreal.

Stolarick et al.'s (2005) and Stolarick and Florida's (2006) recent study of Montreal highlights certain attributes that might be considered as supports of the city's capacity for 'creative connectivity': Montreal is well positioned geographically, is bilingual and multicultural, with a historically grounded 'creative spirit'; knowledge industries are well represented and diverse, with research activities well connected to four international universities; and the city has developed a specific connection between the arts, culture, and technology.

Montreal has developed a certain 'cultural hybridity' that nourishes openness and tolerance within its population as well as the creative spirit of the city (Simon 2002). The population is ethnically diverse and well educated thanks to a highly subsidized/affordable education system, with four major universities. The size of the city, its socio-political history, and its specific status in North America seem to induce a specific cultural intensity, a taste for experimentation, and a strong entrepreneurial drive. From the point of view of cultural production, for instance: 'The fact that a majority of Montreal's population speaks French and English, and that the local market for culture is relatively small, compels the cultural community to continuously create, renew itself, and export its products' (Stolarick et al. 2005, p. 8). The result is that 'the region is also the most diverse in Canada in terms of industries', which is 'an important factor in generating innovation' (p. 12). These specific economic and creative conditions, associated with cheap housing and a good quality of life, attract members of the 'creative class' and specifically members of the 'super creative core'. Stolarick et al. (2005) emphasize the specific 'connections' that the city offers (summarized in Table 9.1).

The evidence compiled by Stolarick et al. and their analysis provide an interesting account of the potential of the city to foster creative endeavour. Critics of this analysis might stress that they fail to acknowledge Montreal's mixed economic results, lagging behind Toronto, Vancouver, or even Calgary. They might also emphasize that 'a potential for connectivity' does not directly convert into economic performance or social development. We acknowledge the need to investigate these issues further

Table 9.1: 'Connections' offered by the city of Montreal

Techno-cultural context: *Art–Culture* ← → *Technology*	• Techno-creative firms (Le Cirque du Soleil, videogames, Mega Brands, etc.) • Techno-creative climate • Festivals • 'Laboratories' for techno-creative creation
Language: *French* ← → *English*	• 53% of Montreal's population speaks both languages • 18% with another 'mother tongue' also speak French or English, or both
Geography: *Montreal* ← → *USA and Europe*	• 'Montreal is closer to Europe than any other major North-American city' • 'Montreal has a culture that is both European and American' • 'Montreal is not simply bilingual – it is bicultural, even multicultural'

Source: Compiled from Stolarick et al. (2005, pp. 12–14).

and to balance the rather optimistic views of Stolarick et al. Yet, in what follows, we consider the 'creative city' approach from a different angle to develop a better understanding of the inner functioning of knowledge flows and sources of creativity.

Our argument is the following: the interplay of multiple creative communities happens through a conjunction of interrelated elements that allow for the development of an absorptive capacity at the city level. As Cohen and Levinthal (1990, p. 131) emphasize:

[A]bsorptive capabilities refer not only to the acquisition or assimilation of information by the organization, but also on the organization's ability to exploit it. Therefore, an organization's absorptive capacity does not simply depend on the organization's direct interface with the external environment. It also depends on transfers of knowledge across and within subunits that may be quite removed from the original point of entry. To understand the sources of a firm's absorptive capacity, we focus on the structure of communication between the external environment and the organization as well as among the subunits of the organization, and also the character and distribution of expertise within the organization.

In line with the views of Cohen and Levinthal, we suggest that the creative city plays the role of an 'organization', and that its creative communities are the 'subunits of the organization', which are the active units of absorptive capabilities. What the creative city provides is a local platform of 'spaces and places' and a centrality of 'projects and events' that favour not only the diversity of creative communities but also the continuous opportunity to intertwine communities, transfer knowledge across and within communities, and accelerate the translation of ideas and practices. As Allen (2000, p. 28) emphasizes:

The translation of ideas and practice as opposed to their transmission, are likely to involve people moving to and through "local" contexts, to which they bring their own blend of tacit and codified knowledge, ways of doing and ways of judging things. There is no one spatial template through which associational understanding or active comprehension takes place. Rather, knowledge translation involves mobile, distanciated forms of information as much as it does proximate relationships.

In Section 9.6 we discuss the issues of 'diversity and proximity' of local KI firms, that allow for the emergence of a significant amount of diverse yet relatively overlapping communities, 'spaces and places' as areas where communities can meet and share knowledge creating 'local buzzes', and 'projects and events' as opportunities to translate and hybridize knowledge through the pressure of enactment and performance, opening on 'global pipelines'.

9.6 The Creative City: Diversity and Proximity, Spaces and Places, Projects and Events

As a metropolis of medium range (three million people), Montreal seems to better fit in the Jacobian model (Jacobs 1968) than in the Marshallian one, with a significant amount of KI firms in different industries. A quick assessment would show a historic concentration of firms in the fields of aerospace/aeronautics, telecommunications, software development, advertising and communication, pharmaceuticals, and in the cultural and clothing/fashion industries. A noticeable characteristic of the Montreal case is that specific industries emerged through a process of the crisscrossing of capabilities. To give but a few examples:

- *CAE Electronics* hires computer-graphic artists to work with software developers and aeronautic experts in flight-simulator conception and development.
- *Ubisoft*, a French-based videogames firm, uses local capabilities in software development and talents from the cultural industries.

241

- *Mon Mannequin Virtuel* mixes capabilities in IT, telecom, computer graphics, and advertising to develop a virtual model for online clothing retail stores.

- *DTi* owns more than 90 per cent of the in-flight entertainment market, using knowledge from the videogame industry and from the aeronautic industry.

All these project-based KI firms shelter diverse communities used in hybridizing knowledge. The relative proximity allows for some boundary-spanning activities, career shifts from one field to another, and entrepreneurial endeavour. If intense knowledge flows between KI firms play a significant role in fostering innovative activities, we would argue that they are supported by the reliance of communities on the sources of knowledge springing from the socio-cultural activities of the city itself.

Montreal itself possesses a dual identity as a bilingual city, and most likely, a multiple identity as a multicultural city (Simon 1999; Stolarick et al. 2005). These multiple identities are also prevalent among members of communities who take on multiple roles: (*a*) as an employee of the firm, with a formal mandate; (*b*) as a member of a community of specialists involved in one module of a project; (*c*) as a generic member of a community of specialists, sharing with co-members involved in other projects, in or outside the organization; (*d*) as an inhabitant, living in the city and absorbing new knowledge as a consumer or spectator; and, (*e*) as a member of an active creative community in the city participating in the creation of new knowledge. Belonging to these multiple communities facilitates boundary-spanning, knowledge-brokering, and knowledge-sharing. More specifically, we argue here that employees of the KI firm actively sharing and processing knowledge in a community of specialists inside the boundaries of the firm may also absorb knowledge from their active or passive participation in one or several creative communities of the city. Next, we discuss the roles of 'spaces and places' and 'projects and events' as loci in the city where communities formally and informally gather, meet, share knowledge, and learn from each other.

9.6.1 *Spaces and places*

The urban structure of Montreal includes areas with well-identified ethnic concentrations and multiethnic areas attracting young professionals, artists, and also couples with children. The city is a patchwork of residential, commercial, and industrial areas with almost no systematic order and allows for natural interactions between residential areas, the business district, tourists venues, and 'abandoned' industrial areas.

Most 'new' economy creative industries have settled in former industrial districts left empty by the disappearance of 'old' economy firms – factories, shops, and warehouses. This is a classical phenomenon, almost a cliché, of this economic transition. Old warehouses offer open spaces that supposedly allow for more 'horizontal' organization of work, with free-flowing communication, improvised meetings, and easier sharing of tacit knowledge. Leases are cheaper, and even the spirit of these zones seems inhabited by the alternative worldviews of the margins of society, communes, squatters, and struggling artists.

Two noticeable cases in Montreal illustrate the importance of 'derelict' spaces and their potential to become 'places' acting as playground for creative activities:

- *La SAT, Société des Arts Technologiques*, started as an interdisciplinary research project in digital arts involving artists and the academia. It evolved as a laboratory for digital arts experimentation, creation, and diffusion. The city provided some help through the allocation of a former bank building abandoned for years a few blocks away from the business district on Montreal's busiest street. This perfect location, next to the building housing a popular music TV channel, one block away from Montreal's most successful 'after-hours' club, two blocks from a museum of contemporary art, and a subway station allowed La SAT to attract people for concerts, from which it secured some revenues, and to introduce some avant-garde creators to a wider audience.

- The province of Quebec profited massively from the success of *Le Cirque du Soleil*, to the point where Montreal officials now introduce activities around the circus arts as a cluster. This physical existence of the cluster followed an initiative from the association representing the interests of circus artists and firms, *En Piste!*, which convinced Le Cirque du Soleil to build its new headquarters on a former dumping ground, close to one of the poorest neighbourhoods in Canada, 'le quartier St-Michel'. A few public leaders promoted the idea of an ambitious threefold project with a cultural, a social, and an environmental mission. Le Cirque du Soleil would settle next to the dump, and would be associated with the National School for Circus arts and a new permanent circus theatre, still to be built. The project would be an opportunity to promote the restoration of the dump with the objective of transforming it into an industrial park with a recycling centre. Finally, the new theatre would hire employees from the multiethnic neighbourhood with a priority for people with psychosocial difficulties. The project would include an art gallery for local underground urban artist and events for the community.

In the aforementioned cases, groups of creative communities decided to take the lead to bring those abandoned spaces back to life. Lobbying and partnering activities followed and allowed for the revitalization of these spaces. The availability of abandoned, 'derelict', free spaces was turned into an opportunity for exploration. Our main point here is that when 'recycled' with a new vocation, these spaces may be transformed into places that become open platforms for projects and events.

Allowing people to invest in unused spaces created a meeting point for members of the community, where they pursued their creative agenda. In specific cases, spaces would become 'places': studios or ateliers for creators, often coupled with a performing stage to exercise and rehearse. These 'playgrounds for creativity', close to the concept of *Ba* (Nonaka and Konno 1998), allow individuals to meet and gather around a common creative platform from which projects can arise. For example, La SAT allowed electronic musicians, digital video artists, and multimedia graphic artists to gather around the idea of digital creation/performance. As such places are generally also coupled with a bar/cafe, they present their creation to an audience mainly composed of typical members of the nightlife urban crowd: 'yuppies', designers, software developers, cultural entrepreneurs, and creators of all kind, often employees of the KI firms. It gives visibility to the creative community and creates some 'buzz' through face-to-face interactions (Storper and Venables 2004). These places can become creative 'hubs' where creative communities not only exercise and experiment, but also perform, showcase their talents, and share with other communities. This can attract spectators, amateurs, and critics who enter into the conversation and feed diversity. The role of cafes, restaurants, and theatres should not be neglected here, as they offer natural occasions to start conversations, develop networks of relationships, and envision new projects (Saxenian 1994). The occupation of free spaces with the vision of developing places as context for encounters and experimentation drives the enactment of creativity, mainly through projects and events.

9.6.2 Projects and events

A creative community usually thrives on an informal generic project to produce and promote work from its members, foster reactions and comments, and stimulate renewed inspiration. This drives members to engage in conversations and to work together in small, informal projects. The settling of specific places dedicated to one or several creative communities is a strong force for the formalization of projects and partly shifts their orientation from purely collective experimentation internal to the community to a performance open to a wider audience. Public performance widens the buzz to other communities and helps to bring the latent creativity to the surface. This could stimulate a process of institutionalization aimed at transforming the project into a product that might appeal to producers/investors and potential consumers (which is what a music band might desire, for instance, or what a painter might expect from a gallery show). It could also help in developing new relationships and reducing the risk of parochialism associated with the small-world phenomenon (Uzzi and Spiro 2005). Active and entrepreneurial boundary spanners play an essential role here (Hargadon and Sutton 1997), in leveraging their hard-won legitimacy in their community of origin to explore new territories and foster translation activities with other communities (Fleming and Waguespack 2005). We might even hypothesize that the dual/multiple identities phenomenon makes knowledge-brokering easier through the translation/recoding of knowledge (Cillo 2005).

As an illustration again, the site of La SAT, introduced earlier, allowed members from the experimental electronic music community to develop internal collaborations and then to perform in front of a mixed audience of video and graphic artists from the contemporary urban visual arts community, contemporary dancers, academics, and 'Intelligent Dance Music' (IDM) aficionados.[3] Gradually, intercommunity creative collaborations began to emerge, as information spread through the networks of the artists, most of who worked during the day in other creative or techno-creative industries. For example, the buzz around IDM and experimentation at La SAT spread, with events announced and promoted at Ubisoft or Cossette.

Another example clearly shows the link between a creative community from the city and a community involved in a specific project in a KI firm. A sound designer and music editor for the videogame company Ubisoft used to attend shows at La SAT and became a fan of 'drum'n'bass', a very rhythmic and abstract genre of electronic music. Since he was also an amateur composer, he became especially interested by the work of a famous Brazilian disc jockey (DJ), making expert use of traditional percussion mixed with computer-generated sounds (interestingly this DJ has now settled in Montreal, attracted by the buzz around electronic music). The music editor shared his interest with other sound designers at Ubisoft and started a small community of interest around the DJ. He then proposed hiring the DJ to compose the soundtrack of one of the company's flagship projects. After some internal consultation, the producer agreed to hire the DJ. A fruitful collaboration followed: the game was partly marketed with a focus on the involvement of the DJ and the DJ launched a new CD inspired by the videogame and co-produced with Ubisoft, making expert use of the skills of the firm's sound engineers. This example shows how knowledge can flow from local creative communities to a formal commercial project in a KI firm. It epitomizes how the dynamics of the city can feed a creative process from the cultural underground up to the completion of a successful commercial project, via the active role of communities.

In this case, it is also interesting to note that the buoyant local community of electronic artists attracted a renowned creator through a 'global pipeline' that opened thanks to the energy generated by events such as music festivals. Although projects usually target local communities, the buzz may expand and reach out to other creative communities located in other creative cities. The scope of the projects may then widen, following public and commercial success, and the community could plan events – festivals, competitions, fairs – that reach a wider local audience and attract people from outside. Such events are essential in reviving and refreshing the creativity of the community because they open 'global pipelines' connecting to distant communities and opening small worlds to new influences (Bathelt et al. 2004).

Many examples can be cited to illustrate this phenomenon. Montreal's International Jazz Festival plays an iconic role in bringing artists in and sending others out. Two recent examples – *Mutek* and *Montréal Electronic Groove* (MEG) – electronic urban-underground music festivals, started out as local, almost hidden events that now tour in different countries. Success brought an interest that allowed the organizers to invite international artists who in turn facilitated the recognition of these events and the development of links outside Montreal. It is worthy of note that both festivals became formal projects with a commercial and promotional focus and developed strong ties with a few other creative places in their field, such as Berlin, Paris, and Barcelona.

To summarize, artists and other creative people belong simultaneously to communities of specialists in KI firms, and to a community of shared interest, for instance, in experimental electronic music, short movies, or the videogames mod scene. Shared interest is enacted in common projects in 'small worlds'. Small projects, like a music band or the filming of a short movie, gets people involved with several possibilities – realizing creative intentions through performance, learning from partners, and gaining social capital and eventually, in the best case, economic capital. 'Places/venues' emerge in open 'spaces' allowing the performance of projects and the development of new creative conversations with other communities that lead to new – intercommunity – projects. The ensuing buzz reinforces this dynamic, making new projects with wider scope and connectivity possible. This recursive dynamic fosters the development of absorptive capacities at the city level, returning to nurture communities of specialists hired by local KI firms.

The link between communities within the KI firm and creative communities from the city is clearly initiated and supported by individuals. Multiple identities allow for boundary-spanning and knowledge-brokering activities. Individuals involved in communities in the KI firm participate in different, more or less active, ways in the creative life of the city. (See Table 9.2.)

It must be emphasized though, that the interplay between the 'creative city' and KI firms, does not only rely on the exploitation of the absorptive 'capacities' through the development of 'creative slack' generated by communities. The creative city is also fuelled by the presence of large KI firms. Such firms are responsible for attracting talent, offering the start to a career, providing an incentive to emerge out of the underground,

Table 9.2: Modes of participation feeding the dynamics of absorption

	Individual, employee of the KI firm	KI firm
Spaces	• Visits • Lives in	• Settles in
Places	• Visits • Animates	• Promotes • Sponsors
Projects	• Initiator • Actor	• Promotes • Sponsors
Events	• Actor • Spectator	• Promotes • Sponsors

and acting as icons of difference. They play the role of pillar firms, around which clusters revolve and evolve (e.g. Le Cirque du Soleil for the performing arts, Ubisoft for videogames, or Cossette for advertising and communication). As shown in Table 9.2, KI firms are not neutral or blind to the creative activities of the city. Like Le Cirque du Soleil, they settle in parts of the city identified as a locus of creative, often underground activities. They also support the development of these creative activities through promotion or direct sponsoring. As an example, managers at DTi strongly encourage its employees to attend theatre or music shows and to visit contemporary art exhibitions as well. Ubisoft heavily sponsor the Fantasia Film Festival, mainly introducing obscure Asian movies of the fantastic genre to a wider audience, literally pushing its own employees to feed their creativity from such 'exotic' pieces of work.

For KI firms, the promotion of the creativity of their internal communities is a subtle issue. As they develop internal processes to harness creativity, they also have to promote participation in external activities without generating too much 'leakage'. In the case of too tight an institutionalization of internal processes, employees might be pushed to express their creativity elsewhere, either through underground activities[4] or through new entrepreneurial activities, often in competition with the large KI firm. For example, the circus act 'Les 7 doigts de la main' (the seven fingers of the hand) was founded by former employees from Le Cirque du Soleil. Their show appeals to an audience looking for something different from Le Cirque. It takes place in La Tohu, the circus theatre mostly founded and funded by Le Cirque, and it is likely that the show also provides inspiration to employees from Le Cirque itself.

To a large extent these flagship companies can be viewed as 'anchor tenants' (Feldman 2003) because their presence enhances the local creative milieu to the degree of sparking local industrial creativity. They 'thicken' the local labour market; a manager thinking of leaving the anchor tenant is more likely to move to a smaller local firm developing a new technology. Progressively, efficient activity by this fringe of smaller firms increases the impact of vertical knowledge spillovers in the local economy.

9.7 Conclusion

Montreal can be seen as a large-scale forum consisting of a myriad of creative communities, a fertile soil for new shoots of creativity. Through their constant curiosity and their continuous search for best practices, communities of specialists in KI firms are unique devices tapping into the external world to bring permanently useful knowledge and creative ideas to the firm. Thus, tracing the sources of creativity in KI firms reveals a maze of creative communities of different size and scope, a 'hidden architecture of creativity', starting from the different elementary communities of specialists in the firm to those also participating in the dynamic socio-cultural life of the city.

More precisely, what our ethnographic analysis suggests is that the sources of creativity for the members of a given community of specialists are manifold:

- Creativity partly results from knowledge activities *within* the community of specialists itself. Members of a given community of specialists, such as game designers or graphic analysts, remain connected to their community on a daily basis. They exchange knowledge about their current practice and interact with other members of their community utilizing both *geographical proximity* with those working in different knowledge domains, and *relational or virtual proximity* with external colleagues working in the same knowledge domain of knowledge.

- Creativity also results from interactions and frictions *with other communities of specialists through the development of projects* for the KI firm (as Brown and Duguid 1991, p. 54) have underlined: 'separate community perspectives can be amplified by interchanges among communities: out of this friction of competing ideas can come the sort of improvisational sparks necessary for igniting organizational innovation'. In such cases, knowledge activities are shaped by the formal organizational structures that could, to a large extent, enable, support, and stimulate the interactions between the communities of specialists.

- Further creativity results from informal and random interactions *with other communities in the fertile soil* of Montreal. What the creative city provides is a local platform of 'spaces and places' and a centrality of 'projects and events' that favour not only the diversity of creative communities but also continuous and ever-renewed opportunities to intertwine communities, transfer knowledge across and within communities, and accelerate the translation of ideas and practices.

What is revealing is that the above three sources of creativity refer to three different activities of knowledge creation:

- Within each community of specialists, members communicate regularly with each other about their practice through a cognitive space that allows for specialists of the same domain to confront ideas, to build daring assumptions, and to validate new creative forms. As a result, step by step, the 'codebook' of the community of specialists is progressively built from these various knowledge activities. This work space is not fully monitored through the formal corporate process, and is not necessarily aligned with corporate goals and strategy. It is also largely disconnected from the daily pressure of producing an efficient output designed for a specific market purpose.

• Between the communities of specialists of a given KI firm, members of a given community who have participated in a project progressively build cognitive links with colleagues in other communities of specialists, and tend to bring this knowledge back into their community through daily interactions. Step by step, the *cultural distance* between the different communities of specialists is reduced and this leads to a reasonable level of mutual understanding, increasing the potential for innovation and creativity. This workspace is essentially monitored through the formal corporate processes, and is mostly codified.

• With access to the multitude of diverse communities that can be met in the places and spaces of Montreal, members of a given community of specialists have the possibility to tap into external sources of knowledge to find new creative ideas or to confront a newly produced piece of knowledge with local experts or local consumers.

Thus, KI firms can grow, and develop innovative projects based on the dynamics of their creative slack by using the creative potential of local communities to provide absorptive capabilities. Through its unique intertwining of spaces and places, events and projects, the creative city offers an efficient platform to enhance and nurture these absorptive capabilities.

However, this 'virtuous' cycle of creativity between KI firms and the creative cities mediated by communities is dependent upon certain conditions. First, it requires the existence and maintenance of a sufficient number of attractive KI firms to activate and enhance the creative potential of the city. Such conditions are never guaranteed since the competition between different cities to attract KI firms is intense and destabilizing. Second, it assumes that the cognitive communities remain within the creative cities and invest in knowledge activities and exchange on a long-term basis. Again, the competition between creative cities may induce drastic movements of communities from one city to the other (as an example, mostly for regulation reasons, communities in the videogame industry have tended to expatriate from Paris and emigrate to Montreal).

To conclude, this chapter has analysed the spatial ontology of creativity in the city of Montreal, where the local and global are interwoven in specific ways, where creativities of various kinds channelled by active communities of specialists nurture and enhance the performance of KI firms, and where, in turn, the main KI firms nourish the creative soil of the city through a flagship or anchor role. Looking beyond this specific example, we would argue that communities (as instruments of mediation between the creative city and the KI firm) can help in opening novel lines of thinking on the interpretation of the creative city and its growing role in the knowledge-based economy.

References

Agrawal, A. and Cockburn, I. (2003). 'The anchor tenant hypothesis: Exploring the role of large, local, R&D-intensive firms in regional innovation systems', *International Journal of Industrial Organisation*, 21(1): 1227–53.

Allen, J. (2000). 'Power/economic knowledges: Symbolic and spatial formations', in J. Bryson, P. W. Daniels, N. Henry, and J. Pollard (eds.), *Knowledge, Space, Economy*. London: Routledge, pp. 15–33.

Bathelt, H., Malmberg, A., and Maskell, P. (2004). 'Clusters and knowledge: Local buzz, global pipelines and the process of knowledge creation', *Progress in Human Geography*, 28: 31–56.

Bilton, C. and Leary, R. (2002). 'What can managers do for creativity? Brokering creativity in the creative industries', *International Journal of Cultural Policy*, 8(1): 49–64.

Boland R. J. and Tenkasi R. V. (1995). 'Perspective making and perspective taking in communities of knowing', *Organization Science*, 6(4): 350–72.

Brehmer, B. (1991). 'Distributed decision making: Some notes on the literature', in Rasmussen et al. (eds.), *Distributed Decision Making: Cognitive Models in Cooperative Work*. New York: Wiley.

Brown, J. S. and Duguid, P. (1991). 'Organizational learning and communities-of-practice: Toward a unified view of working, learning, and innovation', *Organization Science*, 2(1): 40–57.

Ciborra C. (1996). 'The platform organization: Recombining strategies, structures, and surprises', *Organization Science*, 7(2): 103–18.

Cillo, P. (2005). 'Fostering market knowledge use in innovation: The role of internal brokers', *European Management Journal*, 23(4): 404–12.

Cohen, W. M. and Levinthal, D. A. (1990). 'Absorptive-capacity – A new perspective on learning and innovation', *Administrative Science Quarterly*, 35(1): 128–52.

Cohendet, P. and Llerena, P. (2003). 'Routines and communities in the theory of the firm', *Industrial and Corporate Change*. 12(3): 271–97.

Cohendet, P. and Llerena, P. and Simon, L. (2007). 'Playing across the playground: Paradoxes of knowledge creation in the video-game firm', *Journal of Organizational Behavior* (special issue on the paradox of creativity), 28(5): 587–605.

Cowan, R. and Foray, D. (1997). 'The economics of codification and the diffusion of knowledge,' *Industrial and Corporate Change*, 6(3): 595–622.

——David, P. A., and Foray, D. (2000). 'The explicit economics of knowledge codification', *Industrial and Corporate Change*, 9(2): 211–53.

De Fillippi, R. and Arthur, M. (1998). 'Paradox in project-based enterprise: The case of film-making', *California Management Review*, 40(2): 125–39.

——Grahber, G., and Jones, C. (2007). 'Introduction to paradoxes of creativity: managerial and organizational challenges in the cultural economy', *Journal of Organizational Behavior*, 28(5): 511.

Feldman, M. (2003). 'The Locational dynamics of the US biotech industry: Knowledge externalities and the anchor hypothesis', *Industry and Innovation*, 10(3): 311–29.

Fleming, L. and Waguespack, D. (2005). 'Penguins, camels, and other birds of a feather: Brokerage, boundary spanning, and leadership in open innovation communities' (free/open source research community), available at http://opensource.mit.edu/papers/flemingwaguespack.pdf

Florida, R. (2002). *The Rise of the Creative Class*. New York: Basic Books.

Gann, D. M. and Salter, A. J. (2000). 'Innovation in project-based, service-enhanced firms: The construction of complex products and systems', *Research Policy*, 29(7–8): 955–72.

Hargadon, A. and Sutton, R. (1997). 'Technology brokering and innovation in a product design firm', *Administration Science Quarterly*, 42: 716–49.

Jacobs, J. (1968). *The Economies of Cities*. New York: Random House.

Krugman, P. (1991). *Geography and Trade*. Cambridge, MA: MIT Press.

Loasby, B. J. (1991). *Equilibrium and Evolution*. Manchester: Manchester University Press.

Loasby B. J. (1998). 'The organization of capabilities', *Journal of Economic Behaviour and Organization*, 35(2): 139–60.

Lucas, R. E. Jr. (1993). 'Making a miracle', *Econometrita*, 61: 251–72.

Nersessian, N. J. (1992). 'How do scientists think? Capturing the dynamics of conceptual change in science,' in R. N. Giere (ed.), *Cognitiue Models of Science: Minnesota Studies in the Philosophy of Science, XV*. Minneapolis, MN: University of Minnesota Press.

Nonaka, I. and Konno, N. (1998). 'The concept of "Ba": Building foundation for Knowledge Creation', *California Management Review*, 40(3): 40–54.

——and Takeuchi, H. (1995). *The Knowledge-Creating Company*. New York: Oxford University Press.

Nooteboom, B. (1999). 'Innovation, learning and industrial organization', *Cambridge Journal of Economics*, 23: 127–50.

Penrose, E. (1995 [1959]). *The Theory of the Growth of the Firm*, 3rd edn. Oxford: Oxford University Press.

Saxenian, A. (1994). *Regional Advantages: Culture and Competition in Silicon Valley and Route 128*. Cambridge, MA: Harvard University Press.

Scott, A. J. (2005). 'Creative cities: Conceptual issues and policy questions', OECD International Conference on City Competitiveness, Santa-Cruz de Tenerife, Spain, 3–4 March.

Simon, S. (1999). *Hybridité culturelle*. Montréal, Canada: Editions L'île de la tortue.

Simon, L. (2002) 'Le management en univers ludique: Jouer et travailler chez Ubi Soft, une entreprise du multimédia à Montréal (1998–1999)'. Unpublished PhD thesis, HEC Montréal, Montreal.

Stolarick, K. and Florida, R. (2006). 'Creativity, connections and innovation: A study of linkages in the Montréal Region', *Environment and Planning A*, 38: 1799–817.

—— —— and Musante, L. (2005). *Montreal's capacity for creative connectivity: Outlook & opportunities* Working paper. Montreal, Canada: Catalytix.

Storper, M. and Venables, J. (2004). 'Buzz: Face-to-face contact and the urban economy', *Journal of Economic Geography*, 4(4): 351–70.

Uzzi, B. and Spiro, J. (2005). 'Collaboration and creativity: The small world problem', *American Journal of Sociology*, 111: 447–504.

Notes

1. The authors wish to thank Ash Amin, Joanne Roberts, Jean Lave, Paul Duguid, and Philippe Laredo for their comments at the workshop from which this book originates. These have contributed greatly to the improvement of the chapter. The authors also thank Anna Grandori and members of the KGP project, in particular Gernot Grahber, for their useful comments. They also wish to thank Lucy Stojak for her help in editing.

2. We refer to *communities* as a generic term that defines different types of autonomous learning groups of individuals (communities of practice, epistemic communities, and other more or less informal learning groups) united by common beliefs and interests who voluntarily share their resources on a long-term basis in order to create and diffuse knowledge (Boland and Tenkasi 1995).

3. IDM is a genre of abstract electronic music. With a strong focus on content and technological experimentation, IDM is still rhythmic and suitable for dance floors. An iconic artist would be British experimenter Aphex Twin and a representative label Warp Records, also from the UK.

4. In the videogame industry, expert game-designers or programmers would produce 'mods', small 'add-ons' pieces of software – a new map, new characters – usually downloadable on the Internet; that would add some functionality to an official product.

10

Open, But How Much? Growth, Conflict, and Institutional Evolution in Open-Source Communities[1]

Juan Mateos-Garcia and W. Edward Steinmueller

10.1 Introduction

Wikipedia, together with YouTube, Myspace, and Facebook, is one of the main exemplars of the 'Web 2.0' phenomenon, namely, the emergence and growth of web sites filled with content contributed by large numbers of users. The success of these virtual spaces has been explained by resorting to conceptual frameworks borrowed from popular versions of complexity and social network theory such as 'the Wisdom of the Crowds' (Surowiecki 2004; Sunstein 2006), where the activities of decentralized collectives arrive at better outcomes than hierarchically structured organizations.

This family of arguments, intellectual heirs to Adam Smith's 'invisible hand' and Friedrich Von Hayek's analysis of the informational superiority of the market over alternative institutions for the organization of exchange and production activities, parallels Eric Raymond's Linus's Law ('with enough eyeballs all bugs are shallow') that impersonal exchange produces collective value. In the case of several open-source software project outputs, sufficient value is produced to dominate the rationally planned products of some of the largest global corporations in key segments of the software market.[2] The current literature on the organization of open-source software and other collective information good production processes, such as Wikipedia, focuses on elucidating the motivations of individuals for engaging in these unremunerated activities using developer surveys and other methods (e.g. see Ghosh et al. 2002; Lakhani et al. 2002; Lerner and Tirole 2002).

It is our contention that, although these approaches for examining the success and organization of such activities are useful and offer worthwhile findings, they neglect essential – we would argue defining – features of Free/Libre Open Source Software (F/LOSS) developments that reflect the social and organizational characteristics of the communities engaged in them as well as the essential determinants of the quality of their output. In Section 10.2 we offer a conceptual framework for an analysis of the effects of social and organizational community characteristics on the persistence and quality of a community's outputs and apply it in Section 10.3 to analysis of the social dynamics observed in the historical evolution of the Wikipedia open encyclopaedia, as well as reporting on previous research on the Debian GNU/Linux distribution discussed elsewhere (Mateos-Garcia and Steinmueller 2008).

Our goal is to show the usefulness of conceptualizing a particular F/LOSS project as an effort undertaken by an epistemic community comprised of individuals who share a set of normative and causal beliefs and notions about the validity of specific knowledge, and who accept or produce a common set of rules and norms for collective activity. When coupled with an appealing vision or purpose capable of engaging individuals in a creative endeavour, such communities can achieve productive outcomes superior to those of profit-motivated competitors. In contrast to the more optimistic accounts of F/LOSS development, however, our analysis also identifies the dysfunctional processes that can emerge in F/LOSS projects; growth in the number of participants can create tensions between 'output quality' and 'openness to participation', two important attractors for F/LOSS community membership. Our examination of these dynamics highlights the need to augment the currently prominent individualistic exchange-based models of F/LOSS development with a perspective that acknowledges the social and economic aspects of this setting for collective action. This perspective leads us to propose, as a summary and encapsulation of this perspective, the metaphor of the 'museum', which may serve to balance the metaphor of the 'bazaar' frequently encountered in studies of F/LOSS communities.

10.2 Beyond the Systemic and Inside the System: Social Aspects of Online Knowledge Production

Although we have referred to Wikipedia as an exemplar of the 'Web 2.0 phenomenon', and to 'The Wisdom of the Crowds' (Surowiecki 2004) as one of the main accounts of its success, our decision to focus on the 'communitarian aspects' of this project's activities has led us to resort to the more abundant and better-established literature on F/LOSS development to build the theoretical basis of this chapter, and particularly that area which focuses on its organization and day-to-day practice exemplified by Edwards (2001) and Mateos-Garcia and Steinmueller (2002). We contend that analysis of social processes at work in these groups offers a richer foundation for analysing the dynamics, strengths, and limitation of their operation than the procrustean efforts to characterize these processes in terms of exchange and individual resource allocation that occur in the literature (Lerner and Tirole 2002).

We apply a framework especially tailored to the analysis of a specific form of Internet-mediated communities of practice (F/LOSS) to the case of Debian (a project which integrates open-source packages into distributions that create complete software systems) and to Wikipedia, an online encyclopaedia created using the practices and tools of open-source software development. Some would argue that neither of these efforts has sufficient structure to be defined as a 'community of practice'. It is not our primary goal to resolve debates about thresholds or limits distinguishing terminologies such as networks of practice from communities of practice. Doing so appears to us to require deep assessments of the role of practice in the definition of identity, and profound insight into human motivation for which we would acknowledge our limitations. Instead, our aim is to show how the evolution of two communities employing similar practices involves establishing binding rules, coordination mechanisms, and shared goals. The significance of these activities bears upon the challenges that the Debian and Wikipedia projects have recently faced (e.g. for Wikipedia, see Keen 2007), which can be linked to the sluggishness, or outright failure of their leaders to define and implement an institutional structure that would improve the quality and reliability of the project's output. This normative and predictive conclusion of our analysis (elaborated further in the conclusions in Section 10.4) provides a rather different standard for assessing outcomes than exchange and allocation models, which attribute success and failure solely to the enthusiasms of participants for the project's vision. What we intend to demonstrate in this chapter is the relevance of analysing the manifestations of organizational structure and authority in online endeavours, such as Wikipedia, and to identify their linkages to operational performance in terms of output quality, quantity, timeliness, and community sustainability.

This analysis bridges a theoretical divide created by the excessive emphasis that the conventional analyses of F/LOSS development and other Internet-based collective knowledge-production endeavours has placed on voluntary allocation of effort (enabled by free access to information/source code) as the key variable that differentiates these groups from traditional, hierarchically managed organizations. Against this dichotomous conceptualization of the potential ways of organizing knowledge production in the online context, we suggest a continuum of possible structures with organizational shapes determined by the way in which rules for entrance and participation (including the exercise of authority) are defined and put into practice.[3] In order to undertake this characterization we employ a theoretical framework that elaborates and applies the concepts of 'epistemic community', 'legitimate peripheral participation', and 'distributed authority' to the open-source context.[4]

10.2.1 *Foundations for analysing community practice*

The creation of information goods using the tools of computer-intermediated communication involves the construction or collection as well as the integration of information in broad conformance with some overall architecture or design, which provides guidance for those involved in the process about what is desired. This architecture or design can be open in at least two senses. First, it is possible for the nature of the design or architecture to evolve through the processes of participation – in this sense design and architecture are 'snapshots' of an ongoing negotiation over the structure and content of the information being created and assembled. Second, it is possible for the nature and processes of negotiation to be open to revision and amendment – even if constituted in a particular way at the beginning of a project, the way that 'things are done around here' may be subject to discussion and revision over the life of a project. These constituents of 'openness' in community practice are both an opportunity and a threat. They are an opportunity for groups of participants to achieve a collective sense of purpose and a sense of collective ownership of both content and process of a project. At the same time they are a threat to the success of the effort and the stability of the community inasmuch as visions of purpose and process may not coincide or cohere, leading to collective disillusionment and the dissipation of participation. While the scope for invention and discovery of new social mechanisms for resolving these problems is very broad, it seems likely that individuals will turn to their own social backgrounds and experience in attempting to find ways forward (Berdou 2007). In this sense, social experience with the instantiation and governance of 'communities' provides a starting point for the brave new world of computer-mediated collaboration, as does the literature devoted to examining community formation.[5]

10.2.1.1 EPISTEMIC COMMUNITIES AND A SHARED FRAMEWORK FOR F/LOSS DEVELOPMENT

The 'epistemic communities' concept introduced by Haas (1992) in his analysis of international networks of policy experts is particularly suitable for the identification of some essential features of the groups of individuals engaged in F/LOSS development (including efforts such as Wikipedia consciously organized along similar lines). Such groups share normative and causal beliefs and knowledge validity notions, as well as agreed goals to be achieved through the accumulation of a body of knowledge, which, in the case of Haas' subjects of analysis, attempts to influence the policymaking process. The epistemological characterization of a community implicit in this definition underlines the necessity for commonly agreed standards for the validation of knowledge produced by individuals from a diversity of backgrounds, working in very different locations, while the identification of shared goals is important when considering the voluntary participation context of the majority of F/LOSS projects. Agreement on these standards in certain cases (particularly those more tightly linked to the activities of the Free Software Foundation) present important political elements. Even in the absence of these political elements, the shared goal, which at its simplest level could be sketched as the development of software (or more generally information goods) of the highest quality, with the source code (or content) available for anyone to investigate and improve on, makes it possible for the members of the community to focus their efforts.[6]

The elements that define the epistemic community associated with a F/LOSS project facilitate the coordination of members' activities by providing a commonly agreed framework for the performance of development tasks, standard criteria for the assessment of the quality of the knowledge being created, and a definition of purpose. All these elements we assume, given the extraordinary success that some of these projects have enjoyed, make it possible to overcome problems of decentralized software development projects such as those identified by Herbsleb et al. (2000).

10.2.1.2 LEGITIMATE PERIPHERAL PARTICIPATION AND THE REPRODUCTION OF A F/LOSS COMMUNITY

As Edwards (2001) argues, the static picture of relative stability in the day-to-day productive operations of a F/LOSS community needs to be complemented with an explanation of the dynamic processes through which the community manages to reproduce itself, that is, attract new participants and train them in its 'ways' and goals. Lave and Wenger's (1991) legitimate peripheral participation framework constitutes a particularly powerful lens for analysis of the learning dynamics within communities of practitioners. According to these authors, learning can only be understood in the social context of practice, and constitutes an essential element of a novice's initial participation in a community, which is initiated in the periphery (with the undertaking of relatively minor, routine tasks) leading eventually, as experience and knowledge accumulate, to the acquisition of an 'insider identity'. This account highlights the importance of features such as 'spaces for learning' or 'control over access to resources' which can be easily mapped into F/LOSS projects,[7] although the lack of a personal, individualized relationship between master and apprentice (which is seen as fundamental in Lave and Wenger's account) might be construed as limiting its applicability to the virtual context.[8]

Since the epistemic community concept has as one of its defining elements, the shared (political) values and goals of participation, it becomes necessary here to highlight the way in which legitimate peripheral participation might incorporate processes of indoctrination (understood as 'political learning' of those values and goals), and point to acceptance of the communities' values and goals as being a requisite for the development of an 'insider' identity.[9] These indications of the community's direction and purpose might be conceived of as signals about its operations aimed at an audience of potential 'recruits'.[10]

10.2.1.3 THE EXERCISE OF POWER FOR THE IMPOSITION OF GOALS AND RESOLUTION OF CONFLICTS

Conceiving of the social collective engaged in a F/LOSS project as an epistemic community whose operations are regulated by an (often implicitly) agreed set of rules and values and directed towards the achievement of a shared goal to which novices are progressively introduced through processes of legitimate peripheral participation, seems sufficient to explain the stability and persistence of such communities. However, it overestimates the extent to which norms, values, and goals are actually shared by community members, or are sufficient to address the uncertainties of day-to-day development inside a project. It also neglects the processes through which the norms, values, and goals are established and enforced initially. We contend that in an environment where goals are often insufficiently defined to inform actual technical decision-making, or to guarantee that the day-to-day activities of participants are sufficiently coordinated, it becomes necessary for those individuals endowed with decision-making power to exercise it in order to steer the project in the direction they consider desirable, or to resolve controversies which the conventionally accepted methods of online debate are unable to close.[11] While there may be alternatives to this exercise of power that involve some other form of collective decision-making, these alternatives were not evident in the communities that we examined.

The source of this power lies in these individuals' superior knowledge about the project, demonstrated through continuous high-quality contributions. The weight that F/LOSS communities place on technical proficiency makes the opinions of those individuals who have contributed more often (and insightfully) trusted and influential; such trust might elevate them to positions of de facto ownership over areas of the project where they have demonstrated specific expertise. This ownership is usually embodied in the exercise of 'maintenance rights', the authority to decide which contributions from other developers will be integrated into the maintainer's area of responsibility.[12] This role, with its essential quality assurance and coordination functions, can also be thought of as a tool of 'political' or social control – the exercise of maintainer rights makes it possible to exclude undesirable contributions, that is, to restrict the space for participation of those individuals whose development goals or principles do not conform to those of the maintainer, or more broadly, the project. This gate-keeping position makes it possible to enforce rules and values in ways that are limited by what is perceived by the rest of the community to be acceptable.[13]

10.2.2 *Impact on performance of the communitarian F/LOSS modus operandi*

A way of demonstrating the relevance of the framework we have advanced in this section and, more generally, of adopting an organizational lens to analyse the activities of online knowledge production collectives, such as those engaged in F/LOSS development, is to apply it to explain some of the outcomes we observe in these groups. In this subsection we sketch some key processes in the areas of innovation and creativity, which we will illustrate empirically in our discussions of the evolution of Debian and Wikipedia in Section 10.3.

10.2.2.1 THE STRENGTHS OF STRUCTURED POROSITY

It is often argued that the availability of source code for peer review in F/LOSS projects makes it possible to produce more reliable software artefacts than in the closed context of traditional software development.[14] This explanation would seem to make rather optimistic assumptions about the availability of time and skills in the user population (as well as its altruism), and appears to a large extent to be refuted by the available empirical evidence, which shows that most contributions to a project, in terms of code, patches, and bug reports, come from a small number of highly committed developers.[15] In incorporating learning and community-formation issues, our framework is able to address the rich reality of F/LOSS development more accurately than socially dis-embedded accounts – while it is true that the source code is available for anyone to see, only those who understand it will be able to make fruitful contributions to a project. The strengths of the F/LOSS model are that it provides individuals willing to do so with the social structures (and resources) necessary for learning and experimentation, through which they can, at some point, start making useful contributions. These same social structures provide a means for quality-assurance safeguards through the rejection of substandard quality or malicious code in the program being developed.

The 'parallel exploration of the design space', which takes place in a context of openness in F/LOSS development and reduces the risks of a particular project locking in to a 'sub-optimal development path' (Raymond 1999), can also be examined fruitfully as the manifestation of an element of the culture of debate enshrined in the norms and values of F/LOSS communities (Levy 2001), enacted in a social context where some opinions are more trusted and influential than others, depending on the developers' positions in the project (based on their past performance). So, although anyone (including non-members) can express an opinion in the available forums, the community will focus its attention on those utterances that are more likely to be useful and relevant.

The existence of a more or less formalized meritocracy based on situated expertise diminishes the incentives for opportunistic behaviours and makes it possible to arbitrate in cases of deadlock. Also, the porous nature of the boundaries of F/LOSS communities (which reflects the free availability of the source code of their products) favours 'knowledge leakage' in flows that, as Brown and Duguid (2001) argue, are bidirectional and might enhance the breadth of perspectives and knowledge bases brought into development. This also appears linked to the responsiveness of F/LOSS projects to user needs,[16] which dominate accounts related to the existence of 'Horizontal User-Innovation Networks'.[17] In our framework, this strength can be explained, again, as a consequence of the open and fluid social-membership structure of F/LOSS communities, which enables the rapid incorporation of relevant talent and expertise into a project by rewarding individuals who make high-quality contributions with enhanced reputation and decision-making power.[18]

10.2.2.2 THE WEAKNESSES OF ORGANIZATIONAL FUZZINESS

We could summarize the above-mentioned discussion in the statement that a F/LOSS community's main source of strength lies in the way in which its social structure manages to conjugate openness to participation and learning with the presence of rules for the coordination of development activities (including a reward system that encourages high-quality contributions).[19] However, this openness can also become a source of conflict. As mentioned above, project goals in many cases will be insufficiently defined to inform the day-to-day activities of the community. Although this 'vagueness' is another factor that enhances openness inasmuch as it makes it possible for a project to be 'different things' to participants with diverse (even conflicting) aspirations and thus encourages participation at earlier stages of development,[20] it can also become a source of conflict when a project's evolution makes it necessary to define development goals more clearly.[21] Controversies about which goals are to be pursued might be particularly disruptive because the technical debate mechanisms established in F/LOSS communities seem particularly ill-suited to the resolution of arguments that counterpoise incommensurable goals and solutions. It is difficult enough for two parties that support alternative goals to agree without the confusion added by the fact that their discussion is taking place in the sphere of technical solutions (aimed at achieving conflicting goals).

In such situations it might become necessary for individuals endowed with decision-making power to intervene. In the case of projects in which these 'officials' have particular prestige and authority, it might be possible to stabilize the situation, find some sort of compromise, or establish the conditions and goals of participation more clearly (forcing dissenters to exit the project, or perhaps establishing a 'fork' causing different versions of the project to come into existence). On the other hand, if the position of the hierarchy is contested (e.g. when expertise is highly distributed throughout the project), we would expect to witness distracting clashes for the leadership, potentially associated with a stall in the development process, which might demoralize the community and, given the rapidity with which software markets move, make the program being developed irrelevant.

So it seems that the 'reality check' of project growth and advance towards maturity brings to the foreground of the development effort trade-offs between goals that at earlier stages were hidden. Put more dramatically, project and community growth, that is, success, contains the seeds of dissension and potential demise.

The discussion above presents decision-making in F/LOSS development as essentially reactive, that is, action that is taken only when commonly accepted procedures for the resolution of conflicts and the assessment of solutions based on public debate inside the community have failed. Pro-active exercise of leadership in many F/LOSS projects is frowned upon, which might make it difficult to achieve architectural or radical innovation, since such changes would impact on the social structure of a project on a wide range of levels and possibly make obsolete the accumulated expertise of members (which constitutes the source of their reputation and power).[22]

10.3 Empirical Evidence: Debian and Wikipedia

In Section 10.2 we argued that F/LOSS communities present more social and organizational features than most accounts, with their emphasis on decentralized allocation of development resources by atomized individuals, would credit them with. We consider that this dominant depiction in the literature on F/LOSS development is not only imprecise in its neglect of the rich social aspects of the communities engaged in these activities, but also dangerous inasmuch as it might lead to the prescription of overtly simplistic strategies for improvements in the efficiency of knowledge-production activities by, for example, business firms. The main thrust of our argument is that behind the seemingly open façade of a F/LOSS project lies an infrastructure of rules, operational practices, and decision-making hierarchies structuring the activities of its community. Openness is therefore not a dichotomous variable, but a continuous one, and one that appears essentially linked to the organizational structure of a project, its technical architecture, and the outcomes of its activities. In this subsection we first summarize the outcomes of the application of our theoretical framework to the GNU/Debian project as presented in Mateos-Garcia and Steinmueller (2008) before focusing on the case of the Wikipedia community, which lies at the empirical 'core' of this chapter.

10.3.1 Debian

Our analysis of the evolution of the GNU/Linux Debian distribution depicts several situations and processes that correspond to those we have described above, and henceforth support the basic structure and implications of our conceptual framework.[23]

Debian was launched in 1993 with the goal of creating a high-quality Linux distribution. By 1996, individuals strongly committed to the tenets of Free Software had reached positions of authority inside it were faced with confusion regarding the project's political stance. This situation became more acute as the project's popularity grew, and those in authority decided, against the wishes of other members of the community who would have preferred a more pragmatic definition of the project's goals, to define a 'social contract' to explicitly establish the project's moral commitment to the principles of Free Software.

Debian's highly modular architecture presents interesting linkages with the shape of the project's political infrastructure. Unlike some other F/LOSS projects, such as the Linux kernel, which is built bottom-up through contributions submitted to individuals in positions of responsibility (a cadre of 'trusted lieutenants' and, eventually, Linus Torvalds), in charge of assessing and integrating these contributions into official releases, Debian has a flatter, much more decentralized structure with thousands of 'software' packages supported by Debian maintainers. This modular architecture, a result of Debian's larger scale as a software distribution, of which the Linux kernel is only one package, reduces the extent to which individuals in positions of responsibility are able to sustain superior levels of expertise over package maintainers in their specific areas of specialization, and constrains the extent to which they can justify the exercise of authority inside them.[24]

It was precisely a project leader's perceived interference with the internal matters of one of the project's packages that raised the need to establish a Debian Constitution defining the roles and protocols for selection of a class of Debian 'officers' (including the Debian project leader) in order to enhance the legitimacy of the project's decision-making process. The members of this de facto officialdom maintain a tense relationship with another group of developers in positions of responsibility in Debian's technical infrastructure (e.g. the 'FTP-Masters' in charge of assessing the compliance of submitted software packages with the principles of the project).[25] This shows how misalignment between the project's technical and political infrastructure led to the emergence of what appear to be two parallel structures for project governance, sometimes with conflicting goals.[26]

Another example of the tension between openness to participation and quality of output was the establishment in 1998 of a 'New Maintainer Process' in Debian, provoked by an influx of new developers who were perceived to be making low-quality contributions to the project and to be unaware of the project's ideological tenets. The New Maintainer Process established a procedure for the acquisition of membership, including verification of identity and tests of a candidate's technical skills and philosophical stance regarding Software Freedom issues. The result in this case was the codification of the project's goals and development techniques into a lengthy protocol aimed at ensuring that new entrants understood and agreed with its principles. The adoption of this policy attracted criticisms because of its emphasis on compliance with the project's ideology and the time to complete the processes it required, which were perceived as discouraging participation.

The history of Debian seems to support our line of reasoning regarding the main strengths of F/LOSS development, that is, the dynamic leveraging of expertise from a broad range of backgrounds made possible by the existence of relatively open spaces for participation, which are conducive to learning, and an incentive structure that promotes and rewards its exercise, but also the problems that such openness might eventually create. As we have argued, the project's growth and improvement raises the need to make difficult technical (and social) decisions which might antagonize members of the community. In cases such as Debian, where the project's culture (and its technical architecture) discourages the exercise of power by the leadership, it might become exceedingly difficult to put an end to continuous bickering between different factions, which diverts resources and attention from the development process. According to a former Debian project leader:

I think that one of the biggest problems Debian is currently facing is the inability to make decisions. There are so many endless, completely futile (and repetitive) discussions going on. We need someone who comes in, tells people to shut up and makes a decision on behalf of the project. A decision people will follow, even if they personally disagree with it. But seriously, do you think our culture would currently accept such a leader? I can tell you from experience that even people who have been asking for a 'strong' leader won't actually follow a leader who tells them to take a certain course of action.[27]

The lengthy period it has taken Debian to make its last stable release, and competition from the Ubuntu distribution (which is built on top of Debian code, but modified and improved by paid developers for usability in the desktop) indicate some of the limitations of F/LOSS models for software development in projects whose organizational structure (linked to the technical infrastructure, i.e. modularity, regulating know-ledge dispersion, and allocation of decision-making power to individuals) constrains the exercise of authority for conflict resolution and decision-making in critical areas.

10.3.2 *Wikipedia*

This brief summary of some 'moments' in the history of Debian shows how the project's community has had to react to political and organizational 'growth crises' by engaging in processes of institutional redesign aimed at establishing its goals and values more clearly, guaranteeing compliance with them through the institution of membership-acquisition processes, and legitimizing the exercise of decision-making through the creation of a Debian Constitution. We now move to a more detailed analysis of the Wikipedia community, including a description of its organizational structure, a history of its evolution, and discussion of some key events using the framework described in Section 10.2 as an interpretive lens.

10.3.2.1 THE ORGANIZATION OF WIKIPEDIA

Wikipedia is an online encyclopaedia elaborated by a decentralized collective of volunteers who carry out their activities using a wiki soft-ware infrastructure (which permits immediate, user-friendly creation and editing of any page in the web site, by anyone, and interlinking between pages).[28] The aim of the Wikipedia project, as stated by one of its founders, is 'to create and distribute a multilingual free encyclopaedia of the highest possible quality to every single person on the planet in their own language'.[29] Since its inception in January 2001, the English version of Wikipedia has grown to encompass more than 1.9 million articles.[30]

Each of the articles on Wikipedia can be edited openly and is linked to a discussion page where issues, such as what is needed to improve the article, reasons for modifications, etc., are debated, and to a 'history page', which lists the different versions of the article and their authors (identified through their login names or Internet Protocol (IP) addresses). Users can compare versions of an entry in order to assess changes, and redact a new version by reverting the page to a past state. It is also possible for any member of the community to 'nominate' pages by signalling them with special tags that might indicate that they do not belong in the web site (e.g. if they constitute 'original research' or spam), or that they are of a particularly high quality and deserve to become candidates for inclusion in the 'featured articles' category.[31]

Amongst the key roles established in Wikipedia's organization we can count editors (anyone who creates, modifies, or engages in a discussion), administrators selected by community consensus (with special rights and responsibilities, including the power to protect pages from edits, to delete them, or to block users), bureaucrats (responsible for maintaining the socio-technical infrastructure of the site,[32] yearly elected stewards (responsible for managing user access rights and, in some cases, verifying the identity of users in order, e.g. to avoid illegal voting), the Arbitration Committee (which provides binding solutions to disputes that the community has been unable to resolve by consensus, whose members are appointed by the project leader advised by the results of the 'Arbitration Committee' elections),[33] and the project leader, currently the project's founder Jimmy Wales (who has wide-ranging – albeit rarely exercised – powers including the right to appoint members to the Arbitration Committee, make policy proposals, and ban problematic users).

Wikipedia has a set of policies and guidelines that regulate the behaviour of members, the shape of (formal and informal) interactions within the community, and the type of and preferred formats for contributions[34]:

Behaviour – Concerning the conduct of members when participating in the project and interacting with the rest of the community. They are expected to be respectful and civil, to accept that their work might be edited by anyone (there is no such thing as 'article ownership'), and to avoid engaging in 'revert wars' or vandalism.[35]

Content – Related to the type of acceptable contributions (e.g. no original research is to be published in Wikipedia), as well as the approach that should be adopted when portraying controversial topics. In this case, members are expected to adopt a 'neutral point of view policy' (NPOV) that 'represents all significant views fairly and without bias'.[36]

Deletion and enforcing – Includes processes for the deletion of categories and articles, as well as policies related to the enforcement of Wikipedia's norms (i.e. blocking users, protecting articles, or resolving disputes).

Legal and copyright – Related to legal issues such as the copyright status of content that is published in Wikipedia, procedures for reusing content taken from the web site, fair-use matters, etc.

The process through which a behaviour or structure becomes enforceable in Wikipedia, and thus becomes 'policy', is usually one of online discussion, negotiation, and 'consensual' acceptance (or rejection) of proposals.

10.3.2.2 A HISTORY OF WIKIPEDIA

Wikipedia was launched in 2001 as a complement to Nupedia, a peer-reviewed open-content encyclopaedia project that had been launched a year earlier. Wikipedia was initially conceived as a repository of content that Nupedia editors could draw on and subsequently shape following formal peer-review procedures. Unlike Nupedia, whose workflow was based on email exchanges, and whose contributors were certified experts in their subject area, participation in Wikipedia occurs through a Web-based Wiki, and barriers to participation are non-existent (anyone can edit articles in it). Wikipedia grew rapidly, while Nupedia stagnated (its web site was eventually shut down in September 2003).

The former Nupedia 'editor-in-chief' along with other émigrés from the project, became the initial core of the Wikipedia community.[37] Being uncertain about the suitability of different social structures for fulfilment of the project's aims, they tried to adopt a flexible, consensus-based approach to rule-setting: for example, although the editor suggested that Wikipedia members should, generally, 'defer to experts', he also upheld an 'ignore all rules' rule aimed at encouraging new participants to experiment with the project and, above all, contribute. This promoted the emergence of a highly open and decentralized content-creation model with its roots in what the then editor-in-chief referred to as 'the Wiki culture'. A feature of this model, the rejection of 'authority', had two important consequences for Wikipedia. First, a very high tolerance of disruptive behaviours (inasmuch as the exercise of authority would be required to curtail the activities of individuals prone to conflict, or to ban them), and second a lack of deference to 'real-world' expertise and related 'arguments to authority' (since they would go against the community's egalitarian spirit).[38]

In spite of this emphasis on egalitarianism, a small number of essential rules were enforced in order to define and achieve the project's 'primary goal', to create a high-quality online encyclopaedia. The editor-in-chief created policy pages setting out 'What Wikipedia is (and is not)', and defining the 'NPOV' that contributors were expected to adopt in their contributions, as well as several stylistic conventions to standardize the appearance of the web site.

Notice in the media and growing traffic via Google and the Slashdot technical community site generated an influx of participants in Wikipedia, and this made it more difficult to apply the consensual policymaking approach that had been followed during the early days of the community. It also resulted in a surge in the number of problematic (very difficult to expel) users. The editor's efforts to discourage abuses of the system provoked accusations of censorship and 'authoritarianism'.

One of the essential controversies had to do with Wikipedia's 'primary goal': while some members, including the editor-in-chief considered the project's openness as a medium towards the achievement of a goal (a high-quality encyclopaedia) others conceived it as a goal in itself. The editor argued in a short essay that:

The remarkable success of the project so far is in very great measure due to this anarchy, or freedom, or openness, or whatever you'd like to call it. That is undeniable. But we must make sure that the tail doesn't start wagging the dog here, so that the Wikipedia project becomes as much or more a test of the principles of anarchism as it is an encyclopaedia.[39]

This editor eventually resigned at the beginning of 2002 as a consequence of the elimination of funding for his position, and of his frustration at the tolerance towards disruptive behaviours, and the general lack of respect for expertise.[40]

Subsequent population growth made it necessary to implement additional tools and powers (such as IP blocking, protection of pages, and article tracking) to address vandalism, spam, and abuse of the web site to promote partisan points of view. The Arbitration Committee was instituted with the aim of solving ongoing disputes between members of the community.

These modifications have been insufficient to quell concerns about Wikipedia's reliability, especially in the context of the current heavy usage to which it is subject: complaints about incorrect or libellous content in articles, as well as the detection of systematically biased contributions in the web site, have led to discussions about further adjustments that could be applied to the project's content-creation and membership model.[41] These include the requirement for users to register and to login as a precondition to editing articles, and the creation of 'stable/developmental' branches for the project.[42]

10.3.2.3 ANALYSIS

The above-mentioned outline of Wikipedia's institutional evolution illustrates the trade-offs between openness and control of the project that, we have argued, most F/LOSS endeavours face. Whilst the absence of barriers to entry has led to the rapid emergence of a vibrant and active community of contributors, and to extraordinary growth in the breadth and depth of the topics included in the project, it has also made it very difficult to exclude from participation individuals interested in self-promotion, commercial gain, the pursuit of a political agendas, and other goals that clash with the creation of a high-quality 'objective' encyclopaedia. The definition of 'objectivity' is in itself controversial, as an examination of the protracted debates and 'flame wars' raging in the discussion pages of many Wikipedia entries show. Even in the absence of opportunistic individuals trying to profit from the project, we would expect constant, intractable arguments between participants with 'different biases'.

The opposition that parties such as the former editor faced when trying to implement stricter criteria for participation in the project, or to institute an incentive structure that promoted contributions by experts (by giving them ownership over areas where they were particularly knowledgeable) is linked to the community's emphasis on values such as openness, decentralization, or disregard for credentials. As the former editor points out in his account of Wikipedia's early days:

So Wikipedia began as a good-natured anarchy, a sort of Rousseauian state of digital nature. I always took Wikipedia's anarchy to be provisional and purely for purposes of determining what the best rules, and the nature of its authority, should be. What I, and other Wikipedians, failed to realize is that our initial anarchy would be taken by the next wave of contributors as the very essence of the project – how Wikipedia was 'meant' to be – even though Wikipedia could have become anything we the contributors chose to make it.[43]

We have already indicated that the 'norms and values' of a F/LOSS epistemic community (as, e.g. codified in a 'vision statement' or a 'social contract') and its 'membership-acquisition process', define its boundaries and constitute signals to attract potentially productive participants, and to dissuade from entrance others who do not understand or disagree with the project's values and goals. They also circumscribe a space where novices can learn about the community, its norms, goals and operation, and eventually acquire insider status.

At the beginning of the Wikipedia project, in order to promote participation and thus avoid the fate of Nupedia, institutions were scarcely defined. Norms were non-existent and the acquisition of insider status, without the need to engage in any sort of peripheral participation process, was immediate.[44] This approach enhanced population growth, but also attracted problematic users to the project, with the consequences of malicious or ill-informed contributions and constant bickering: the polemic about the primary goal of Wikipedia quoted earlier is but an example of conflict that emerged from the misalignment between the project founders' goals and values and those of new entrants.

With respect to Wikipedia's governance structure, the third institutional pillar we described for F/LOSS projects, the project's flat hierarchical set-up (where only a small number of members are endowed with special powers, only to be exercised in cases of exceptional disruption) can be explained as a consequence of its highly decentralized socio-technical configuration. The use of Wiki software promotes an extreme form of knowledge (and authority) dispersion, with all participants enjoying absolute undifferentiated control over articles (modules), and the right to start new ones with negligible effort: hierarchical approaches to content supervision within this model seem very costly and difficult to scale.[45] Quality-assurance tasks are distributed throughout the community, whose members have the right to edit, revert, and report contributions, which, in their opinion, do not comply with the values of the project. This application of 'Linus's Law' to Wikipedia has major limitations. The claim that 'given enough eyeballs all bugs are shallow' should not hide the possibility that some eyeballs will see bugs where some others do not, particularly in the context of the controversial subjects continually sprouting in Wikipedia. This explains the constant arguments, that are aggravated by misunderstandings regarding the meaning of the 'NPOV' policy.

In addition to the previously mentioned egalitarian culture, Wikipedia's document-centric approach to participation, which discourages claims of 'article ownership', together with the immediacy of the editing process, and the contestable nature of the content being created, weakens justifications for the exercise of authority based on expertise or credentials. This has resulted in the emergence of an incentive structure that does not appear to adequately reward participation by experts.

Summarizing, it seems that the three institutional features used to coordinate development in F/LOSS projects, the 'norms and values' of the associated epistemic community, the processes of 'membership acquisition' involving legitimate peripheral participation, and the 'governance' process involving structures for decision-making and conflict-resolution are weakened by Wikipedia's egalitarian culture and the dispersion of knowledge (and authority) throughout the project. This results in constant controversies among participants in the project, a factor that can be positive when it contributes to the elaboration of more comprehensive entries encompassing a broad range of points of view, but can also detract from its quality (especially at a particular moment in time). It can also create an environment of constant bickering, which might lead to participant burnout and exit. Efforts to balance these conflicting tendencies include implementation of required registration for Wikipedia editors, as well as ongoing discussions regarding the possible creation of two Wikipedia 'branches' (one stable and the other experimental, mirroring the approach adopted by many F/LOSS projects).

10.4 Conclusions

10.4.1 *Institutional dimensions of online communities*

In this chapter we have elaborated a framework that focuses on three main characteristics of F/LOSS communities, that is, rules and norms for the coordination of development activities, social dynamics for participation and learning, and governance structures. To analyse the former two we resorted, following Edwards (2001), to the concepts of 'epistemic community' and 'legitimate peripheral participation'. We contend that these two social mechanisms are insufficient to guarantee stability in online communities, and that governance is indeed exercised (in spite of claims regarding the horizontal nature of F/LOSS projects) by individuals who have been endowed with the responsibility (reputation) by initiating the project or making similarly crucial contributions to its development.

Our examination of Debian and Wikipedia has revealed evidence of the presence of these structures, lending support to our contention, first that the social processes that unfold in F/LOSS projects appear inextricably linked to their social structure, which is of relative openness to participation and allocation of rewards according to norms that place particular worth on technical expertise. And second, that conflict and tension emerging from dissensions over 'destinations' (goals) and 'paths' (technical decisions to achieve those goals) are addressed through processes of institutional redesign. The codification of community norms and practices in online documents and frequently asked questions (FAQs), and of protocols that have to be followed in order to achieve membership rights, constitute attempts to enforce a minimum level of alignment or agreement among project participants in order to avoid continuous bickering and stalled development. However, adoption of these strategies raises new problems, insofar as they may reduce the attractiveness of participation for novices (who might be doubtful about the extent to which a community of volunteers has the right to require such levels of commitment) and harm its sustainability; or result in political conflict (and constitutional crisis) by bringing to the fore trade-offs between the preferred goals of different participant constituencies.

Although there are clear differences between Debian and Wikipedia, we have focused throughout this chapter on the processes within them that present clear parallels. We hope that our highlighting of these similarities will stand as a warning to practitioners, academics, and commentators who at times seem excessively optimistic about the extent to which technical discussions in open-source software projects can be resolved objectively compared to other activities employing open-source principles (such as Wikipedia), which are sometimes derided as inherently subjective.[46] We have argued that although it is easier to assess the quality of the code (it 'either runs or not') being incorporated into Debian than to assess an entry in Wikipedia, there is space for discussion and controversy regarding the implementation, maintainability, legal status, size, and many other attributes of code, which on occasion will be conflicting – code is almost never perfect, and different code implementations are better for different purposes, which opens up possibilities for debate, which are exacerbated in a context of uncertainty.

On the other hand, a feature of both projects where there are important differences is the allocation of reputation to participants who make sustained contributions.[47] The document-centric approach adopted by Wikipedia, where individual ownership over specific articles is 'hidden' and relegated to their discussion pages, would seem to reduce the incentives for quality contributions. This model, and the accelerated processes of acquisition of 'insider status', promote openness to participation, but also give rise to internal strife among participants (who disagree constantly about epistemic norms for validation of knowledge such as the 'NPOV' principle), which harms the quality and reliability of Wikipedia's content and creates participant burnout. So what we find is that the definition of these institutional variables or dimensions is associated with different outcomes, which might be more suitable for communities and social groups, depending on their purposes. This finding highlights the need to consider institutional issues during the design and management of F/LOSS communities, something particularly relevant for companies interested in establishing 'hybrid models' for software development (Berdou 2007).

10.4.2 *The F/LOSS museum*

We conclude this chapter by arguing that instead of thinking of F/LOSS projects as Raymondian bazaars, an idealized and inherently flawed metaphor because of its focus on individual exchange rather than collective construction of a stable structure, perhaps it would be more useful to conceive of them as public museums. Museums are spaces that anybody can enter (in that sense, open), in which the right to hang artwork from the walls is granted by a curator (i.e. the project leader or integrator) depending on more or less objective criteria of quality, the museum's values, coherence with other contributions, the experience or even status of the would-be exhibitor, etc. Museums also contain many 'hidden' resources and processes including the infrastructures for security, archiving of works not currently on display, and activities associated with restoration and refurbishment of artefacts retained by the museum. We think that this metaphor as opposed to that of the bazaar, accommodates much better the integration elements of F/LOSS development, the complex structure 'behind the scenes', and the possibility of participation as a form of self-expression (not precluding vandalism, graffiti, and sabotage). It also conveys the public-good aspects of accessibility by the general public. Thinking about this F/LOSS museum in architectural terms also makes it possible to conceptualize the difficulties that fast growth represents for coordination and quality assurance, inasmuch as a visitor might decide to hang his or her own picture from the wall in a distant, rarely visited room, regardless of rules, regulations, or the presence of 'security guards'.[48]

More generally, museums face the continuous challenge of establishing their relevance for a contemporaneous public. While some of those involved with museums see inherent value in the historical and cultural processes that generated the artefacts it houses, others would argue that these artefacts only provide the foundations upon which engaging and relevant 'displays' can be constructed. How those displays are constructed, and more particularly *who* makes the key decisions regarding theme and expression, are a central feature governing the attractiveness and ultimately resource (in terms of patrons) of the museum, and of the open-source project. Of course, there are also differences. The processes by which museums set their acquisition policies is even more hierarchical and less open than the control processes that we have described as occurring in open-source communities. The 'open museum' is a conceptual category with a fictive address.

Employing this category, however, allows us to suggest that there is a continuum that goes from the open museum to the medieval cathedral, with which Eric Raymond originally compared proprietary software companies. In this continuum, there is room for the bazaar as a complex social network built upon relationships of trust in the context of repeated exchange, as well as communities that more reflexively constitute the rules and norms of their practice. The methodologies for constructing F/LOSS efforts are instantiations from the universe of possible social configurations for software development. These instantiations arise from policy decisions ('more or less open', 'more or less managed') made by project participants, the diverse character and social experience of the participants, and the evolving 'audience' for the efforts of participants (including their own needs). This metaphor makes it possible to understand the emerging diversity of institutional arrangements established (or evolved) in F/LOSS communities as a consequence of the effort to find a balance between the achievement of different, sometimes conflicting goals (such as stability versus innovation, or appropriability versus community goodwill). We suggest that our proposal does not constitute a mere redefinition or renaming of a phenomenon, but a useful and necessary reconceptualization that should contribute to a better understanding of its nature.

References

Andriopoulos, C. (2001). 'Determinants of organizational creativity: A literature review', *Management Decision*, 39(10): 834–40.

Berdou, E. (2007). 'Managing the bazaar: Commercialization and peripheral participation in mature, community-led free/open source software projects', unpublished DPhil thesis, London School of Economics and Political Science, Department of Media and Communications, London.

Brown, J. S. and Duguid, P. (2001). 'Knowledge and organization: A social-practice perspective', *Organization Science*, 12(2): 198–213.

Christensen, C. M. (1997). *The Innovator's Dilemma*. Cambridge, MA: Harvard University Press.

Coleman, E. G. (2005). 'Three ethical moments in Debian', available at http://papers.ssrn.com/sol3/papers.cfm?abstract_id = 805287 (accessed 18 August 2007).

Dougherty, D. (1992). 'Interpretive barriers to successful product innovation in large firms', *Organization Science*, 3(2): 179–202.

Edwards, K. (2000). 'When beggars become choosers', *First Monday*, 5(10), available at http://www.firstmonday.org/issues/issue5_10/edwards/index.html (accessed 18 August 2007).

—— (2001). 'Epistemic communities, situated learning and open source software development', Working paper available at http://opensource.mit.edu/papers/kasperedwards-ec.pdf#search = %22kasper%20edwards%20epistemic%22 (accessed 18 August 2007).

Ghosh, R., Glott, R., Krieger, B., and Robles, G. (2002). *Free/Libre and Open Source Software: Survey and Study Final Report. Deliverable D* 18. *Part IV: Survey of Developers*, available at http://www.infonomics.nl/FLOSS/report/Final4.htm (accessed 18 August 2007).

Haas, P. M. (1992). 'Introduction: Epistemic communities and international policy coordination', *International Organization*, 46(1): 1–36.

Herbsleb, J., Mockus, A., Finholt, T. A., and Grinter, R. E. (2000). *Distance, Dependencies, and Delay in a Global Collaboration: Proceedings of the 2000 ACM Conference on Computer Supported Cooperative Work*. Philadelphia PA: ACM Press, available at http://portal.acm.org/citation.cfm?id = 359003&coll = portal&dl = ACM (accessed 18 August 2007).

Keen, A. (2007). *The Cult of the Amateur: How Today's Internet is Killing Our Culture and Assaulting Our Economy*. London: Nicholas Brealey.

Klincewicz, K. (2005). 'Innovativeness of open source software projects', Working paper available at http://opensource.mit.edu/papers/klincewicz.pdf (accessed 18 August 2007).

Koch, S. and Schneider, G. (2000). 'Results from software engineering research into open source development projects using public data', Working paper available at http://wwwai.wu-wien.ac.at/~koch/forschung/sw-eng/wp22.pdf (accessed 18 August 2007).

Lakhani, K., Wolf, B., Bates, J., and DiBona, C. (2002). *The Boston Consulting Group Hacker Survey*, available at http://www.bcg.com/opensource/BCGHackerSurvey OSCON24July02v073.pdf (accessed 18 August 2007).

Lave, J. and Wenger, E. (1991). *Situated Learning: Legitimate Peripheral Participation*. Cambridge: Cambridge University Press.

Lerner, J. and Tirole, J. (2002). 'Some simple economics of open source', *Journal of Industrial Economics*, 52: 197–234.

Levy, S. (2001). *Hackers*. New York: Penguin.

Mateos-Garcia, J. and Steinmueller, W. E. (2002). 'The open source way of working: A new paradigm for the division of labour in software development? SPRU Electronic Working paper, available at http://www.sussex.ac.uk/Units/spru/publications/imprint/sewps/sewp92/sewp92.pdf (accessed 18 August 2007).

———— (2008).'The institutions of open source software: Examining the Debian community', forthcoming in *Information Economics and Policy*.

O'Mahony, S. (2006). 'Developing community software in a commodity world', in M. Fisher and G. Downey (eds.), *Frontiers of Capital: Ethnographic Reflections on the New Economy*. Durham, NC: Duke University Press, pp. 237–66.

—— and Ferraro, F. (2003). 'Managing the boundary of an "open" project', prepared for the Santa Fe Institute (SFI) Workshop on the Network Construction of Markets, available at http://opensource.mit.edu/papers/omahonyferraro. pdf#search = %22o'mahony%202002%20debian%22 (accessed 18 August 2007).

Raymond, E. S. (1999). *The Cathedral and the Bazaar: Musings on Linux and Open Source by an Accidental Revolutionary*. Sebastopol, CA: O'Reilly.

Sanger, L. (2005). *The Early Story of Wikipedia and Nupedia: A Memoir*, available at http://features.slashdot.org/article.pl?sid = 05/04/18/164213 (accessed 16 November 2007).

Schiff, S. (2006). 'Know it all: Can Wikipedia conquer expertise?' *New Yorker*, 27 April, available at http://www.newyorker.com/archive/2006/07/31/060731fa_fact?currentPage = 5 (accessed 18 August 2007).

Sunstein, C. (2006). *Infotopia: How Many Minds Produce Knowledge*. Oxford: Oxford University Press.

Surowiecki, J. (2004). *The Wisdom of Crowds: Why the Many Are Smarter Than the Few and How Collective Wisdom Shapes Business, Economies, Societies and Nations*. New York: Random House.

Von Hippel, E. (2005). *Democratizing Innovation*. Cambridge, MA: MIT Press.

Notes

1. The research reported in this chapter could not have been undertaken without the financial support received by the Stanford Institute for Economic Policy Research (SIEPR) Project on the Economics of Free and Open Source Software in the form of grant awards by the National Science Foundation program on Digital Technology and Society: IIS-0112962(2001–04) and IIS-0329259(2003–05) (see http://siepr.stanford.edu/programs/OpenSoftware_David/OS_Project_ Funded_Announcmt.htm).

2. Arguably, Free/Libre Open Source Software (F/LOSS), precursors to the 'Web 2.0' phenomenon, and the source of many of the technologies that enable it.

3. Since these structures might lead to differences in performance depending on the area they operate in (e.g. highly creative versus routinized tasks, incremental versus architectural innovation), particular attention should be paid to the conditions for their emergence during processes of organizational design and implementation. We hope this acknowledgement of a heterogeneity of 'degrees of openness' with different organizational manifestations provides a more finely nuanced account of the strengths of F/LOSS development than claims that present 'crowd-sourcing' and other buzzword-led strategies as 'silver bullets' to resolve the conundrums that companies engaged in complex knowledge-production activities face on a day-to-day basis.

4. Section 10.2.1 is an abbreviation of the account presented in Mateos-Garcia and Steinmueller (2008).

5. A common conundrum in the use of the word 'community' is the existence of human settlements with deep social, cultural, and ethnographic foundations established well before living memory. It should be apparent from the context that the primary contribution of communities of this type is to provide a store of preconceptions and understandings that may or may not prove useful in the rather different context in which the term community is employed in this chapter, and more generally in the consideration of virtual communities.

6. The importance of this shared purpose might perhaps appear attenuated in the case of communities that emerge in geographically co-located contexts (e.g. members of a department located in the same office) or in the presence of financial incentives for participation. In these cases the dynamics of daily interaction in the workplace might contribute to create the social bonds giving rise to the emergence of a community.

7. These two aspects could be exemplified respectively by forums and other public areas where novices can present potential solutions to problems and discuss their merits and shortcomings with more experienced developers, learning in the process, and by the existence of project areas and actions that can only be entered/exercised by individuals with the suitable authorization.

8. We acknowledge this limitation, but in the spirit of 'methodological pragmatism' informing the elaboration of this chapter we argue that the explanatory power of the 'legitimate peripheral participation' concept in this specific area warrants its application.

9. Not necessarily for initial participation, given the openness of most spaces for communication in these projects: we could, for example think of 'trolls' as participants who do not agree with a community's values and goals.

10. It is important to note that the 'goals' are in many cases operational and related, for example to building a technologically excellent software program. In these cases it is the project itself that attracts participants to the community.

11. Consider, for example that the goal of 'creating the highest-quality program' might be insufficient to select a development path in areas characterized by trade-offs between program attributes, such as number of features and usability, both of which are desirable, but often conflicting.

12. See Mateos-Garcia and Steinmueller (2002) for a detailed description of the organizational structure of F/LOSS projects and the roles within them.

13. The volunteer nature of F/LOSS development and the special characteristics of F/LOSS licences makes it possible for any disgruntled participant to exit the community and start a new development branch using the project's code base. It is often argued that this possibility keeps those individuals in positions of power 'in check' and responsive to the needs and aspirations of the community.

14. Again, what has been referred to as 'Linus's Law' (Raymond 1999).

15. See Koch and Schneider (2000) for an empirical analysis of contribution patterns. What is more, it appears that in many cases bug reports and other contributions made by well-intentioned technically illiterate outsiders can stress a project's informational infrastructure.

16. At least in the case of technically savvy users.

17. The users inside these 'Horizontal Innovation Networks' decide to reveal freely the innovations they have developed internally on the basis of a 'cost–benefit analysis', which, it is argued, in the case of software programs tends to favour free sharing (von Hippel 2005). In this framework, issues related to the need to assess the quality of these contributions, or to integrate them into larger aggregates are generally neglected.

18. The extent to which a F/LOSS project is embedded in the myriad communities to which its developers belong might make it possible to raise awareness about its existence in groups with the expertise required for development. We can think of a F/LOSS community as a community of practice that overlaps with a broad range of institutions (companies, academia, hobbyist groups) to which its developers belong as part of, for example their professional activities.

19. The voluntary nature of participation, the self-allocation of effort to those areas in which an individual is more interested, and the admiration of expertise give rise to a system of intrinsic and extrinsic incentives conducive to productivity and creativity enhancements (see Andriopoulos 2001 for an overview of some organizational determinants of creativity). This reward system can be linked to the 'motivational stream' of the F/LOSS literature in order to provide a synthetic framework that explains participation in projects for individuals with a wide range of aspirations (see Mateos-Garcia and Steinmueller 2002).

20. Establishing the goals of a project might discourage potential volunteers: agreement on these goals, when made explicit, constitutes a criterion for (or perhaps in some cases a barrier to) participation. See Edwards (2000) and Mateos-Garcia and Steinmueller (2002).

21. An illustration of this would be the controversies in the GNU/Linux project regarding whether the goal should be reliability and high performance (essential in a server environment) or functionality and usability (necessary for growth in the desktop area).

22. Klincewicz (2005) presents this lack of decisiveness as an explanatory factor for the relatively low innovativeness in a sample of 500 F/LOSS papers he analyses. In a way, F/LOSS communities find themselves facing their own special version of the 'innovator's dilemma' (Christensen, 1997).

23. See Mateos-Garcia and Steinmueller (2008) for a more detailed discussion of Debian's evolution inside this conceptual framework, and O'Mahony and Ferraro (2003), O'Mahony (2006), and Coleman (2005) for a discussion of Debian's history.

24. We could say that Debian's knowledge structure favours a 'federal' organizational structure.

25. Differently from Debian's officers, these developers have reached their position of power outside Debian's sanctioned political process.

26. Debian's officialdom appears concerned with maintaining a steady cycle of releases, and favouring the incorporation of innovative packages in the project, while FTP Masters focuses on stability and making sure that buggy packages, or packages with a dubious legal status are not included in a release. These differences seem to mimic those found by Dougherty (1992) in her analysis of 'worldviews' as barriers to innovation inside firms.

27. Post in his blog available at http://www.cyrius.com/journal/2006/03/09# being-dpl (accessed 18 August 2007).

28. See http://www.wikipedia.org and http://www.wiki.org (both accessed 18 August 2007). Wikipedia currently comprises ten projects in different languages, although throughout this chapter we will mostly focus on the English language Wikipedia (http://en.wikipedia.org/, accessed 18 August 2007).

29. http://en.wikipedia.org

30. As of 6 August 2007. See http://en.wikipedia.org/wiki/Wikipedia:Overview_ FAQ (accessed 18 August 2007).

31. See http://en.wikipedia.org/wiki/Wikipedia:Articles_for_deletion and http:// en.wikipedia.org/wiki/Wikipedia:What_is_a_featured_article%3F (both accessed 18 August 2007). respectively.

32. This should not be confused with the role of maintaining and developing the software on which Wikipedia relies, a task undertaken by the Wikimedia Foundation (http://wikimediafoundation.org/wiki/, accessed 18 August 2007).

33. In addition to the Arbitration Committee, there is a less formal Mediation Committee, which assists users engaged in disputes, and an Association of Members Advocates, which provides users with assistance and advice (e.g. by explaining relevant policies or representing users in an arbitration process).

34. Format issues are mostly addressed through more flexible guidelines, which are not the focus of this chapter.

35. Revert wars occur when two parties engaged in a dispute about an article start reverting automatically any changes made by the opponent.
36. http://en.wikipedia.org/wiki/Wikipedia:Neutral_point_of_view (accessed 18 August 2007).
37. For simplicity, we will henceforth refer to this individual as the 'editor' even though he rejected such a title.
38. This 'anti-elitism', which would later be criticized by the former editor in http://www.kuro5hin.org/story/2004/12/30/142458/25 (accessed 18 August 2007). concurs with some of the basic tenets of the 'Hacker ethic' as summarized by Levy (2001).
39. http://meta.wikimedia.org/wiki/Is_Wikipedia_an_experiment_in_anarchy (accessed 18 August 2007).
40. See http://www.kuro5hin.org/story/2004/12/30/142458/25 for his opinions on the matter. He has since moved on to found Citizendium, an encyclopaedia project styled after Wikipedia, but with an organizational structure of quality assurance based on 'real-world' credentials (http://en.citizendium.org/wiki/Main_Page, accessed 18 August 2007).
41. See Keen (2007), http://www.usatoday.com/news/opinion/editorials/2005–11–29-wikipedia-edit_x.htm and http://news.bbc.co.uk/2/hi/technology/4695376.stm (both accessed 18 August 2007). for examples of both problems.
42. The latter strategy is to be implemented as a 'pilot' in the German Wikipedia: the 'stable development branch' would be vetted by privileged members of the project and visible to non-logged-in users (who would not be allowed to edit), while the 'development' branch could be edited by anyone logged in the web site. See http://news.bbc.co.uk/2/hi/technology/5286458.stm (accessed 18 August 2007).
43. Sanger (2005).
44. This also implies that all participants, in principle, had the same status and rights regardless of their past record.
45. Given the sheer size of the project and the absence of 'vantage points' (or an integration locus) from which to perform such an assessment.
46. 'Schiff (2006) recounts an interview with Eric Raymond whose work, schiff notes 'inspired Wales'. Schiff states, 'In his view, the site is "infested with moonbats" (Think hobgoblins of little minds, varsity division.)'. Schiff further quotes Raymond as saying, 'The more you look at what some of the Wikipedia contributors have done, the better Britannica looks … ' According to Schiff '[Raymond]' believes that the open-source model is simply inapplicable to an encyclopaedia. For software, there is an objective standard: either it works or it does not. There is no such test for truth'.
47. For example when extolling the advantages of software projects over Wikipedia as loci for the implementation of open methods for development, Wikipedia's former editor-in-chief does not make any reference to the actual subject of development, but to the different approaches different groups

have taken to the definition of expertise. See http://many.corante.com/arch-ives/2006/09/20/larry_sanger_on_me_on_citizendium.php (accessed 18 August 2007).

48. A practice undertaken by the graffiti artist 'Banksy' in venues such as New York's Metropolitan Museum of Art and Museum of Modern Art, http://news.bbc.co.uk/2/hi/americas/4382245.stm (accessed 18 August 2007)

Epilogue: *Situated Learning* and Changing Practice[1]

Jean Lave

Situated Learning: Legitimate Peripheral Participation (Lave and Wenger 1991) was a short manifesto for learning as an apprentice-like part of all social practice. The concept of 'communities of practice' emerged as an informal label for a knot of ideas developed in the process. The label stuck, the book brought the concept to the table, and it has travelled to places, and for purposes, that we did not envision at the time. In the process it has taken on a life of its own, sometimes in felicitous and generative ways, but at other times in ways that give me pause. The ideas worked out in *Situated Learning* were intended as both a critique of conventional theories of learning, doing, and social change and as a means of *analysing* situations of all kinds in which learning was of interest to researchers – not just schools, and not only in schoolish terms. It was specifically *not* intended as a normative or prescriptive model for what to do differently or how to create better classrooms or businesses. Many who use the concept of 'communities of practice' now seem ignorant of the original intent (and its limitations), and simply assimilate it into conventional theory. Perhaps revisiting that radical (though by no means new) vision would be useful. The present book offers a good opportunity to reflect on the concept of 'communities of practice' 15 years later, in the form of a review of *Situated Learning: Legitimate Peripheral Participation*.

Revisiting *Situated Learning*

Situated Learning formulated a general question, 'how are we to understand learning as an integral part of ongoing practice?'. Etienne Wenger and

283

I argued that all practices involve learning. Learning is situated activity, indeed, legitimate peripheral participation (lpp). All learning and every-day life have some aspects of apprenticeship about them. This is a social phenomenon – newcomers can only become old-timers by participating in communities of practitioners. Legitimate peripheral participation is a way to speak about *relations* between newcomers and old-timers, activities, identities, artefacts, and communities of practice. Each of the five ethnog-raphies of apprenticeship that illustrated our argument was concerned with apprentices *mastering* practice, and we enclosed this in a glove called a community of practice whose structure and purpose was acting master-fully. At the same time we were trying to say that the development of identity in relation to the identities of others was more fundamental than knowledge or mastery.

We had other reasons for concentrating on apprenticeship: I had been working on craft apprenticeship among Vai and Gola tailors in Liberia for a long time, convinced a close analysis of apprenticeship would help illu-minate the limitations of academic theorizing on learning. Etienne Wen-ger had just finished a book on intelligent tutoring systems. Situated learning as lpp offered an alternative to the dualist assumptions of cogni-tive theories (e.g. Lave and Wenger 1991, p. 52; cf. Lave 1988) and theories of education that made pristine distinctions between things like mind and body, person and world, the individual and the social, and thought and action. Further, we felt that theories of learning trivialized the life – and person-transforming character of learning (ch. 5, p. 121).

The Relation of Legitimate Peripheral Participation and Communities of Practice

'Community of practice' was a way to give scope in time/space to an understanding of 'practice' so as not to reduce social life to only its interpersonal transactions, interactions, and problem-solving activities. Similarly, learning as 'lpp of newcomers becoming old-timers' was inten-ded to open out 'learning' to broader historical, cultural, and political relations and larger scopes of time and place.

We rejected the notion of learners as immobile recipients of informa-tion, instead focusing on centripetal movement, changing locations and ways of participating, and a notion of how knowledgeability changes in these circumstances. We suggested that value (complexly, contradictorily, positive, and negative) is created by/for all participants through their engagements in practice. 'Identity' was a concept whose purpose was to insist that increasing knowledgeable skill is only a small part of the broader social being of newcomers becoming old-timers.[2]

We began to explore how to parse a community's day-to-day practice with respect to its involvement in producing 'old-timers' out of 'newcomers'. These last terms were intended to move away from abstract notions of the 'universal person' or 'individual', and to emphasize that they exist in their relations with each other. Also, we were trying to get away from too-tight conventional assumptions that all 'old-timers' are teachers (and no newcomers) and all 'newcomers' are novices. 'Old-timers' and 'newcomers' left open just what, besides relative length of participation, differentiated participants from one another. 'Communities of practice' was likewise an attempt to move away from an abstract universal notion of group or social category to emphasize that people are mutually engaged in *doing* things together. This doing is necessary to sustain for participation by a 'next generation', the cultural practices that they make over and into their lives. But both old-timer–newcomer relations and relations among differently situated participants embody tensions that help to generate the conceptual complexities of 'lpp'.

'Legitimate peripheral participation', we said, was to be taken as one indivisible concept. Or at least its parts should never be taken one at a time. In spite of this the concept invited a polarizing vision of illegitimate, or central, or non-participation. Why it was hard to grasp as 'a textured landscape of participation' may have had more to do with two problems running through the essay than with the three-part term itself. One problem was the notion of moving from peripheral to full participation, part of a broader argument that I now reject (see below). This strongly suggested a polar contrast, even as we said that was not what we meant. Second, on a more positive note, legitimate peripherality was the most problematic of the pairwise permutations of lpp (legitimate participation and peripheral participation were more straightforward) because it pointed to ambiguities of power, to difference and struggle over the changing participation of newcomers becoming old-timers. Though we acknowledged this we really did not get into it. Arguably it might have swamped the project. This would have been a good test of our conception of lpp. Because we stopped short of pursuing its conflicting (not simply opposed) implications we made it easier to dismember the concept of lpp in simple abstract terms. We should have made clearer that (and how) institutions, capital, and forces of production give people power over legitimacy, peripherality, and participation without dividing one from another.

I am not certain the word cognition never appears in *Situated Learning*, but such was our intention – that, and the desire that every use of the term 'participation' could be read twice – both as 'a person participating' and as a 'practice participated in'. So lpp described the practice of persons with respect to communities of practice. Likewise, from the other side of this relation, communities of practice consist in part of their participants. This ubiquitous double meaning was the key to our efforts to refuse to divide person from world:

Lpp is intended as a conceptual bridge – as a claim about the common processes inherent in the production of changing persons and changing communities of practice. This pivotal emphasis, via lpp, on relations between the production of knowledgeable identities and the production of communities of practice, makes it possible to think of sustained learning as embodying, albeit in transformed ways, the structural characteristics of communities of practice. (*Lave and Wenger* 1991, p. 55)

Our perspective, then, was a relational one. So we began the conclusions by saying:

The concept of lpp obtains its meaning, not in a concise definition of its boundaries, but in its multiple, theoretically generative interconnections with persons, activities, knowing and the world. (p. 121)

Ethnography and Theory

We went about our project from two directions: by inquiring into historically specific exemplars of apprenticeship and by creating an analytic framework for addressing practices of apprenticeship. In thinking about what the book did convincingly it is useful to pay attention to where the examples exemplify the points we were trying to make, and where the points are not pushed by ethnographic instances. The latter could not have had the same dramatic weight as the former, and perhaps they had not equal significance for us either.

What the examples were good at: The Yucatec midwives and Vai and Gola tailors showed how learning happens without didactically overriding ongoing practice. Dramatically this supported a different view of learning (e.g. learning curricula are different from teaching curricula; near peers are primary pedagogical resources rather than masters; e.g. p. 113.). We also showed through ethnographic examples, for instance the Vai and Gola tailors, that work processes and learning processes are structured differently. This matters for an argument about *changing* practice:

Dissociating learning from pedagogical intentions opens the possibility of mismatch or conflict among practitioners' viewpoints in situations where learning is going on. These differences often must become constitutive of the content of learning. (pp. 113–14)

The ethnographic account of butchers' apprenticeship was about the dark side of access – legitimate peripherality denied, sequestration by management interested in labour at the expense of learning, the exception that proves the rule; apprentices learned more about conditions of labour in supermarkets, among other things, than about butchering practices. The Alcoholics Anonymous example helped to underline the importance of analysis of genres of changing linguistic participation, talking within and about the practice, war stories, and more, all as part of practice. The ethnographic examples pointed to peers and practice as structuring resources for learning in practice. Motivation seemed to inhere in movement towards full participation in community practice in which apprentices also had a future and were developing identities.

Difficulties of *Situated Learning*

There were two problems with our analysis, with multiple effects. One concerned a too single-minded focus on identities of mastery requiring trajectories of increasing knowledgeability. Even as we pushed out the boundaries of examples of apprenticeship, *Situated Learning* concentrated on social processes aimed at producing experts – apprenticeship construed as coming to be knowledgeably skilled at work *in situ*. We assumed that we were talking about the telos of becoming masters, mastery, increasing knowledgeable skill (e.g. p. 94), and masters as exemplars of what apprentices were becoming (e.g. p. 95) – rather than complex co-participants. It was a short step to the notion of apprentices becoming full practitioners (e.g. p. 95) rather than participants – so that again a telos of mastery is implied, along with a community of masters (and comers). This left 'mastery' as too complete and duplicative a vision of old-timers and their practice.[3] But it was a difficult step away from the particulars of apprenticeship to a theory of learning that involved moving from mastery (and the implied novitiate) to degrees of participation.

The second problem involved leaving out the political economic and institutional structuring that partially determines communities of practice and their changing participants.[4] It is difficult to imagine the differences

it makes in talking about 'learning' to examine the interconnected political economic and cultural forces at work, beyond the immediate.
What follows might be an object lesson on what happens when you
ignore them: for without working on the political economic historical
relations, we fell back on some ahistorical assumptions about social
order, containerized single communities of practice, a tensionless equation of mastery and membership, and a language of forms.[5] These points
require elaboration.

It strikes me now that we chose four examples of apprenticeship far from
late capital, in spirit at least, and only one example set squarely in contemporary conditions of training for wage labour. Only the butchers'
example situated learning in its alienated, commoditized relations in
contemporary life. We did touch on teaching in terms that suggest an
analysis of alienated practice in the present (e.g. p. 112), but that just
meant that in some sense we equated teaching with alienated relations
of capital and romanticized learning as unalienated authentic activity. We
are not alone – this is something I notice and object to in the work of
many psychologists who romanticize learning and choose their examples
accordingly. Our desire to do justice to the richness of learning belongs
squarely in that box. I no longer look on learning as having a predetermined value, any more than I would assign abstract value to the practices
and participants of which it is a part.

Situated Learning discussed communities of practice as sites of conflict,
difference, and change in ways that still seem sensible. But these were
intertwined with themes of social order ('the concept of lpp provides a
framework for bringing together theories of situated activity and theories
about the production and reproduction of the social order', p. 47), *forms*
of culture, learning, communities, and practice; *a* community of practice;
progress towards mastery (still some residual aspects of knowledge 'accumulation' here), and identities of membership. These did not engage with
conceptions of conflict, difference, or change, nor with the exception of
the butchers' example did the ethnographic material on apprenticeship
make conflict and difference central to an analysis of everyday life. We
did not intend to oppose a homogenized 'communal' community to a
community whose commonalities (and differences) are produced through
its contradictions, but *Situated Learning* has all too often been read as
painting a view of social life as closed, harmonious, and homogeneous,
so that participants are 'members'. This conventional view framed a
sequence of theoretical connections that run through the book: person

is a person-in-the-world, that is, the social world, composed of communities, that is, communities of practice, in which lpp leads centripetally to full participation and a new identity of membership as a member of a community of practice. There are no contradictions or tensions here to set social life, multiple institutions, forces, and communities of practice in motion. Establishing the political economic, historical, and institutional context and forces at work would have prevented a slip into homogeneous, enclosed, and unchanging readings of communities of practice taken one at a time and made it easier to see that the question of what constitutes communities of practice takes much of its urgency from questioning whether, how, and how much official communities, official practices, and formal organizations in fact define the working nexus of living, culturally productive social practice.

In the lives we study there are no doubt culturally identified moments of communality and occasionally 'membership'. There is widespread belief and longing for such a state of affairs along with massive work to deny their absence (cf. Raymond Williams'(1976) discussion of 'community'). These are part of the everyday present that furnishes our lives; but they are not very helpful in explaining those lives, for they obscure the contradictory processes by which they are produced. We should be able to take them into account along with everything else.

Contradiction and Change

Situated Learning introduced notions of lpp in communities of practice as contradictory, shaping, and shaped by differences and constitutive tensions among changing persons, activities, and circumstances. Let us begin with the central notion of access: There were specific points of conflict in legitimate peripherality, in its ambiguities and uncertainties, in its struggles between newcomers' access to practice, and sequestration from it. The butchers' example showed (and the tailors' as well) the conflict between masters and apprentices over whether apprentices should engage in short-term contributions of labour sequestered from arenas of mature practice (meat-package wrapping, working the master tailor's farm upcountry) or in activity with peripheral participatory possibilities, but perhaps not as immediately useful to the master (working with journeyman meat cutters, practicing cutting on fabric scraps). Old-timers and newcomers have conflicting stakes in desirable scopes of access and control over them, both within themselves and between them. We concluded – a crucial point – that learning must always be such a problematic process. Further, this meant 'communities of practice are engaged in the generative process of producing their own future' (both points pp. 57–8).

A central contradiction in communities of practice with respect to lpp is that of continuity and displacement.[6] There is a fundamental contradiction in the meaning to newcomers and old-timers of increasing participation by the former; for the centripetal development of full participants, and with it the production of a community of practice, also implies the replacement of old-timers (p. 57):

Conflicts between masters and apprentices (or, less individualistically, between generations) take place in the course of everyday participation. Shared participation is the stage on which the old and the new, the known and the unknown, the established and the hopeful, act out their differences and discover their commonalities, manifest their fear of one another, and come to terms with their need for one another. Each threatens the fulfillment of the other's destiny, just as it is essential to it. (p. 116)

The dilemma for newcomers is that they need to engage in the existing practice, but also have a stake in its development as they begin to establish their own identity in its future (p. 115). Old-timers find it useful to draw in newcomers to exploit their labour even as it is in some ultimate sense necessary to make newcomers into legitimate co-participants if the practice is to survive. One guaranteed dilemma for old-timers especially is that 'granting legitimate participation to newcomers with their own viewpoints introduces into any community of practice all the tensions of the continuity-displacement contradiction' (p. 116).

Probably the most frequent, and irritating, question from readers of *Situated Learning* has been, 'how do I know I've got a community of practice?' (especially since they do not bother to ask with equal bewilderment about what is a family or a neighbourhood, school, race, culture, gender, or society). There is, of course, no such species in the world, recently discovered, that we can now set out to capture. It is a way of looking, not a thing to look for. Carsten Osterlund (personal communication 1999) observes that about 85 per cent of articles that discuss communities of practice begin with the notion of a (homogeneous, harmonious, unchanging) community. A search for one of these is likely to be very long indeed. About 15 per cent begin with the notion of complicated doings and the question that puzzled us in the first place: How is it that a heterogeneous practice, with different participants, engaged differently as part of the practice, with different stakes, places, locations, and histories, can become a site that requires and makes possible succeeding generations of participants, indeed a community of practice?

There is a striking silence in most community of practice studies about social class or race or ethnicity as their relations shape corporations, communities of practice, and everything else. This provides a good illustration of the difference between analytic and prescriptive ways of taking up notions like 'communities of practice'. Analytically: investigating communities of practice on the ground, the identities that participants walk through the door with and which help to account for the complex heterogeneity of communities of practice, surely crucially involve relations of gender, race, and class and participants thoroughly inscribed thereby. Prescriptively: projects that undertake to start a community of practice seem to rely on assumptions that making this new thing does not involve already existing social relations. But the main point is that they always already exist: participants assembling to do something in sufficiently sustained ways that bringing along next generations of participants has to be part of the project, are already members of multiple communities of practice, including some that may exclude each other. Getting participants to take up what they are doing (in circumstances that permit this) as part of who they are across multiple contexts of their lives is what confirms and sediments changed identity and knowledgeability. That makes race, class, and gender (among other historically, socially relevant) identities not a special or optional topic, but always centrally relevant to analyses of communities of practice.

Situated Learning proposed that we pay attention to the process by which communities of practice are produced and produce themselves, asking what newcomers are becoming part of, rather than looking for a community of practice as a product. It is clearer to me now than it was then, that the object is to ask how communities of practice are produced and, since 'how' is in many ways the question of 'what', what contradictory practices are produced, partially, by whom, with whom, in what circumstances across one or more series of old-timer–newcomer relations. Asking how and what continuity is being produced (in contradictory processes of struggle) and what and how displacements are being produced across 'generations', is a useful way to focus attention on a central and interesting question: Just what complex practice is under production?

Knowledgeability and Spatiality

No concept exists by itself – 'communities of practice' is not a theoretical problematic. To say (at the beginning of this epilogue) that the perspective of *Situated Learning* might be radical but not new reflects this point: Social practice theory has philosophical roots in Marx, Gramsci (see accounts by R. J. Bernstein 1971; Ollman 1971), more recently Stuart Hall, and the Birmingham Center for Contemporary Cultural Studies (see Lave et al. 1992), and critical social psychology (Dreier 2008). It is a complex of interrelated assumptions, analytic questions, concepts, and analytic practices through which 'communities of practice', lpp, and other interrelated concepts have been derived. This includes conceptions of knowledge, space, and their interrelations. They surely matter for discussions of a 'knowledge society'. It might be useful to consider how conceptions of knowledge and space are implicated together in our account of 'communities of practice'.

The conception of 'communities of practice' in a social-practice theory perspective is an analytic tool built on a careful argument against taking the world to be an epistemological project. In *Situated Learning* (in a section called 'Places of Knowledge', pp. 94–8), we proposed that knowledgeability changes through lpp (not inductively or deductively, but rather spatially, in motion, in relation to diverse others, participating differently, and through differences the apprentices' own changing practice). To speak of 'knowledgeability' rather than 'knowledge' implies that whatever it is, knowledge is always knowledge in persons in practice. Thus, 'knowledge' is not reducible to something distinct from other aspects of practice which would include its locations and its situated production. It is not knowledge that produces social life or *is* social life but rather, it is praxis, the making and doing of social life that produces changing knowledgeabilities as part of ongoing practice. At its most general, social-practice theory argues that social life is a matter of the social ontology of human praxis, not its epistemology, and certainly not the epistemological production of social life. Further, since much takes place in the world in the name of solid, non-reactive, transmittable knowledge, or in the name of a knowledge society or knowledge economy, the social analyst's challenge is to come to understand how these effects are created in practice – not to assume their existence *sui generis*.

The core issue in the present book is whether communities of practice are a 'driver of innovation and creativity'. Do communities of practice lead to innovation and the creation of knowledge? A second question might well be what happens to communities of practice if they do? I wonder if some 'community of practice' studies do not naively assume the unmitigated good and politically benign character of social processes of innovation and competition. But consider those perilous contradictions of continuity and displacement between old-comers and new timers. Think of innovators as knowledge whistle-blowers questioning old knowledge – that is old knowledgeabilities, existing knowing in practice. (It is a piece of common wisdom that entrepreneurs get fired more often than others.) It would not be implausible to suggest that any community of practice that was an engine of innovation would shortly go up in flames. Which raises an interesting question: If not, why not? To address such questions may require a more nuanced vocabulary of modes of difference, disagreement, antagonism, agonism, dissent, etc., than we usually apply to everyday life (cf. Jason Delborne, 2008).

It is interesting to consider the variety of assumptions about spatial relations that inform 'communities of practice', for there are indeed assumptions about the production of space implied in the theory of which a concept of 'communities of practice' is a part. The problems discussed above, as we misused common spatial metaphors about 'communities of practice', suggest care in taking up 'a community' as a closed and local, or virtually local, entity. Other hazards include assuming without noticing or exploring boundaries, when these are implied, for example in distinguishing between 'within a community of practice' and 'between communities of practice', and taking up common notions of nested units – 'little units compose bigger units'. These geometric spatial formalisms stand at odds with geographer Henri Lefebvre's (1974, trans. 1991) theory of social practice. If we can argue that skulls only provide illusions of closed spaces for what in fact are complex relations between subjects, others, embodied knowledgeabilities, etc.; we can argue similarly about rooms, buildings, institutions – and virtual worlds. The seminar tables we sit around so frequently in our practices also create illusions of closed spaces. The members of a virtual community hunkered down at computers facing cyberspace may make the latter too easy to conceptualize as a virtual seminar table. If not, what instead? How about trajectories of persons in practice through multiple communities of practice?

Conclusion

In what sense were the intentions of *Situated Learning* 'radical?' I have tried to show throughout this brief discussion that social practice theory makes different, conflicting assumptions about the nature of social existence than the common theoretical problematic of the academy. Accordingly, the meanings, relations, and analytic uses of concepts like 'communities of practice' part company from conventional theory as well. Maybe the most puzzling thing about all this is why the concept ever migrated into the worlds of business and education (but not anthropology) in the first place and what it is doing there, while the 'it' has lost the differences of analytic practice that gave it energy in the first place (but see Prologue by Duguid, this volume, and Brown and Duguid (1991) for enlightenment). I am struck by the accounts of practitioners, in, for example public health or city management bureaucracies who seem to have found the notion efficacious in changing, making more room for, and developing their practices. They have successfully argued the necessity as well as ability of heterogeneous groups of interconnected participants to produce a sustained variety of socially valuable projects at different levels in governmental, non-governmental, and corporate organizational settings.

Readers can judge for themselves whether and how the theoretical perspective that generated a concept like 'communities of practice' has informed the empirical studies and their theoretical underpinnings in the contemporary work discussed in this book. From my point of view, there is more connection than merely a shared catchy phrase with two unrelated 'lives'. I find common ground in the focus on heterogeneity, complexity, and conflict as generative in (and of) communities of practice. There is a good deal about learning as an ordinary part of the give and take implied by heterogeneous everyday practice. Where research examples are on offer they seem to be fairly intensive studies, tending towards the ethnographic. I notice interesting issues concerning spatiality in this book – working on the broader political economic, including institutional, structuring of communities of practice, and raising issues of scale, from global forces on the one hand, to social relations of 'proximity', along with mediating spatial relations, including cities, and regions (cf. Holland and Lave 2002).

In taking up the opportunity so kindly extended by Amin and Roberts to learn first hand about contemporary work on 'communities of practice' in the field of management studies, I have repeatedly had the fun of being surprised (both delighted and shocked) at the changing employment of 'communities of practice'. In my own work I have continued to pursue the path we began to set out in *Situated Learning*. Clearly I believe our 'take' on communities of practice was part of a powerful and productive approach to social analysis. But it is also clear that this is now just one conception of communities of practice among others. So go changing knowledgeabilities-in-practice.

References

Bernstein, R. J. (1971). *Praxis and Action: Contemporary Philosophies of Human Activity*. Philadelphia, PA: University of Pennsylvania Press.

Brown, J. and Duguid, P. (1991). 'Organizational learning and communities of practice: Towards a unified view of working, learning, and innovation', *Organization Science*, 2(1): 40–58.

Delborne, J. A. (2008). 'Transgene transgressions: Scientific dissent as heterogeneous practice', forthcoming in *Social Studies of Science*.

Dreier, O. (2008). *Changing Persons Across Places*. New York: Cambridge University Press.

Duguid, P. (2006). 'What *talking* tells us', *Organization Studies*, 27(12): 1794–804.

Holland, D. and Lave, J. (eds.) (2002). *History in Person: Enduring Struggles, Contentious Practice, Intimate Identities*. Santa Fe, NM: SAR Press.

Lave, J. (1988). *Cognition in Practice: Mind, Mathematics and Culture in Everyday Life*. Cambridge: Cambridge University Press.

Lave, J. and Wenger, E. (1991). *Situated Learning: Legitimate Peripheral Participation*. New York: Cambridge University Press.

Lave, J., Duguid, P., Axel, E., and Fernandez, N. (1992). 'Coming of age in Birmingham: Cultural studies and conceptions of subjectivity', *Annual Reviews in Anthropology*, 21: 257–82.

Lefebvre, H. (1974). *The Production of Space* (trans. 1991). Oxford and Cambridge: Blackwell.

Ollman, B. (1971). *Alienation: Marx's Conception of Man in Capitalist Society*. Cambridge: Cambridge University Press.

Wenger, E. (1998). *Communities of Practice: Learning, Meaning and Identity*. New York: Cambridge University Press.

Williams, R. (1976). *Keywords: A Vocabulary of Culture and Society*. New York: Oxford University Press.

Notes

1. Thanks to Ash Amin and Joanne Roberts for the enormous effort they dedicated to producing a lively and successful workshop in November 2006 and for their serious imprint on the development of the book that emerged from the conference.

2. I will return to this issue later, for it seems central to any conversation today that incorporates 'communities of practice' into discussions of a 'knowledge society'.

3. I think Etienne Wenger was bothered by the characterization of 'full participation' and the way we limited lpp to newcomers (except in a suggestive sentence at the end of ch. 4 that everyone is a peripheral participant in each other's doings). I reacted with a notion of core-blindness – that there is no simple accumulation of knowledgeable skill, but rather changing knowledgeability (and viewpoints, and erasures, and losses of possibilities of coming to know as participants change). Etienne Wenger (1998) in his book *Communities of Practice* reacted by an inspired insistence that everyone engaged in a practice is changing with respect to that practice, and so lpp is not confined to newcomers. Further, he explores ambiguities in 'legitimate peripherality', distinguishing peripheral and marginal participation. He may have been trying to escape from the strong reification of learning as lpp in insisting that 'reification' itself is a part of all participants' activities. We have gone on in different directions: Etienne towards what might be called a sociology of meaning, I towards a social theory of changing practice.

4. This critical (in both senses) observation is Paul Duguid's (2006). He points out that analysis focused exclusively on lpp and communities of practice cannot address crucial questions about the institutional structures and practices which are the conditions of possibility for communities of practice (among other things). This is crucial, further, to addressing another critical flaw in our argument: Instead of 'a community of practice' we should have insisted that communities of practice do not exist in isolation from each other and should be examined in their relations.

5. I suspect that the perverse side of the popularity of 'communities of practice' lies here, in the too-short distance we had moved away from conventional functionalist theorizing.

6. We called it a contradiction in meaning. I would now call it a contradiction in practice, including relations of meaning.

Index

Note: page numbers in *italics* refer to tables and figures.

Index

CLASS (Clockless Logic Analysis, Synthesis and Systems) project 181–2, 190
clock-based (synchronous) logic 183, 190
clock time 91
club goods 52
Codetronix 190
codified knowledge 74–6, 213
cognition 125, 129–30
  activity theory of 126–8
  embeddedness of 126–7
cognitive distance 129–31, 138, 139
  between communities 233–4
  collaboration and 130, 132
  optimal 130, 209
Cohen, W. M. 126, 129, 237, 240
Cohendet, P. 191, 207–8
Coleman, J. S. 89 n. 25
collaboration 27, 131, 134, 140, 211
  and cognitive distance and 130, 132
  international 218, 219
  in Montreal 245–6
  projects and 158–9, 167
  within/between CoPs 138–9, 140, 141, *214*
collective knowledge 131
communities
  actor-networks 38–9
  blockage tendencies 51, 52, 57, 58, 61
  cognitive distance between 233–4
  economic geography of 55–63
  and global integration 57–9
  loss of 56
  negative views of 37
  positive views of 38
  role in projects 231–5
communities of practice, *see* CoPs
communities of specialists 231–3
  and creativity 248–50
community learning 155
competence 139, 141
connotations 127–8
contractual theories of the firm 134–5
control 112
convergence 99
coordination
  and exploitation/exploration 137–8
  levels of *137*
CoPs (communities of practice) *139*
  and breakthrough innovation 191–2
  characteristics of *12*, *153*
  cognitive distance in 139
  collaboration within/between 138–9, 140, 141, *214*
  definitions 1–2, 9, 124
  history of 2–4

and knowledgeability 292–3
learning theory 1–8
  and legitimate peripheral participation 284–6, 288–90
  multiple 155
  and spatiality 293
corporate culture 211
Cosgrove, D. 108
Cowan, R. 71–2, 232
creative cities 227–8
  and absorptive capabilities, development of 238–41
  and KI firms 247–8, 249–50
  projects and events 244–8, *247*
  spaces and places 242–4, *247*
  see also Montreal
creative slack: as source of growth 228, 231, 235–8
creativity
  communities of specialists and 248–50
  KI firms 231–5

Damasio, A. R. 127
DARPA (Defence Advanced Research Projects Agency) 181–2, 190, 192, 194
data flow organization 198–9 n. 9
David, P. A. 71–2
De Beistegui, M. 99
de Certeau, M. 3
De Fillippi, R. 235
De Laat, B. 187
Debian project 256, 264–6
  decision-making 265–6
  New Maintainer Process 265
decision-making 49, 135
  Debian project 265–6
  F/LOSS communities and 260, 262–3, 264, 265–6
  mental accounting theory 42
  prospect theory 42
decisive moments 94–7
Defence Advanced Research Projects Agency (DARPA) 181–2, 190, 192, 194
design tools 189–91
differentiation 132–3, 140
distance paradox 235
distanciated learning 204, 207–8, 216–21
  advanced manufacturing technology case study 217–18
  drug development case study 217, 219
  industrial software development case study 217, 218
  and knowledge type 212–16
diversity 27, 48–9, 57–60, 61–3, 229

298

Index